# THE OFFICIAL®

# 1996
# BLACKBOOK
# PRICE GUIDE OF
# UNITED STATES
# PAPER
# MONEY

## TWENTY-EIGHTH EDITION

## BY MARC HUDGEONS, N.L.G.

HOUSE OF COLLECTIBLES • NEW YORK

© 1995 by Random House, Inc.

All rights reserved under International and Pan-American Copyright Conventions.

Published by: House of Collectibles
201 East 50th Street
New York, New York 10022

Distributed by Ballantine Books, a division of Random House, Inc., New York, and simultaneously in Canada by Random House of Canada Limited, Toronto.

Manufactured in the United States of America

ISSN: 0195-3540

ISBN: 0-876-37934-X

Cover design by Kristine Mills
Cover photo by George Kerrigan

Twenty-Eighth Edition: July 1995

10 9 8 7 6 5 4 3 2 1

# TABLE OF CONTENTS

# OFFICIAL BOARD OF CONTRIBUTORS

# PUBLISHER'S NOTE

*The Official ® Blackbook Price Guide of United States Paper Money* is designed as a reference aid for collectors, dealers, and the general public. Its purpose is to provide historical and collecting data, as well as current values. Prices are as accurate as possible at the time of going to press, but no guarantee is made. We are not dealers; persons wishing to buy or sell paper money, or have it appraised, are advised to consult collector magazines or the telephone directory for addresses of dealers. We are not responsible for typographical errors.

# NOTE TO READERS

All advertisements appearing in this book have been accepted in good faith, but the publisher assumes no responsibility in any transactions that occur between readers and advertisers.

# 1996
# BLACKBOOK
# PRICE GUIDE OF
# UNITED STATES
# PAPER
# MONEY

# MARKET REVIEW
## by W. R. "Bill" Rindone

The 1990s find more and more collectors entering into the hobby of collecting paper money. This upward spiraling interest comes from many sources. First, there is an inward appreciation of the engravers' art and the outstanding designs exhibited on U.S. currency. Secondly, the notes have a great deal of historical significance. Individual notes represent billboards of their time. Lincoln's appearance on the 1862 $10 note, issued during his tenure in office, tended to bolster public sentiment for the northern war effort. The one dollar issue of the same period bore the portrait of Salmon Chase, Secretary of War, under Lincoln, who by rumor and inuendo was linked to Lincoln's assassination. Another interesting example is the 1880 series $10 note. It is known amongst collectors as a Jackass Note, because the eagle appearing on the face was intentionally designed by the engraver to represent a jackass when inverted. The eagle was later acknowledged as a political statement by one of the parties in Congress.

Among the other substantial reasons for collecting is the thrill of discovery. Many notes are yet to be "discovered." They are still lying around in desk drawers, old attics, or hidden in the walls of early buildings. I was once asked how so many notes survived in such nice condition. The answers are varied. Many were placed in baby books at birth or in the case of some hoards, they were actually the booty taken from early train robberies or bank holdups. There is one major accumulation existing today that was a residue of Wells, Fargo and Company holdings. It is said to be quite substantial (over $100,000 face value) and has sat dormant for over sixty years. The owners were simply unaware of its value.

The field of collectible paper money continues to attract history students, but they have been joined by other serious collectors who are willing to spend substantial sums to further their chosen field of collectibles. This bodes well for the hobby in general and is part of a continuing rise in interest that started in the 1970s. Prices are, of course, rising steadily as would be expected of any market where the demand continues to increase. Dealer tables at last year's major paper money shows were generally sold out well in advance. The current complaint of dealers is the difficult problem of keeping a well-rounded inventory in stock. Auction attendance and bidding also reached an all-time high last year and indications are that it will continue to do so for several months, if not years, to come.

On the bright side, although more collectors have moved into the field, it is still possible for individuals with a modest income to collect an outstanding array of "type" notes. Unlike other major collecting areas, paper money has not been artificaly promoted and is still mainly the domain of collectors rather than investors. Because the hobby is collector based, the values we have today are representative of the "true" rarity and liquid value of a given note. Individual prices steadily rise, as they should, in direct relationship to rarity and demand. It should also be noted that new paper money clubs are springing up over widespread geographical areas. This signifies the vibrant growth evident within today's collecting community.

## LARGE SIZE CURRENCY 1862–1928

All but the rarest notes are still available to collectors entering the hobby today. An ever-increasing demand for more material has caused several major collections to be sold both by auction and to established dealers in notes. Ironically, these were quickly absorbed by the influx of new collectors and by those who had waited several years to acquire a particular note. Some "finest known" notes brought astronomical prices during the last year. The finest (AU) 1880 $50 Legal Tender Note (Roscrans-Nebeker) brought $17,000 at open auction. Only nine examples of this note have been recorded and, of those, three are escounced in museums. Although the Smithsonian has a fine currency collection that is certainly worth viewing, they have only a counterfeit of this great rarity. Other notes, of which fewer than a dozen examples are known, found new homes in the $500 to $1,500 range. Unlike coin collecting, true rarities are still within the reach of the average collector. How much longer this will exist remains to be seen.

## SMALL SIZE TYPE NOTES 1928–PRESENT

Interest is currently at an all-time high. With the current rumor of new currencies being issued by the federal government, interest will undoubtedly be spurred to new heights. Over recent months the stock of collectible small size notes has drastically dwindled. Once thought to be "endless," we now know that the availability of early notes is a great deal smaller than anyone had previously thought. Many of the true rarities in this field are just beginning to be identified. Wise collectors are putting together comprehensive collections, while these early notes are still available at very little over face value. Because of the relatively low cost, the heavy emphasis is on acquiring uncirculated examples. The existing stock of these notes will drop drastically over the next year or two. A great deal of variety exists in field with the items such as Hawaii Overprints, North African Invasion Notes, Gold Certificates, Red Seal Legal Tenders, Silver Certificates, Federal Reserve Bank Notes, National Currency, and numerous experimental issues, etc. This area of collecting is quickly emerging as one of new interest and certainly should be considered by new collectors.

# THE FIRST AMERICAN PAPER MONEY

## PAPER MONEY BORN OF NECESSITY

Prior to the American Revolution some individual colonies issued paper currency. This was done on a limited basis in order to supply a temporary medium of exchange, pending the arrival or availability of specie (gold or silver coins). These issues were used primarily to finance military expeditions and were repudiated or declared null and void after brief circulation and acceptance.

The Massachusetts Bay Colony issued paper money in 1690 to pay troops for participation in a foray into Canada during King William's War (1689-97).

South Carolina issued paper money to pay for military activities against Spanish and Indian neighbors in Florida in 1703. New York, New Hampshire, Connecticut, New Jersey, Rhode Island, and North Carolina all followed in issuing paper money to defend their frontiers from Indian raids.

## INFLATION AND DEPRECIATION

Experience with these early issues of paper money in America demonstrated that the value of the hastily issued notes varied widely from hand to hand and was not universally or cheerfully accepted. Without exception, paper money lost its value with the passage of time and with the increase in distance from place of issue. Depreciation was the order of the day where paper currency was concerned. The Massachusetts issue of 1702 went down in value to less than one-eighth of face value before payment was refused. Paper money was a "hot potato."

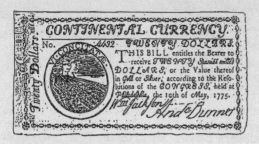

**CONTINENTAL CURRENCY,** 1775
Issued by Continental Congress
Philadelphia (Obverse)
Vi Concitate
"Driven By Force"

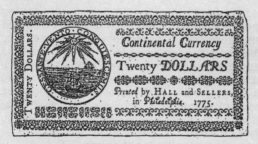

**CONTINENTAL CURRENCY,** 1775
Printed by: Hall & Sellars
(Successors to B. Franklin, Printer) (Reverse)
Cessante Vento Conquies Cemus
"When the Wind Dies Down We Rest"

## CONTINENTAL CURRENCY

In 1775 the Continental Congress began issuing paper currency that would amount to a total of over *two hundred forty million dollars*. Continental currency was widely distributed and accepted and was supposed to be backed by "Spanish Milled Dollars," as so stated on each note.

**GEORGIA CURRENCY**
Issued by Georgia Congress
Savannah
Backed by *Spanish Milled Dollars*
Sustine Rectum
"Support What's Right"

Individual former colonies (now states) such as Georgia followed suit and promptly authorized and printed paper money "backed by Spanish Milled Dollars," the money most preferred and trusted by all.

## "NOT WORTH A CONTINENTAL" = WORTHLESS

As a matter of convenience, individual states issued paper money in 1776 denominated in dollars and backed by "Continental Currency." The currency was not backed by "Spanish Milled Dollars," as so stated. This was similar to depositing a large check into your bank account, then writing checks based on the assumption that the funds you deposited were good. What happens when the check you deposited is returned "NSF-Not Sufficient Funds"? That is what happened to the states that issued notes backed by "Continental Currency."

Guess who was left holding the bag: John Q. Public!

## "NO GREATER EVIL"

When the Revolutionary War was won, troops were paid with paper money that could not be spent. George Washington voiced his opinion of paper money: "I know of no greater evil for the working man than a paper currency." Eventually, the troops that did not discard the currency were able to redeem it for unsettled raw land. The citizenry of our new nation trusted coins of gold and silver issued by other nations rather than accept paper money.

## THE BANK OF THE UNITED STATES

Our fledgling nation tried to copy its Anglo master by creating the Bank of the United States. This private institution served as a central bank to the United States until its charter was revoked by President Andrew Jackson. The Bank of the United States issued paper money and had branch banks in the major cities of the day. The issue of paper money by banks and other institutions was controlled and regulated by the banking commission in each state of issue. Paper money issued by the Bank of the United States became worthless in 1837 when its charter lapsed. The Bank of the United States currency cannot be redeemed at face value today. The failure of the Bank of the United States plunged the nation into the worst depression to date.

## HARD TIMES

The lapse of charter of the central bank resulted in the closing of banks throughout the land. Many private banks dealt extensively with the Bank of the United States. Its failure caused issues of their paper money to lose their value and eventually cease circulation. "Hard Money," in other words, coins, was the only acceptable currency. There was such a shortage of coins that industrious individuals began to issue their own coins. These coins often reflected political or satirical sentiments such as "Millions for Defense—not ONE CENT—for tribute," carried by a copper token that circulated as a large cent. Other cent tokens depicted President Jackson as King Andrew the First or as Caesar of the Republic.

## BUSINESS AND BANKING CARRY ON

Time and tide for no man wait, nor does business. As a result of the massive collapse of the banking infrastructure, a replacement had to be created to fill the void. Bank notes were printed from woodcut type, metal type, copper plate engraving, steel plate engraving, and a new lithography process. Bank note salesmen called at every stop to display their design specimens for bank notes in any denomination a customer desired to print.

## "TWO BITS—FOUR BITS—SIX BITS—A DOLLAR"

The widespread acceptance of the Spanish dollar caused the popularity of its fractional units ($3\frac{1}{8}$¢, $6\frac{1}{4}$¢ and $12\frac{1}{2}$¢):

> Spanish Milled Dollar = 8 Reales or Bits
> $\frac{1}{2}$ Spanish Milled Dollar = 4 Reales or Bits
> $\frac{1}{4}$ Spanish Milled Dollar = 2 Reales or Bits
> Real or Bit = $12\frac{1}{2}$ Cents ($\frac{1}{8}$th Dollar)
> $\frac{1}{2}$ Real or Bit = $6\frac{1}{4}$ Cents ($\frac{1}{16}$ Dollar)
> $\frac{1}{4}$ Real or Bit = $3\frac{1}{8}$ Cents ($\frac{1}{32}$ Dollar)

These denominations became the basis for quotes on our infant stock exchange. Today, quotes in the *Wall Street Journal* of stock prices still reflect this heritage. Notes from this period are often referred to as "Broken Bank Notes" or "Wildcat Notes." Most are no longer redeemable, although many are worth more than face value as collectors' items.

## ANTEBELLUM BOOM TIMES

The national economy restructured itself rapidly as the United States expanded to the West and as industrial and agricultural production increased.

Steam power had now come to America. In addition to speeding the westward movement with locomotives and steamships, this new development powered the engines of industry, including the printing presses of our currency printers. Paper money poured forth as never before from banks, railroads, canal companies, toll roads, insurance companies, and mercantile houses—but not from the federal government.

Each state still controlled the issue of paper money within its sovereign territory.

## THE WAR BETWEEN THE STATES

The first shot fired on Fort Sumter signaled the first issue of paper money by the government of the United

States of America since its infamous Continental Currency debacle. An issue of *sixty million dollars* in paper money was authorized by congress in the summer of 1861. The "Demand Notes," as they were designated, were printed on both sides, which was unusual in that most currency of the day was printed on the front only. The back impression was printed in a distinctive green ink, and they came to be called "Greenbacks." The name stuck and this price guide includes all known issues of "Greenbacks" from 1861 to date.

Robert W. Cornely, Sr.
Historical Numismatic Consultant
Professional Numismatist
4665 Lower Roswell Road
Marietta, GA 30068   FAX 404/565-6213

# THE SECURITY FEATURES THAT SAFEGUARD U.S. CURRENCY

*Reprinted with permission of the Department of the Treasury, Bureau of Printing and Engraving.*

Treasury Secretary Nicholas F. Brady announced on July 25, 1991, two new features designed to protect U.S. currency against counterfeiting by advanced copier, scanner, and computer-based printer equipment.

"The introduction of these new features is well ahead of the widespread accessibility of advanced copier and printer technology," Secretary Brady said, "but we must be vigilant and continuously provide protection against emerging counterfeit threats. A secure currency is the foundation of the nation's economy and important to every American. With over 50 percent of U.S. dollars held outside the country, security from counterfeiting is also essential to a sound global economy."

The Bureau of Engraving and Printing is now producing Series 1990 $100 notes with a security thread and microprinting. These will be closely followed by security-enhanced $50 notes. When the Federal Reserve System puts the Series 1990 $100 notes into circulation, enhanced notes will slowly replace existing notes which will continue to circulate without recall. Enhanced $50 notes will be introduced in a similar manner.

Because the two security enhancements are almost invisible to the naked eye, U.S. currency will look much the same. But they give the public and cash handlers two additional means of checking notes if they suspect a counterfeit. The security safeguards are:

**Security thread.** A polyester strip is embedded in the paper on the left side of the note's face in the clear field between the border and the Federal Reserve seal. The letters USA and the denomination (e.g. USA 100) are printed on the strip in an alternating up-and-down pattern. Easily seen when held to a light, the strip cannot be reproduced in the reflected light of copiers.

**Microprinting.** "THE UNITED STATES OF AMERICA" is printed repeatedly along the sides of the portrait. The letters, at six to seven thousandths of an inch, appear like a thin line to the naked eye. They can only be read with a magnifier and cannot be distinctly reproduced by advanced copiers.

These features were chosen after extensive research and testing for effectiveness in deterring counterfeiting, durability and subtlety.

**Q. Why are these changes necessary?**
**A.** Advanced color copiers, graphic computers, color laser scanners, and printers that permit high quality reproduction are expected to be widely available within a few years. This would have created a new counterfeiting threat to U.S. currency, but because we have developed the security enhancements well ahead of the widespread availability of this technology, we have full confidence in all American currency.

**Q. What exactly is this new copier and printer technology, and how does it work?**
**A.** Advanced copier and printer technology improved dramatically during the 1980s and is expected to continue to mature during the remainder of the 20th century. Some of this equipment is capable of accurately reproducing the colors and fine line detail of security documents and is seen as a threat to United States currency.

Market surveys indicate that as quality, affordability, and availability increase, advanced equipment will become the standard in offices, copy centers, and printing facilities. Industry analysts forecast that up to 1.7 million color copiers and 1.8 million color printers will be in use by the end of 1994. The color copier of the '90s has been compared to the color television of the '70s, when color became the standard rather than the exception.

Of the new technologies, advanced copiers, electronic scanners, and color workstations are the primary threats to currency. They do not require extensive expertise to operate and are expected to become widely accessible. Of these, only about 30 percent pose a serious threat because of high quality, high resolution capabilities.

## ADVANCED COLOR COPIERS

There are two types of advanced color copiers: analog or optical imaging systems and digital imaging systems. Analog imaging systems scan the image optically and directly or indirectly make an image on paper. These systems include photographic, electrophotographic, and Cycolor. Digital imaging systems optically scan an image and convert it by computer into digital signals used to make an image on paper. Digital systems include thermal transfer, ink jet, and also an advanced electrophotographic.

**Photographic—(Analog/optical).** Photographic based color copiers at under $20,000 offer exceptionally high quality reproductions using photographic paper. This technology, even with improvements for less specialized use, is not a threat to security documents since copies are readily identifiable by the special photographic paper.

**Cycolor—(Analog/optical).** This light activated analog imaging technology has a unique process using microencapsulated prima color dyes. The color copier is relatively inexpensive at under $10,000. The color quality is considered good, but the special paper requirements reduce the threat to currency security.

**Thermal Transfer—(Digital).** Color thermal copiers, usually associated with computer digital printers, are priced around $10,000. The copiers produce shiny, waxy copies in the lower quality range and are not viewed as a major counterfeit threat.

**Color Ink Jet—(Digital).** Designed for the engineering/ scientific area, this technology is capable of making good quality, oversize copies at 400 dots-per-inch with plain paper copying. Priced at approximately $95,000, it is not widely available and does not pose a current risk to currency security.

**Electrophotography—(Analog/optical and digital).** The electrophotographic process provides a high quality plain paper copy at high copy speeds (up to 23 copies per minute) and a per copy cost of from 7 to 15 cents. High end digital copiers of this type can faithfully reproduce the fine detail of currency, and, as the price lowers below the $20,000 point, these copiers are expected to pose an increasing threat to currency security. Market surveys project conservatively that 40,000 electrophotographic copiers will be placed in the United States by 1993.

## ELECTRONIC SCANNERS

Scanner equipment electronically scans an image or text on an original document and digitizes it into a computer-readable form. The image may be displayed on a screen, changed, or combined with other images. The edited image can then be stored, printed on a color output device, or used to make offset or gravure printing plates. Medium quality scanners can scan or read 100 dots per inch (dpi). High quality 400 dpi scanners can read very small one point type as well as half tones. Advanced copiers and printing equipment using this technology are considered a security threat because of flexible editing capabilities and fine detail reproductions.

Scanner equipment is mostly found in large graphic design firms. One thousand dpi color scanners are priced at $25,000; 400 dpi units are less. As prices drop, this technology will become increasingly available in design, printing, and advertising organizations.

## COLOR WORKSTATION

A color workstation combines the latest personal computer, software, printer/copier, and video camera/scanner tech-

## NEW FEATURES

TO DETER COUNTERFEITING WITH ADVANCED COPIERS, SCANNERS, AND PRINTERS.

**FEDERAL RESERVE SEAL**

Issuing Federal Reserve Bank. Code letter same as first letter in two serial numbers.

**SECURITY THREAD**

Embedded polyester strip with repeated USA 50 or USA 100 in an up-and-down pattern. Visible when held to light. Cannot be reproduced in reflected light of copiers. In new Series 1990 $50 and $100 notes.

**MICROPRINTING**

"The United States of America" printed repeatedly on sides of portrait. Letters too small to read without a magnifier or for distinct copier reproduction. In new Series 1990 $50 and $100 notes.

**PORTRAIT**

Lifelike portrait distinct from fine, screenlike background.

**PAPER**

Cotton and linen rag paper has strong, pliable "feel." No watermarks.

## SERIAL NUMBERS

Two serial numbers distinctively styled and evenly spaced. Ink color same as Treasury seal. No two notes of *same series* and denomination have same serial number.

## BORDER

Border's fine lines and lacy, web-like design distinct and unbroken.

## FIBERS

Tiny red and blue fibers embedded in paper.

## TREASURY SEAL

Sawtooth points sharp, distinct, and unbroken. Seal's color same as two serial numbers.

## ENGRAVED PRINTING

Engraved plate printing gives new note embossed "feel."

## DENOMINATION

Note's value on corners same as over Treasury seal.

nologies. The data or image can be stored indefinitely on magnetic floppy disks or other media and copied later on a color output device. A document scanned in one location can be printed on any compatible printer. Output quality depends on the dpi resolution and scanner and printer capabilities. Printer resolution is of greater importance because scanner input can be edited to enhance quality.

By the middle of 1990, it is anticipated that the personal computer will be linked to a digital copier to produce high quality, inexpensive copies directly from the digitized information in the personal computer. With the trend to use charts, graphs, and illustrations (many of which are now generated by computers) in presentations and reports, it is expected that color workstations will soon be commonly found in business operations.

**Q. Are these changes to U.S. currency only to deter advanced copier or printer counterfeiters?**

**A.** Yes. The security thread and the microprinting will provide extra protection to deter counterfeiting on easily operated copier and printer equipment which is expected to soon be widely accessible in offices, copy centers, and printing operations. Professional counterfeiters will also be hindered by the difficult, costly, and time consuming task of producing genuine looking threaded paper or reproducing microprinted text. Existing security features still offer protection against other means of counterfeiting.

**Q. Is counterfeiting a serious economic problem?**

**A.** No, it is not a serious problem now. Traditionally, about 90 percent of known counterfeits are believed to be seized before being passed to the public. In fiscal year 1990, that amounted to $66 million; $14 million was seized in circulation. This totals less than one-tenth of one percent of total currency production of $77 billion in genuine notes produced during that time, or the estimated $268 billion in circulation worldwide. As a criminal activity, however, counterfeiting endangers the financial well being of everyone who holds or uses U.S. currency.

**Q. Are counterfeits from advanced copiers and printers a problem?**

**A.** Counterfeits from advanced copiers and printers

totaled only about $2 million in fiscal year 1990—double that of fiscal year 1988—but still only two percent of the dollar amount of all fiscal year 1990 counterfeits.

Copiers and printers with the capability of making high quality counterfeits exist in small numbers today. But by 1994, with improved quality and lower cost, industry analysts forecast 1.8 million color copiers and 1.7 million color printers will be in use in offices, copy centers, and printing facilities.

### Q. Why are the changes being introduced now?
**A.** The government is responsible for maintaining the integrity and security of United States currency—the most widely held currency in the world. The time required for research and development, production, and distribution through domestic and international financial markets makes it necessary to stay well ahead of counterfeit threats.

### Q. Who decided to make the changes?
**A.** The Four Nation Group, established in 1978 and comprised of the United States, England, Canada and Australia, studied the potential counterfeit threat from reprographic technology advancements along with currency protection options. In response to the Group's 1981 report, the Secretary of the Treasury established an Advanced Counterfeit Deterrence Steering Committee chaired by the U.S. Treasurer. Other members represent the Federal Reserve System and Treasury's Bureau of Engraving and Printing and U.S. Secret Service. After studying numerous security features, the Committee recommended that the security thread and microprinting be adopted. The Secretary of the Treasury, who has the legal authority to determine currency design, approved these options.

### Q. Why were the security thread and microprinting chosen?
**A.** Numerous other devices, many of which are used successfully by countries with lower currency production and circulation demands, were evaluated. These included holograms, thin films, multiple defraction grating, metameric inks, watermarks, and color tints. After the criteria of effectiveness, cost, durability, and adaptability to the traditional design were applied, the security thread and micro-

printing were determined to be the most appropriate security devices for U.S. currency. This was confirmed in a comprehensive 1986 National Science Foundation study.

## EVALUATION CRITERIA

**Effectiveness.** Counterfeit deterrent effectiveness was tested by reprographic equipment manufacturers and government scientists. The ease of public and cash handler recognition and use was also considered.

**Durability.** Durability was tested under the rigors of normal circulation. Tests included crumpling, folding, laundering, and soaking in a variety of solvents such as gasoline, acids, and laundry products.

**Cost.** Production tests were conducted to determine if a feature would adversely affect production or cost, which in 1989 amounted to 7 billion notes at 2.6 cents per note.

**Appearance.** Features were evaluated on their compatibility with the traditional design of U.S. currency.

## DEVICES/FEATURES EVALUATED

**Holograms.** These three-dimensional, laser-generated image devices undergo color or image shifts when tilted. Although commonly used on credit cards, holograms were too expensive and fragile for U.S. currency applications. Simulated circulation tests (folding, crumpling, and chemical soaks) destroyed the image.

**Multiple Diffraction Gratings.** Diffraction gratings have different line spacings that are superimposed to break up light into various color patterns. This produces image and color shifts depending upon the viewing angle. These devices were expensive for large production demands and did not survive simulated circulation testing.

**Thin Film Interference Filter.** This multilayer reflective device produces a distinct and controlled color shift when tilted (gold to green or red to blue). The device evaluated for U.S. currency, more durable than holograms or diffraction gratings, would require major currency production changes. It also did not survive simulated circulation testing.

**Watermarks.** Watermarks applied during the paper manufacturing process produce a distinct design that can be seen in transmitted light. This security feature, common in other world currencies, would require a complete redesign to give sufficient clear space for U.S. currency effectiveness.

**Latent Image.** An image is created by multidirection engraved lines that are visible when viewed at a specific angle. Effectiveness is based on the three-dimensional effect of intaglio printing. The device rapidly degraded and was difficult to detect after simulated U.S. currency circulation.

**Background Color Tints.** Complex color tints (rainbow tints) are commonly used in security documents to provide subtle, difficult-to-produce color gradations. Useful against older copiers and photographic reproduction equipment, the tints were not as effective against advanced copiers or scanners. A redesign would be required to successfully utilize this type of deterrent in U.S. currency.

**Metameric Pairs.** Two inks, appearing the same color under normal light, appear different under intense copier and scanner lights. Copies show color differences. Some foreign currencies have this feature. For U.S. currency, a significant redesign would be required to provide the large area of metameric colors necessary for effectiveness.

**Security Threads.** Several variations of security threads were evaluated, such as windowed, solid, and denominated. These devices have a continuous filament or ribbon embedded into the base paper during manufacture. They can also be manufactured with identifying information, such as the denomination.

The security thread, determined to be the most effective counterfeit deterrent for U.S. currency, is visible when held to the light and invisible in the reflected light of copiers or scanners. It is durable, cost effective, and can be incorporated into the traditional design.

**Microprinting.** Text is printed too small (6 to 7 thousandths of an inch) to be accurately copied by reprographic equipment. Microprinting is inexpensive, durable, and can be incorporated into the current U.S. currency design. After the original engraving, it is reproduced as part of the normal printing operation.

**Q. How is the security thread inserted in the note?**
**A.** The security thread is inserted in the currency paper during the papermaking process. The vendor uses a highly innovative technique that was developed specifically to produce threaded paper which meets stringent Bureau of Engraving and Printing requirements. The U.S. security thread is unique in the world in that it is wider, the graphics are easy to read, and it is virtually invisible in the reflected light of copiers.

**Q. Why will the new features only be in $100 and $50 notes?**
**A.** The higher value notes are being introduced first because they naturally pose the greatest risk of loss from counterfeiting. The two notes also only amount to about four percent of yearly currency production, which allows for an easily managed start-up of initial production and circulation.

Other notes will be introduced with the security features over the next five years, with the probable exception of $1 notes, which do not pose a great risk. The security thread will read USA FIVE, USA TEN, and USA TWENTY, depending upon the denomination.

**Q. Which note will have the security thread added next?**
**A.** Production of an enhanced Series 1990 $50 note began in late 1991. The $20 note is expected to have a security thread added next, probably within a year-and-a-half. The $20 note amounts to about 30 percent of the yearly currency production.

**Q. Will existing currency be taken out of circulation?**
**A.** No recall or "demonetization" of existing currency is planned. The Federal Reserve will introduce the security enhanced currency as replacement notes in the normal cir-

culation process. However, when the Federal Reserve has sufficient inventories of the enhanced Series 1990 $100 notes, it plans to replace the old series $100 notes, regardless of their condition, in order to provide the public with security enhanced notes as early as possible.

**Q. Why won't existing currency be withdrawn altogether if the purpose is to prevent counterfeiting?**
**A.** The integrity of the U.S. dollar is based on its stability and sound backing. Regardless of when first issued, any currency authorized by the U.S. government is still legal tender.

**Q. What will keep counterfeiters from copying currency without the enhancements?**
**A.** Advanced copier and printer technology capable of producing authentic-looking currency is still not widely available. As advanced equipment placements increase, we also expect security enhanced currency to become predominant. As older currency becomes scarce, the public will pay more attention to checking bills without the new security features. Counterfeiters do not want to draw attention to themselves or bogus bills. The new features create a greater risk of detection and apprehension by law enforcement agents.

**Q. How much will these changes cost?**
**A.** Approximately $460 thousand per year was spent by the Bureau of Engraving and Printing over a five-year period (total of $2.3 million) to evaluate and test the security thread. This is equivalent to about 20 percent of the $2½ million yearly budget for ongoing research and development on currency inks, paper, and printing techniques.
When the security thread is added to all denominations, with the probable exception of the $1 bill, the increased cost per note is expected to be about two-tenths of a cent more than the current cost of three cents per note.

**Q. Who pays for the costs associated with new security features?**
**A.** The Bureau of Engraving and Printing is a customer-funded agency. It is reimbursed by the Federal Reserve System for the capital, research and development, and

printing costs for currency production. The Bureau does not receive funds through the Congressional budget process and is not taxpayer funded.

**Q. What good does the microprinting do if you can't read it?**
**A.** The microprinting provides an additional way of authenticating a suspect note. It is a low-cost security feature in that once the printing plate has been engraved there are no additional costs. If there is concern about a note, a simple magnifying glass can help in further scrutiny.

**Q. How long does currency usually stay in circulation?**
**A.** In the normal system of currency replacement, the Federal Reserve estimates the following approximate life cycles:

| | |
|---|---|
| $1 | 1½ years |
| $5 | 1¼ years |
| $10 | 1½ years |
| $20 | 2 years |
| $50 | 5 years |
| $100 | 8½ years |

(This is an estimated extrapolation based on 1990 Federal Reserve Board statistics on currency received from circulation, paid into circulation, and destroyed.)

**Q. How much currency is in circulation worldwide?**
**A.** According to the Department of the Treasury's Financial Management Service Quarterly Report of March 31, 1991, approximately $268 billion in U.S. currency is in circulation worldwide. Of that amount, some Federal Reserve researchers have estimated that $80-$110 billion is supporting domestic spending and $110-$160 is offshore or domestically held.

**Q. Will the enhanced currency last as long as existing notes?**
**A.** We expect the enhanced currency to be as durable as existing dollars. The average $1 note can be folded 6,500 times before it wears out and has a life span of

18 months—about 35 percent more than it was in the 1940s. This increase is due to improved presses and paper composition.

**Q. Can either the security thread or microprinting be machine read? Will the new features affect change machines, ATMs, or can they be used to track a private citizen's use of money?**
**A.** The new features have no special qualities that can be picked up by sensors, such as airport metal detectors. The enhancements will not affect the use of money in any way except to protect it from counterfeiting by advanced copiers and printers.

**Q. With enhanced and existing currency both circulating, won't it be confusing to anyone trying to determine whether the new features should be in the note or not?**
**A.** A simple way to check the currency is to look first at the series year found to the left of the Secretary of the Treasury's signature. All $100 and $50 notes Series 1990 or later should have the security thread and microprinting. Series 1988A and earlier will not. (There is no Series 1989.)

**Q. When was U.S. currency last changed?**
**A.** The last major change in currency was over 60 years ago in 1929 when the size was reduced by a quarter and uniform designs were adopted. In 1955, the addition of "In God We Trust" was required by Congress. It first appeared on Series 1957 $1 Silver Certificates and was then gradually phased in on all other paper currency denominations and classes. The English inscription Treasury seal was introduced initially with the Series 1966 $100 U.S. notes and was later phased in for all currency.

# THE HISTORY OF
# U.S. PAPER MONEY

*Reprinted with permission of the Department of the Treasury, Bureau of Printing and Engraving.*

In the early days of the nation, before and just after the Revolution, Americans used English, Spanish, and French money.

**1690 Colonial Notes.** The Massachusetts Bay Colony issued the first paper money in the colonies which would later form the United States.

**1775 Continental Currency.** American colonists issued paper currency for the Continental Congress to finance the Revolutionary War. The notes were backed by the "anticipation" of tax revenues. Without solid backing and easily counterfeited, the notes quickly became devalued, giving rise to the phrase "not worth a Continental."

**1781 Nation's First Bank.** Also to support the Revolutionary War, the Continental Congress chartered the Bank of North America in Philadelphia as the nation's first "real" bank.

**1785 The Dollar.** The Continental Congress determined that the official monetary system would be based on the dollar, but the first coin representing the start of this system would not be struck for many years.

**1791 First U.S. Bank.** After adoption of the Constitution in 1789, Congress chartered the First Bank of the United States until 1811 and authorized it to issue paper bank notes to eliminate confusion and simplify trade. The bank served as the U.S. Treasury's fiscal agent, thus performing the first central bank functions.

**1792 Monetary System.** The federal monetary system was established with the creation of the U.S. Mint in Philadelphia. The first American coins were struck in 1793.

**1816 Second U.S. Bank.** The Second Bank of the United States was chartered for 20 years until 1836.

**1836 State Bank Notes.** With minimum regulation, a proliferation of 1,600 local state-chartered, private banks now issued paper money. State bank notes, with over 30,000 varieties of color and design, were easily counterfeited. That, along with bank failures, caused confusion and circulation problems.

**1861 Civil War.** On the brink of bankruptcy and pressed to finance the Civil War, Congress authorized the United States Treasury to issue paper money for the first time in the form of non-interest bearing Treasury Notes called Demand Notes.

**1862 Greenbacks.** Demand Notes were replaced by United States Notes. Commonly called "greenbacks," they were last issued in 1971. The Secretary of the Treasury was empowered by Congress to have notes engraved and printed, which was done by private banknote companies.

**1863 The Design.** The design of U.S. currency incorporated a Treasury seal, the fine line engraving necessary for the difficult-to-counterfeit intaglio printing, intricate geometric lathe work patterns, and distinctive linen paper with embedded red and blue fibers.

**1865 Gold Certificates.** Gold certificates were issued by the Department of the Treasury against gold coin and bullion deposits and were circulated until 1933.

**1865 Secret Service.** The Department of the Treasury established the United States Secret Service to control counterfeits, at that time amounting to one-third of circulated currency.

**1866 National Bank Notes.** National Bank Notes, backed by U.S. government securities, became predominant. By this time, 75 percent of bank deposits were held by nationally chartered banks. As State Bank Notes were replaced, the value of currency stabilized for a time.

**1877 Bureau of Engraving and Printing.** The Department of the Treasury's Bureau of Engraving and Printing started printing all U.S. currency, although other steps were done outside.

**1878 Silver Certificates.** The Department of the Treasury was authorized to issue Silver Certificates in exchange for silver dollars. The last issue was in the Series of 1957.

**1910 Currency Production Consolidated.** The Department of the Treasury's Bureau of Engraving and Printing assumed all currency production functions, including engraving, printing, and processing.

**1913 Federal Reserve Act.** After 1893 and 1907 financial panics, the Federal Reserve Act of 1913 was passed. It created the Federal Reserve System as the nation's central bank to regulate the flow of money and credit for economic stability and growth. The system was authorized to issue Federal Reserve Notes, now the only U.S. currency produced and 99 percent of all currency in circulation.

**1929 Standardized Design.** Currency was reduced in size by 25 percent and standardized with uniform portraits on the faces and emblems and monuments on the backs.

**1957 In God We Trust.** Paper currency was first issued with "In God We Trust" as required by Congress in 1955. The inscription appears on all currency Series 1963 and beyond.

**1990 Security Thread and Microprinting.** A security thread and microprinting were introduced, first in $50 and $100 notes, to deter counterfeiting by advanced copiers and printers.

# COLLECTING PAPER MONEY

Paper money can be a fascinating hobby. Though of more recent origin than coinage, U.S. paper money exists in enormous varieties and can be collected in many ways.

Potential specialties are numerous. The following is not by any means a complete list.

**1. Series collecting.** Here the collector focuses upon a certain series of notes, such as the $5 1863–75 National Bank Notes, and attempts to collect specimens showing each of the different signature combinations, points of issue, seal colors, or whatever varieties happen to exist in the series. This may sound restrictive but, as an examination of the listings in this book will show, most series are comprised of many varieties. Generally, the older the series, the more difficult or expensive will be its completion, while certain series include great rarities beyond the budget range of most collectors. The cost can be brought down somewhat if one does not demand the finest condition but is content to own an example of the note in whatever condition he can reasonably afford. It should be pointed out, though, that in reselling paper money there is generally a greater loss—or smaller profit—on notes whose condition is less than Very Fine.

**2. Set collecting.** Sets are groups of notes of different denominations, issued at the same time (or approximately the same time), which were in current circulation together.

**3. Place or origin collecting.** Collecting notes by the city whose Federal Reserve Bank issued them.

**4. Signature collecting.** Collecting one specimen of every note bearing the signature of a certain Secretary of the Treasury.

**5. Confederate currency collecting.** The notes issued for use within the Confederate States of America during the Civil War.

**6. Portrait collecting.** By the individual or individuals depicted on the note. This is sometimes known as topical collecting.

**7. Freak and oddity collecting.**

**8. Fractional currency collecting.**

Imagination, especially if placed into use in a coin shop well stocked with paper money, will suggest further possibilities. All is fair; there are no strict rules on what makes a worthwhile collection, so long as the material included is not seriously defective or of questionable authenticity.

Don't expect to build a large collection rapidly. Paper money is not comparable to stamps, where a beginner can buy a packet of 1,000 different stamps and instantly have a sizable collection. Nor should the size of a collection be regarded as a mark of its desirability or worth. Many prizewinning collections contain fewer than a hundred pieces; some consist of only two or three dozen. Direction and quality count much more in this hobby than weight of numbers. Collectors seeking to own a large collection generally end up with one whose only recommendation is its size. It may impress beginners but is not likely to be regarded highly by more experienced collectors.

# Pcda

# PROFESSIONAL CURRENCY DEALERS ASSOCIATION

Looking for a reliable paper money dealer? . . . Collecting rare paper money can be an enjoyable hobby. Imagine being able to own an example of fractional currency printed during the Civil War era, or a National Bank Note issued by a financial institution in your own state.

Whatever your collecting interests, the members of the Professional Currency Dealers Association will be pleased to assist and guide you. The members of this prestigious trade association specialize in virtually all the areas of paper money collecting.

Once you've started to collect, it can sometimes be a challenge to locate a dealer with a significant inventory. Members of the Professional Currency Dealers Association are the market makers for currency collectors. Whatever your interest, a PCDA member is certain to be able to supply you. Whether you are a beginner on a limited budget or an advanced collector of many years' experience, you can be certain that you'll find fair, courteous, and reliable treatment with a member of the Professional Currency Dealers Association.

For a free copy of the PCDA membership directory, write to:

Professional Currency Dealers Association
P.O. Box 573
Milwaukee, WI 53201

Your personal copy of the PCDA directory, listing members by their specialty areas, will be sent to you promptly via first class mail.

# THE SOCIETY OF PAPER
# MONEY COLLECTORS

The Society of Paper Money Collectors invites you to become a member of our organization. SPMC was founded in 1961 with the following objectives: encourage the collecting and study of paper money and all financial documents; cultivate fraternal collector relations; furnish information and knowledge; encourage research about paper money and financial documents and publish the resulting information; promote legislation favorable to collectors; advance the prestige of the hobby of numismatics; promote rational classification of exhibits and encourage participation by our members; encourage realistic and consistent market valuations.

The bimonthly magazine *Paper Money* is issued to all members. For a sample copy and membership information, write to:

Ron Horstman
P.O. Box 6011
St. Louis, MO 63139

# RECOGNIZING THE VALUABLE NOTES

Every note ever issued by the United States government is worth, at minimum, its face value. This applies even to notes of which one-third is missing. Whether a note is worth *more* than its face value—to collectors and dealers in paper currency—depends chiefly upon its age, condition, scarcity, and popularity among hobbyists.

All obsolete notes (such as Silver Certificates) are worth more than face value when the condition is "crisp uncirculated" (or CU as it is called by collectors). Many notes, hundreds in fact, have premium value even in lower grades of condition due to their scarcity. The premium on a collectible note may be double or triple face value or more. There are early $1 notes worth more than one thousand times face value. While 19th-century notes tend to be more valuable, as fewer were printed and saved, notes of considerable value did occur among those of the 20th century.

A note may be valuable as the result of belonging to a series in which all had limited printings, such as the historic 1862 United States Note. This type of valuable note is, of course, the easiest for a beginner to recognize, as the notes look very different compared to those of the present day.

Conveniently, notes have dates on them, and an early date is yet another indicator of possible value. But even without dates and size differences there would be little difficulty in distinguishing an early note. The earlier the note, the more it will differ in design, color, and other details from later currency. It may picture an individual no longer shown on notes, such as Robert Fulton, Samuel Morse or James Garfield. It may have the portrait on the back instead of the front. The portrait may be to one side rather than centered. The serial numbers may not be where they are normally found. Such notes are instantly recognizable as being very old. They, in fact, look so unlike modern currency that some non-collectors take them for stock or bonds or something other than legal tender.

A non-collector often believes that the value of old paper money is linked to its serial numbers. While a serial number can contribute to value, it is well down the list of ingredients for valuable notes. Among specimens of very high value, the serial number is hardly ever of consequence.

What is? Quite often the signatures. The signatures on a note play a very considerable role in the collector's world. If notes did not carry signatures, or if the signatures were never changed, the paper money hobby would be a mere shadow of what it is today. To cite just one example, the 1902 series of $10 National Bank Notes without dates yielded fifteen different varieties for the hobbyist to collect. Every one of them is a signature variety! Take away the signatures and all would be identical. Nothing changed but the signatures, yet they changed fifteen times. A rarity was created, too: the Jones-Woods combination is worth about three times as much as any of the other fourteen. If you did not look at the signatures and were unaware of the rarity of this particular combination, you would surely fail to pick this note out of a batch of 1902 $10 National Bank Notes. There is absolutely nothing remarkable by which to notice it.

There are many other notes on which the signatures are vitally important. The 1875 Bruce-Jordan combination on the $5 National Bank Note is so rare that pricing it is difficult. The other eight signature combinations from this series, while definitely of value, are not in that class.

The color of the seal, which has varied on notes in the 19th and 20th centuries, is seldom a major factor in value. In most cases where it appears to be a factor, some other element is, in fact, responsible for the note's value. An example of this is the $2 United States Note of 1878 with red seal and signatures of Scofield and Gilfillan. It is quite a bit more valuable than any $2 U.S. Note with a brown seal, leading many people to think that the seal color is a factor in its value. The rarity of this note derives from the signature combination. Another was issued with the same date and same red seal, but with signatures of Allison and Gilfillan. Its value is less than one-tenth as much.

However, there are a few cases in which the seal color makes a great difference in value, so it should not be totally dismissed. The $1 United States Note of 1878 with a maroon seal is valuable, while the same note with a red seal—identical in all other respects—is worth sharply less.

The date appearing on a note can be a value factor, not just by indicating the note's age. There may be two or more variations of the note that are distinguished by the date. In the case of Federal Reserve Notes (the only notes still being printed), the district of origin can influence their value. In some series there were not as many printed for Kansas City or Dallas as for New York or Chicago, and the scarcer ones have gained an edge in collector appeal and value. This applies to an even greater extent among National Bank Notes, which involved literally thousands of local banks across the country.

It's safe to say that paper money should be carefully examined. When examined by a person who knows what he's looking for, there is little chance of a rarity slipping by undetected.

# BUYING PAPER MONEY

Browsing in coin shops is the usual way in which beginners start buying paper money. Just about every coin dealer—and many stamp dealers—stock paper money to one degree or another, from a single display album with elementary material to vaults filled with literally millions of dollars worth of specimens. Be observant of condition when shopping from dealers' stocks. There is really no excuse for unsatisfactory purchases from shops—the buyer has ample opportunity for inspection. Don't buy in a rush. Get to know the dealer and become familiar with his grading practices. Some dealers will grade a specimen higher than another dealer, but this may be offset by the fact that they charge a lower price.

**Bargains.** Is it possible to get bargains in buying paper money? To the extent that prices vary somewhat from dealer to dealer, yes. But if you're talking about finding a note worth $100 selling at $50, this is unlikely to happen. The dealers are well aware of market values, and the slight price differences that do occur are merely the result of some dealers being overstocked on certain notes or, possibly, having made a very good "buy" from the public. What may appear to be a bargain will generally prove, on closer examination, to be a specimen in undesirable condition, such as a washed bill on which the color has faded.

**Auction sales.** Many coin auctions feature selections of paper money, and there are occasional sales (mostly of the postal-bid variety) devoted exclusively to it. There is much to be said for auction buying if you have some experience and know how to read an auction catalog.

**Shows and conventions.** Paper money is offered for sale at every coin show and exposition. These present excellent opportunities to buy, as the dealers exhibiting at such shows are generally out-of-towners whose stock you would not otherwise have a chance to examine. As many sellers are likely to be offering the same type of material, you have the opportunity to make price and condition comparisons before buying.

# CARING FOR YOUR COLLECTION

Paper money is not at all difficult to care for, store and display attractively. It consumes little space and, unlike many other collectors' items, runs no risk of breakage. Nevertheless, it is important that the hobbyist give some attention to maintenance, as a poorly kept collection soon becomes aimless clutter and provides little enjoyment.

There is not much question that albums are the favorite storage method of nearly all paper money enthusiasts. In the days before specially made albums with vinyl pocket-pages, collectors used ordinary scrapbooks and mounted their specimens with philatelic hinges or photo corners. This, of course, may still be done, but such collections do not have the advantage of displaying both sides of the notes. Furthermore, the use of gummed hinges may leave marks upon removal, whereas specimens may be removed and reinserted into vinyl-page albums without causing the slightest blemish. We especially recommend the albums and "currency wallet" sold by Anco Coin & Stamp Supply, P. O. Box 782, Florence, Alabama 35630.

**Faded color.** There is no known restorative for faded color.

**Holes.** It is suggested that no effort be undertaken to repair holes, as this will almost certainly result in a further reduction in value.

**Missing corners.** Missing corners can seldom be restored in a manner that is totally satisfactory. The best that can be done is to secure some paper of approximately the same color and texture, trim a small piece to the proper size, and glue it in place as described below. If a portion of printed matter is missing, this can be hand-drawn, in ink, after restoration. Obviously, this kind of repair is not carried out to "fool" anybody, but simply to give a damaged specimen a less objectionable appearance.

**Repairs to paper money.** Repair work on damaged or defaced paper money is carried out strictly for cosmetic purposes; to improve its physical appearance. Repairs, even if skillfully executed, will not enhance the value of a specimen, as it will still be classified as defective. Amateurish repair efforts can very possibly make matters worse.

**Tears.** Tears can be closed by brushing a very small quantity of clear-drying glue to both sides of the tear, placing the note between sheets of waxed kitchen paper and setting it under a weight to dry. A dictionary of moderate size serves this function well. Allow plenty of drying time and handle gently thereafter.

**Wrinkles.** Wrinkles, creases and the like can sometimes be improved by wetting the note (in plain water) and drying it between sheets of waxed paper beneath a reasonably heavy weight—five pounds or more. This should not be done with a modern or recent specimen if there is danger of losing crispness.

Many ills to which paper money falls prey result from not being housed in a suitable album, or any album at all. Framing and mounting present some risk, as the item may then be exposed to long periods of direct sunlight, almost sure to cause fading or "bleaching" of its color.

# SELLING YOUR COLLECTION

**Selling to a dealer.** All dealers in paper money buy from the public, but not all buy every collection offered to them. Some are specialists and are interested only in collections within their fields of specialization. Some will not purchase (or even examine) collections worth under $100, or $500, or whatever their line of demarcation happens to be. Obviously, a valuable collection containing many hard-to-get notes in VF or UNC condition is easier to interest a dealer in than a beginner-type collection. If a dealer is interested enough to make an offer, this is no guarantee that another dealer would not offer more. In the case of a collection worth $50,000, offers from several dealers might vary by as much as $5,000. This is not an indication that the dealer making the lowest offer is unscrupulous. Dealers will pay as much as the material is worth to them, and one dealer may be overstocked on items that another badly needs. Or one dealer may have customers for certain material that another doesn't. For this reason it makes good sense, if you choose to sell to a dealer, to obtain several offers before accepting any. But should you sell to a dealer at all? The chief advantage is quick payment and reduced risk. The price may not be as high as would be obtained at auction, however, depending on the property's nature and pure luck.

**Selling by auction.** Auction selling presents uncertainties but at the same time offers the possibility of gaining a much better return than could be had by selling to a dealer. It is no easy matter deciding which route to follow. If your collection is better than average, you may be better advised to sell by auction. This will involve a waiting period of, generally, four to six months between consigning the collection and receiving settlement; over the summer months it may be longer. However, some auctioneers will give a cash advance, usually about 25 percent of the sum they believe the material is worth. In special circumstances a larger advance may be made, or the usual terms and conditions altered. One auctioneer paid $100,000 under a special contract, stipulating that the money was not to be returned regardless of the sale's outcome or even if no sale took place. But this was on a million-dollar collection. Auctioneers' commissions vary. The normal is 20 percent, but some houses take 10 percent from the buyer and 10 percent from the seller. This would appear to work to the seller's advantage, but such a practice may discourage bidding and result in lower sales prices.

**Selling to other collectors.** Unless the owner is personally acquainted with a large circle of collectors, this will likely involve running ads in periodicals and "playing dealer," which runs into some expense. Unless you offer material at very favorable prices, you are not apt to be as successful with your ads as are the established dealers, who have a reputation and an established clientele.

# INVESTING

**1.** Buy only specimens in V.F. (Very Fine) or better condition.

**2.** Be sure the notes you buy are properly graded and priced in accordance with their grade.

**3.** Avoid Federal Reserve Notes of the past thirty years. These have been stockpiled by dealers to such an extent that their value is not likely to show dramatic increase.

**4.** For investment purposes it is usually wise to avoid the very highly specialized types of notes. Investment success depends on continued growth of the hobby, and most new collectors will buy the standard items.

**5.** Do not seek quick profits. It is rare for an investment profit on paper currency to occur in less than five years. When holding five years or longer, the possibility of a profit is much greater.

**6.** Notes recommended by their sellers as investments are sometimes the worst investments. Learn about the paper money market and make your own selections.

**7.** Do not invest more than you can afford. Tying up too much capital in investments of any kind can be hazardous.

# GLOSSARY

## BROKEN BANK NOTE (sometimes referred to as "obsolete notes")

Literally, a broken bank note is a note issued by a "broken" bank—a bank that failed and whose obligations could therefore not be redeemed. It may be presumed, by those who recall passing of legislation establishing the Federal Deposit Insurance Corporation, that banks failed only in the financial panic of 1929. During the 19th century, bank failures were common, especially in western and southwestern states. These were generally small organizations set up in frontier towns which suffered either from mismanagement or a sudden decline in the town's fortunes. Some collectors make a specialty of broken bank notes.

## DEMAND NOTES

Demand Notes have the distinction of being the first official circulating paper currency of this country, issued in 1861. There are three denominations: five, ten and twenty dollars, each bearing its own design on front and back. Demand Notes arose out of the coinage shortage brought about by the Civil War. A total of $60,000,000 in Demand Notes was authorized to be printed, amounting to several million individual specimens. Though this was an extraordinary number for the time, it was small compared to modern output, and only a fraction of the total survived. These notes were signed not by any specially designated Treasury Department officers, but a battery of employees, each of whom was given authority to sign and affix his name by hand in a slow assembly-line process, two signatures to each note. Originally the spaces left blank for signatures were marked "Register of the Treasury" and "Treasurer of the United States." As the persons actually signing occupied neither of these offices, they were obliged to perpetually add "for the . . ." to their signatures. In an effort to relieve their tedium, fresh plates were prepared reading "For the Register of the Treasury" and "For the Treasurer of the United States," which required nothing but a signature. This created a rarity status for the earlier specimens, which are now very desirable collectors' items.

## ENGRAVING

Engraving is the process by which designs are printed on U.S. paper money. Engraving involves the use of a metal plate, traditionally copper, into which the design is drawn or scraped with sharp-bladed instruments. Ink is smeared over the surface and allowed to work into the grooves or lines comprising the design. The ink is then cleaned away from raised portions (intended to show blank in the printing). The engraving is pressed against a sheet of moistened paper, and the ink left in these grooves transfers to the paper, resulting in a printed image. When done by modern rotary press, it's a fast-moving process.

## FEDERAL RESERVE BANK NOTES

Federal Reserve Bank Notes were issued briefly in 1915 and 1918. Like National Bank Notes they were secured by bonds or securities placed on deposit by each Federal Reserve Bank with the U.S. government. While issued and redeemable by the member banks of the Federal Reserve system, these notes are secured by—and are obligations of—the government.

## FEDERAL RESERVE NOTES

Federal Reserve Notes, the notes in current circulation, were authorized by the Federal Reserve Act of December 23,

1913. Issued under control of the Federal Reserve Board, these notes are released through twelve Federal Reserve Banks in various parts of the country. Originally they were redeemable in gold at the United States Treasury or "lawful money" (coins) at a Federal Reserve Bank. In 1934 the option of redemption for gold was removed.

## FREAK AND ERROR NOTES

Bills which, by virtue of error or accident, are in some respect different from normal specimens. See the section on Freak and Error Notes.

## GOLD CERTIFICATES

When gold coinage became a significant medium of exchange, the government decided to hold aside quantities of it and issue paper notes redeemable by the Treasury Department. The first Gold Certificates for public circulation were released in 1882. The series lasted until the era of small-size currency, ending in 1928. In 1933 all were ordered returned to the Treasury Department for redemption, including those in possession of collectors. A new law in 1964 permitted their ownership by collectors, though they can no longer be redeemed for gold.

## LARGE-SIZE CURRENCY

Large-size currency is the term generally used to refer to U.S. notes issued up to 1929, which were somewhat larger in size than those printed subsequently. The increased size permitted more elaborate design, which seldom fails to endear large-size currency to beginners. Some of the earlier examples (especially of the 1870s, 1880s, and 1890s) are works of art. Though economic considerations were mainly responsible for the switch to a reduced size, there is no doubt that today's notes are far more convenient to handle and carry. Large-size notes are sometimes referred to as "bedsheet notes."

## NATIONAL BANK NOTES

This is the largest group of notes available to the collector. They were issued from 1863 to 1929 and present collecting potential that can only be termed vast. More than 14,000 banks issued notes, in all parts of the country. While the approach to collecting them is usually regional, sets and series can also be built up, virtually without end. The National Banking Act was instituted in 1863, during the Civil War, to permit chartered banks to issue and circulate their own currency. Printing was done at the U.S. Government Printing Office and the designs were all alike, differing only in names of the banks, state seals, bank signatures and the bank's charter number. Each charter bank was limited to issuing currency up to 90 percent of the value of bonds that it kept on deposit with the government. Charters remained in force for 20 years and could be renewed for an additional 20 years. National Bank Notes circulated in the same fashion as conventional currency and, thanks to the bond-deposit system, gained public confidence. The financial panic of 1929, which brought ruin or near-ruin to many banks, put an end to National Bank Notes.

## NATIONAL GOLD BANK NOTES

These notes were issued exclusively by California banks during the 1870s under the same terms as ordinary National Bank Notes, their values backed by bonds deposited with the government. Events surrounding their origins form a unique chapter in the history of American economy. Following the discoveries of substantial quantities of gold in California in the late 1840s, that metal soon became the chief medium of local exchange, largely because it was more readily available in that remote region than coinage. Later, when gold coins and tokens began to circulate heavily in California, banks became so swamped with them that they petitioned Washington for authority to issue Gold Notes that could be substituted for the actual coinage. On July 12, 1870, Congress voted favorably on this meas-ure, giving the right to issue such notes to nine banks in California and one in Boston. The Boston bank, Kidder National Gold Bank, appears not to have exercised its right, as no Gold

Notes of this institution have been recorded. The California banks wasted no time in exercising their authority, the result being a series of notes ranging from five to five hundred dollars in denomination. All were printed on yellow-toned paper so as to be instantly identifiable. The banks issuing these notes were permitted to redeem them in gold coins.

## REFUNDING CERTIFICATES

Refunding Certificates, a sort of hybrid between currency and bonds or securities, were issued under a Congressional Act of February 26, 1879. These were notes with a ten-dollar face value which could be spent and exchanged in the fashion of ordinary money but drew interest at the rate of 4 percent per year. The purposes behind Refunding Certificates were several. They were chiefly designed to encourage saving and thereby curb inflation, which even at that time was becoming a problem. Also, they provided a safe means of saving for persons who distrusted banks (safe so long as the certificates were not lost or stolen), and, probably more important, were readily obtainable in areas of the country not well served by banks. In 1907 the interest was halted. Their redemption value today, with interest, is $21.30.

## SERIAL NUMBER

The serial number is the control number placed on all U.S. paper bills, appearing below left-center and above right-center. No two bills in the same series bear repetitive serial numbers. The use of serial numbers is not only an aid in counting and sorting bills as printed, but a deterrent to counterfeiting.

## SIGNATURES

The inclusion of signatures of Treasury Department officials on our paper bills, a practice as old as our currency (1861), began as a mark of authorization and as a foil to counterfeiters. The belief was that the handwriting would be more difficult to copy than an engraved design. Persons whose signatures appear on notes did not always occupy the same office. From 1862 to 1923, the two signers were the Treasurer and the Register (or Registrar as it appears in old writings) of the Treasury. Subsequently, the Treasurer and the Secretary of the Treasury were represented. These signatures are of great importance to collectors, as some notes are relatively common with certain combinations of signatures and others are rare. A "series" collection is not considered complete until one obtains every existing combination, even though the specimens may be in other respects identical.

## SILVER CERTIFICATES

Silver Certificates were authorized in 1878. America's economy was booming at that time, and the demand for silver coinage in day-to-day business transactions outdistanced the supply. Silver Certificates were not intend-ed to replace coinage but to create a convenient medium of exchange, whereby the government held specific quantities of Silver Dollars (later bullion) and agreed to redeem the notes or certificates against them. In 1934 the Treasury Department ceased redemption of these notes in Silver Dollars, and on June 24, 1968, redemption in all forms was ended. The notes are still, however, legal tender at their face value. When printing of Silver Certificates was discon-tinued, a flurry of speculation arose and many persons began hoarding them. This was done not only in hope of eventual redemption for bullion but the belief that such notes would become valuable to collectors. Though Silver Certificates are popular with hobbyists, they have not increased sufficiently in price to yield speculators any great profits—especially since many collectors saved specimens in circulated condition.

## STAR NOTES

United States Notes, Silver Certificates, and Gold Certificates sometimes have a star or asterisk in place of the letter in front of the serial number. Federal Reserve Notes and Federal Reserve Bank Notes have it at the end of the serial number. These notes are known as "Star Notes."

When a note is mutilated or otherwise unfit for issue, it must be replaced. To replace it with a note of the same serial numbers would be impractical, and "Star Notes" are therefore substituted. Other than having their own special serial number and a star, these notes are the same as the others. On United States Notes and Silver Certificates, the star is substituted for the prefix letter; on Federal Reserve Notes, for the suffix letter. All defective notes are accounted for and destroyed by burning them in an incinerator.

Large stars after the serial number on the 1869 series of United States notes, and 1890 and 1891 Treasury Notes, do not signify replacement notes as are known in later and present day "Star Notes."

Serial numbers on early large-size notes were preceded by a letter and were ended by various odd characters or symbols. These characters are not known to have any significance, except to show that the number was terminated, and prevented any elimination or addition of digits. The suffix characters were replaced by alphabet letters on later issues of notes.

## TREASURY OR COIN NOTES

Treasury Notes were authorized by Congress in 1890. Their official title was Coin Notes, as they could be redeemed for silver or gold coins. The series did not prove popular and was discontinued after the issue of 1891.

## TREASURY SEAL

The Treasury Seal is the official emblem of the U.S. Treasury Department, which has appeared on all our currency since 1862. It is missing only from the early Demand Notes, issued in 1861, and some Fractional Currency. Two versions have been employed, distinguished readily by the fact that one (the original) bears a Latin inscription, while the current Treasury Seal is in English. The basic motif is the same, a badge displaying scales and a key. The original Seal, somewhat more decorative, was in use until 1968.

# UNITED STATES NOTES

Also known as Legal Tender Notes, this substantial and ambitious series followed Demand Notes and constitutes the second earliest variety of U.S. paper currency. There are five distinct issues, running from 1862 to 1923. Though United States Notes are all "large size" and their designs not very similar to those in present use, they show in their successive stages the evolutionary advance from this nation's first efforts at paper money to its currency of today. The first issue is dated March 10, 1862. Denominations are $1, $2, $5, $10, $20, $50, $100, $500, $1,000, $5,000 and $10,000. Individuals portrayed included not only Presidents but other government officials: Salmon P. Chase (Lincoln's Secretary of the Treasury), Daniel Webster, and Lewis and Clark. Some of the reverse designs are masterpieces of geometrical linework. A number of rarities are to be found among Legal Tender Notes, but in general the lower denominations can be collected without great expense.

# WILDCAT NOTES

Wildcat notes are the notes that were issued by so-called "Wildcat Banks," in the era of State Bank Notes before the Civil War. Numerous banks sprang up around the middle part of the 19th century, mostly in the west and southwest, operated by persons of questionable integrity. Some never had capital backing and were instituted purely as a front for confidence swindles. After issuing notes, the bank shut down, its directors disappeared, and owners of the notes were left with worthless paper. As news traveled slowly in those days, the same persons could move from town to town and work the scheme repeatedly. Notes issued by these banks, or any banks that became insolvent, are also called Broken Bank Notes. Apparently the origin of the term "wildcat" derives from public sentiment of the time, which held that owners of such banks had no greater trustworthiness than a wild animal. "Wildcat" may also refer to the rapid movement of swindling bank officials from one locality to another.

# CURRENCY TERMS

Check Letter and Quadrant Number

Federal Reserve District Seal

Serial Number

Treasury Seal

District Numbers

Serial Number

Series

Check Letter and Plate Check Number

# DEPARTMENT OF THE TREASURY, BUREAU OF ENGRAVING AND PRINTING

*Reprinted with permission of the Department of the Treasury, Bureau of Printing and Engraving.*

## THE U.S. GOVERNMENT'S SECURITY PRINTER

- Since October 1, 1877, all United States currency has been printed by the Bureau of Engraving and Printing, which started out as a six-person operation using steam powered presses in the Department of Treasury's basement.
- Now 2,300 Bureau employees occupy 25 acres of floor space in two Washington, D.C. buildings flanking 14th Street. Currency and stamps are designed, engraved, and printed 24 hours a day on 30 high-speed presses. A new state-of-the-art Fort Worth, Texas, Western Currency Facility adds to the nation's currency production capacity.
- In 1990, at a cost of 2.6 cents each, over 7 billion notes worth about $82 billion will be produced for circulation by the Federal Reserve System. Ninety-five percent will replace unfit notes and five percent will support economic growth. At any one time, $200 million in notes may be in production.
- Notes currently produced are the $1 (45 percent of production time), $5 and $10 (12 percent each), $20 (26 percent), $50 (2 percent), and $100 (3 percent).
- The Bureau also prints White House invitations and some 500 engraved items, such as visa counterfoils, naturalization documents, commissions, and certificates for almost 75 Federal departments and agencies.

## TOURS

- The Bureau of Engraving and Printing is one of the most popular tourist stops in Washington—over 500 thousand visit the printing facility each year.
- Free 20-minute, self-guided tours may be taken Monday through Friday, 9 A.M. to 2 P.M., except for Federal holidays and the week between Christmas and New Year's. Tours start on Raoul Wallenberg Place (formerly 15th Street).
- Visitors can see press runs of 32-note currency sheets, Federal Reserve and Treasury seals applied, examiners ensuring high-quality notes, and 4,000 note "bricks" readied for distribution to Federal Reserve banks.

## VISITORS CENTER

- At the Visitors Center, history, production, and counterfeit exhibits showcase interesting information about United States currency.
- Many unique items, such as uncut currency sheets of 32, 16, or 4 one dollar notes; $1 bags of $150 worth of shredded currency; engraved collectors' prints; souvenir cards; and Department of the Interior Duck Stamps, may be purchased at the sales counter.

## MAIL ORDER SALES

- Persons wishing to receive notices on new Bureau products or to order by mail can write: Mail Order Sales, Bureau of Engraving and Printing, 14th and C Streets, S.W., Room 602-11A, Washington, D.C. 20228.

# THE FEDERAL
# RESERVE BANKS

The Federal Reserve system is divided into 12 Federal Reserve districts, in each of which is a Federal Reserve Bank. There are also 24 branches. Each district is designated by a number and the corresponding letter of the alphabet. The district numbers, the cities in which the 12 banks are located, and the letter symbols are:

| | | |
|---|---|---|
| 1-A—Boston | 5-E—Richmond | 9-I—Minneapolis |
| 2-B—New York | 6-F—Atlanta | 10-J—Kansas City |
| 3-C—Philadelphia | 7-G—Chicago | 11-K—Dallas |
| 4-D—Cleveland | 8-H—St. Louis | 12-L—San Francisco |

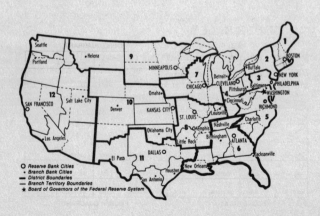

○ Reserve Bank Cities
• Branch Bank Cities
— District Boundaries
— Branch Territory Boundaries
★ Board of Governors of the Federal Reserve System

# 32 SUBJECT SHEET LAYOUT

All United States currency is now printed with 32 subjects (notes) to a large sheet. The first printing is the green back. The second printing is the face of the note, in black. This includes the portrait and border, the series year, the check letter and quadrant number, two signatures and the face plate number. The sheet is then cut in half vertically for the third printing. This includes the black Federal Reserve seal, the four Federal Reserve district numbers, the green Treasury seal and two green serial numbers.

The 32 subject sheet is divided into four quarters called quadrants for numbering and other controls. Each quadrant has its own numbering sequence for the eight notes, with serial numbers advancing by 20,000 to the next note. The quadrant number and check letter in the upper left section indicate the first, second, third or fourth quadrant and the

| FIRST QUADRANT | | | | THIRD QUADRANT | | | |
|---|---|---|---|---|---|---|---|
| A1 | | E1 | | A3 | | E3 | |
| A00000001A | A100 | A00080001A | E100 | A00320001A | A100 | A00400001A | E100 |
| B1 | | F1 | | B3 | | F3 | |
| A00020001A | B100 | A00100001A | F100 | A00340001A | B100 | A00420001A | F100 |
| C1 | | G1 | | C3 | | G3 | |
| A00040001A | C100 | A00120001A | G100 | A00360001A | C100 | A00440001A | G100 |
| D1 | | H1 | | D3 | | H3 | |
| A00060001A | D100 | A00140001A | H100 | A00380001A | D100 | A004600001A | H100 |
| A2 | | E2 | | A4 | | E4 | |
| A00160001A | A100 | A00240001A | E100 | A00480001A | A100 | A005600001A | E100 |
| B2 | | F2 | | B4 | | F4 | |
| A00180001A | B100 | A00260001A | F100 | A00500001A | B100 | A00580001A | F100 |
| C2 | | G2 | | C4 | | G4 | |
| A00200001A | C100 | A00280001A | G100 | A0050001A | C100 | A00600001A | G100 |
| D2 | | H2 | | D4 | | H4 | |
| A00220001A | D100 | A00300001A | H100 | A00540001A | D100 | A00620001A | H100 |

SECOND QUADRANT      FOURTH QUADRANT

position of the note in the quadrant. In the lower right corner the position letter is shown again with a plate number. On the back of the note the same small number in the lower right is the back plate number.

# THE NUMBERING SYSTEM
# OF UNITED STATES
# PAPER CURRENCY

The system of numbering paper money must be adequate to accommodate a large volume of notes. For security and accountability purposes, no two notes of any one class, denomination and series may have the same serial number. The two serial numbers on each note have a full complement of eight digits and an alphabetical prefix and suffix letter. When necessary, ciphers are used at the left of the number to make a total of eight digits.

Whenever a numbering sequence is initiated for United States Notes or Silver Certificates, the first note is numbered A 00 000 001 A; the second A 00 000 002 A; the hundredth A 00 000 100 A; the thousandth A 00 001 000 A; and so on through A 99 999 999 A. The suffix letter A will remain the same until a total of 25 groups, or "blocks" of 99 999 999 notes are numbered, each group having a different prefix letter of the alphabet from A to Z. The letter "O" is omitted, either as a prefix or as a suffix, because of its similarity to zero. The 100 000 000th note in each group will be a Star Note, since eight digits are the maximum in the mechanical operation of numbering machines.

At this point, the suffix letter changes to B for the next 25 groups of 99 999 999 notes, and proceeds in the same manner as the suffix letter. A. A total of 62,500,000,000 notes could be numbered before a duplication of serial numbers would occur. However, it has never been required to number that many notes of any one class, denomination and series.

The Federal Reserve Notes printed for the 12 districts are numbered in the same progression as United States Notes and Silver Certificates, except that a specific alphabetical letter identifies a specific Federal Reserve district. The letter identifying each district is used as a prefix letter at the beginning of the serial numbers on all Federal Reserve Notes and does not change. Only the suffix letter changes in the serial numbers on Federal Reserve currency.

# PORTRAITS AND BACK DESIGN ON SMALL-SIZE NOTES

| DENOMINATION | PORTRAIT | BACK DESIGN |
|---|---|---|
| $1.00 | Washington | Great Seal of the United States |
| $2.00 | Jefferson | Monticello |
| $5.00 | Lincoln | Lincoln Memorial |
| $10.00 | Hamilton | United States Treasury |
| $20.00 | Jackson | The White House |
| $50.00 | Grant | United States Capitol |
| $100.00 | Franklin | Independence Hall |
| $500.00 | McKinley | "FIVE HUNDRED" |
| $1000.00 | Cleveland | "ONE THOUSAND" |
| $5000.00 | Madison | "FIVE THOUSAND" |
| $10,000.00 | Chase | "TEN THOUSAND" |
| $100,000.00 | Wilson | "ONE HUNDRED THOUSAND" |

# DATING U.S. CURRENCY

Unlike coins, the date is not changed each year on United States currency.

The date appearing on all notes, large or small, is that of the year in which the design was first approved or issued. For instance, large-size One Dollar United States Notes of the series 1880 were issued with the same date until the new series of 1917 was issued. There was no further date change until the series of 1923.

The same rule applies to small-size notes. However, in this case a letter is added after the date to designate or indicate a minor change in the main design or probably a change in one or both of the signatures. For example: the One Dollar Silver Certificate of 1935 was changed to 1935-A because of a change in the size of the tiny plate numbers appearing in the lower right corners of the face and back of the note. It was changed again from 1935-A to 1935-B in 1945 when the signatures of Julian/Morganthau were changed to Julian/Vinson. Subsequent changes in signatures continued in the 1935 series to the year 1963 when the signatures of Smith/Dillon terminated the issue with the series of 1935-H. Therefore, these notes were issued for 28 years bearing the date 1935.

# NEW TREASURY SEAL

**FORMER DESIGN:**
The former design had the Latin inscription: "Thesaur. Amer. Septent. Sigil.," which has several translations. It was the Seal of the North American Treasury.

**NEW DESIGN:**
This new design drops the Latin and states "The Department of The Treasury, 1789." First used on the $100 Note of the Series of 1966.

# GRADES AND CONDITIONS OF PAPER MONEY

## CONDITION

The physical condition of a note or bill plays an important role in determining its value. There are many notes that have no premium value beyond face value in ordinary condition but are valuable or moderately valuable when uncirculated. Even in the case of scarce early specimens, the price given for an "average" example is generally much less than that commanded by Fine or Very Fine Condition.

## Defects encountered in paper money include:

**Creases, folds, wrinkles.** Generally the characteristic that distinguishes uncirculated notes from those that almost—but not quite—qualify for such designation is a barely noticeable crease running approximately down the center vertically, resulting from the note being folded for insertion into a wallet or billfold. It may be possible, through manipulation or storage beneath a heavy weight, to remove evidence of the crease; but the knowledge that it once existed cannot be obliterated.

**Discoloration.** Discoloration is not as easy to recognize as most defects, but it must be classed as one. A distinction should be made between notes printed from underinked rollers and those which originally were normally colored but became "washed out." Sometimes washing is indeed the cause; a well-intentioned collector will bathe a note, attempting to clean it, with the result that its color is no longer strong. This should not happen if warm water is used, without strong cleanser. Atmospheric conditions may play some part in discoloration.

**Foxing.** Fox spots may sometimes be observed on old notes, especially those of the pre-1890 era, just as on old paper in general. They seem more common to foreign currency than American, but their presence on our notes is certainly not rare. These are tiny brownish-red dots, caused by an infestation of lice attacking the paper fibers.

**Holes.** Holes are more likely to be encountered in early paper money than specimens of recent origin. In early years it was customary for federal reserve banks to use wire clips in making up bundles of notes for distribution to banking organizations, and these clips or staples often pierced the bills. Another common occurrence years ago was the practice of shop clerks and cashiers in general to impale notes upon holders consisting of nails mounted on stands.

**Missing pieces.** Missing pieces are a highly undesirable defect which, except in the case of rare specimens, renders the item valueless to collectors. Even if only a blank unprinted corner is torn away, this is called a missing-piece note and hardly anyone will give it a second glance.

**Stains.** Notes sometimes become stained with ink or other liquids. If the specimen is commonplace and easily obtainable in VF or Uncirculated condition, it will be worthless with any kind of stain. In a note of moderate value, its price will be hurt to a greater or lesser degree depending on the stain's intensity, size, nature, and the area it touches. A stain in an outer margin or at a corner is not so objectionable as one occurring at the center or across a signature or serial number. Ink stains, because of their strong color, are generally deemed the worst, but bad staining can also be caused by oil, crayon, "magic marker" and food substances. Pencil markings, which frequently are found on bank notes, will yield to ordinary erasing with a piece of soft "artgum" worked gently over the surface and brushed away with an artist's camel-hair brush. Most other stains cannot be so easily removed. With ink there is no hope, as any caustic sufficiently strong to remove the ink will also injure the printing and possibly eat through the paper as well. Oil stains can sometimes be lightened, though not removed, by sprinkling the note on both sides (even if the stain shows only on one) with talcum powder or other absorbent powder, placing it between sheets of waxed kitchen paper, and leaving it beneath a heavy weight for several days in a room where the humidity is not unduly high.

**Tears.** Tears in notes are very common defects, which may be minute or run nearly the whole length of the bill. As a rule the paper on which American currency is printed is fairly rugged and will not tear as readily as most ordinary paper, but given careless or hurried handling anything is possible. An old worn note is more apt to tear in handling than a new one. Repaired tears are more common in the world of paper money collecting than may be generally supposed. A clean tear—one which does not involve loss of surface—can be patched up so as to become virtually unnoticed, unless examined against a light or through a strong magnifying glass. X-ray examination will reveal repairs when all else fails.

## CONDITION STANDARDS

The following condition standards have been used throughout this book and, with slight variations depending upon individual interpretation, are generally current in the trade.

**Uncirculated—UNC.** A specimen that for all appearances has not been handled or passed through general circulation; a crisp fresh note in "bank" condition. There may be minor blemishes, such as a finger smudge or pinhole, but if these are in any respect severe the condition merits description as "almost uncirculated." There is not much satisfaction to be taken in a note fresh and crisp that has gaping holes and fingerprints. Obviously, an 1870 "uncirculated" note should not be expected to match a 1970 in appearance or feel.

**Almost Uncirculated—A.U.** In the case of modern or semi-modern notes, this is generally taken to mean a specimen that shows no evidence of having passed through general circulation but because of some detraction fails to measure up to a rating of "uncirculated." The problem may be finger smudges, counting crinkles, a light crease, a fold along one or more of the corners, or pinholes. But if more than one of these impairments is present, the item would surely not deserve a classification of "almost uncirculated."

**Extremely Fine—X.F.** A note exhibiting little evidence of wear from handling, but not so perfect or near-perfect as to qualify for a rating of "uncirculated" or "almost uncirculated." On a used note issued before 1900 there may be clear evidence of circulation, but no disfiguring marks.

**Very Fine—V.F.** A very fine note has experienced some circulation but escaped without "being mangled." It is still clean and crisp, and its creases are not offensive.

**Fine—F.** Here the scale begins sliding down. It is obvious that, being the fifth in rank of condition grades, "fine" notes are quite a good deal removed from "uncirculated." They have been handed around pretty thoroughly and suffered the normal consequences, but still are without serious blemishes such as tears, missing corners, serious stains or holes.

**Very Good—V.G.** A well-circulated note bearing evidence of much folding, creasing and wrinkling. It may possibly be lightly stained, smudged or pin punctured, but major defects—such as a torn-off corner—would drop it into an even lower category.

**Good—G.** Heavily circulated, worn notes that are possibly stained or scribbled on, edges could be frayed or "dog-eared." There may be holes larger than pin punctures, but not on the central portion of design. This is the lowest grade of condition acceptable to a collector, and only when nothing better is available. Unless very rare, such specimens are considered space-fillers only.

**A.B.P.—Average Buying Prices.** The average buying prices given here are the approximate sums paid by retail dealers for specimens in good condition. As selling prices vary, so do buying prices, and, in fact, they usually vary a bit more.

# ABOUT THE PRICES
# IN THIS BOOK

Prices shown in the *Official Blackbook Price Guide of United States Paper Money* are compiled from offerings made by dealers and from auction sale results. In all cases (except for the Average Buying Price) the prices are retail selling prices. While prices are current at the time of publication, the market can be influenced by buying or selling trends, causing prices to change. All prices, except in the case of seldom offered rarities, are averages, calculated from numerous sales. The actual prices charged by any individual currency dealer may be slightly higher or lower than those indicated in this book. In any given sale various factors play a role, such as whether the seller is overstocked on notes of that type.

# HOW TO USE THIS BOOK

The *Official Blackbook Price Guide of United States Paper Money* provides a convenient reference to prices of all standard U.S. currency, old and new, as well as many unusual issues.

Notes are divided into section by denomination. Within each section can be found the various series of notes for that denomination. The series are arranged chronologically and will vary slightly from section to section, as some notes were issued in one series and not in another. An index page is provided at the beginning of each section.

To price a note correctly, it is necessary that it be accurately identified and graded. The illustrations will aid in identification, and a grading guide has been provided. In the case of some notes, particularly very old ones, the value depends upon minor details. In all such cases these details have been clearly noted.

Listings include the following information:

**Date.** This is the "series date," as it appears on the note, and may bear no relation whatsoever to the year in which the note was actually issued. The date of actual issue is not of importance to collectors. If the series date on the note carries a suffix letter, such as 1935A, it will be so indicated in the listing.

**Seal.** The color of the Treasury Seal will be noted, along with other information if relevant.

**Signatures.** All U.S. notes carry two signatures, and the names of each signer are given for every note listed. If different signature combinations exist for your note, be sure you refer to the correct signature combination. The listings will show you whether there is just one set of signatures for that note or more than one.

**Type.** In a small minority of cases, notes were issued in more than one type. For example, a slight change was made in the paper or printing. All recorded types are identified in the listings.

**Issuing Bank.** This information is provided for Federal Reserve Notes and Federal Reserve Bank Notes only. Check the Federal Reserve seal on your note to identify the issuing bank. In some instances there is a difference in value depending on where the note originated. Space prevents us from listing the numerous local banks issuing National Bank Notes.

**A.B.P.** The first price column is the A.B.P. or Average Buying Price. This is the approximate sum being paid by dealers for a specimen in the lowest listed grade of condition. The lowest listed grade of condition is the column next to the A.B.P. If the next column is headed "Good," the A.B.P. is for a specimen in Good condition. In all cases the A.B.P. includes the face value of the note. This is an important consideration insofar as U.S. notes, regardless of their age or physical condition, can still be spent as legal tender.

**Current Selling Prices.** The current selling prices are given in two or three different grades of condition, as indicated at the top of each price column. Different groups of notes are priced in different condition grades, owing to market availability. Some are virtually unobtainable in uncirculated condition, so it would be pointless to give such a price. Others are of no premium value in less than V.F., hence V.F. is the lowest grade shown.

# RECORD KEEPING

For your convenience, we suggest you use the following record-keeping system to note condition of your paper money in the checklist box:

| | | | |
|---|---|---|---|
| ☒FAIR | ☒VERY GOOD | ☐VERY FINE | ☒ALMOST UNC |
| ☒GOOD | ⊟FINE | ☒EXTREMELY FINE | ■UNCIRCULATED |

# ONE DOLLAR NOTES

**ONE DOLLAR NOTES** (1862) UNITED STATES NOTES
(ALSO KNOWN AS LEGAL TENDER NOTES)
(Large Size)                                    **NOTE NO. 1**

**Face Design:** Portrait of Salmon Portland Chase (1808-1873), Secretary of the Treasury under Lincoln, red Treasury Seal, signatures of Chittenden and Spinner, lower right.

**Back Design:** Large circle center with legal tender obligation.

| SERIES | SIGNATURES | SEAL | A.B.P. | GOOD | V. FINE | UNC. |
|--------|-----------|------|--------|------|---------|------|
| 1862 | Chittenden-Spinner | | | | | |
| ☐Type I-National Bank Note, American Bank | | | | | | |
| Note without Monogram | | Red | 50.00 | 90.00 | 250.00 | 650.00 |
| ☐Type II-National Bank Note, American Bank | | | | | | |
| Note with Monogram ABNCO | | Red | 50.00 | 75.00 | 200.00 | 675.00 |
| ☐Type III-National Bank Note, National Bank | | | | | | |
| Note without Monogram | | Red | 40.00 | 65.00 | 180.00 | 595.00 |
| ☐Type IV-National Bank Note, National Bank | | | | | | |
| Note with Monogram ABNCO | | Red | 40.00 | 65.00 | 220.00 | 750.00 |

## ONE DOLLAR NOTES (1869) UNITED STATES NOTES
## (ALSO KNOWN AS LEGAL TENDER NOTES)
(Large Size)                                               **NOTE NO. 2**

**Face Design:** Portrait of President Washington in the center, large red seal to the right. Scene of Columbus in sight of land to left; also called "Rainbow Note" because of the many colors used in printing. Black ink for main design, red seal and serial numbers, green background for the serial number, green shading in upper-half and blue tint in paper left of portrait to deter counterfeiting.

**Back Design:** Green, "ONE DOLLAR" and "ONE" over "1" center, letters U.S. interwoven to left. Legal tender obligation to right of center.

| SERIES | SIGNATURES | SEAL | A.B.P. | GOOD | V. FINE | UNC. |
|--------|-----------|------|--------|------|---------|------|
| ☐1869 | Allison-Spinner | Red | 60.00 | 110.00 | 350.00 | 950.00 |

## ONE DOLLAR NOTES (1874-1917)
### UNITED STATES NOTES
### (ALSO KNOWN AS LEGAL TENDER NOTES)

(Large Size)                                          **NOTE NO. 3**

**Back Design:** Large green "X" with United States of America in the center. Legal tender obligation and counterfeiting warning to right.

**Face Design:** No blue or green shading and tinting.

| SERIES | SIGNATURES | SEAL | A.B.P. | GOOD | V. FINE | UNC. |
|---|---|---|---|---|---|---|
| ☐1874 | Allison-Spinner | Red Sm. | 30.00 | 50.00 | 110.00 | 450.00 |
| ☐1875 | Allison-New | Red Sm. | 30.00 | 40.00 | 90.00 | 350.00 |
| ☐1875 | Same Series A | Red Sm. | 30.00 | 60.00 | 180.00 | 575.00 |
| ☐1875 | Same Series B | Red Sm. | 30.00 | 60.00 | 180.00 | 550.00 |
| ☐1875 | Same Series C | Red Sm. | 30.00 | 75.00 | 215.00 | 725.00 |
| ☐1875 | Same Series D | Red Sm. | 50.00 | 110.00 | 310.00 | 725.00 |
| ☐1875 | Same Series E | Red Sm. | 70.00 | 150.00 | 310.00 | 910.00 |
| ☐1875 | Allison-Wyman | Red Sm. | 25.00 | 40.00 | 70.00 | 210.00 |
| ☐1878 | Allison-Gilfillan | Red Sm. | 25.00 | 40.00 | 90.00 | 300.00 |
| ☐1878 | Allison-Gilfillan | Maroon Sm. | 150.00 | — | — | 925.00 |
| ☐1880 | Scofield-Gilfillan | Brown Lg. | 20.00 | 50.00 | 90.00 | 260.00 |
| ☐1880 | Bruce-Gilfillan | Brown Lg. | 20.00 | 40.00 | 70.00 | 260.00 |
| ☐1880 | Bruce-Wyman | Brown Lg. | 20.00 | 40.00 | 60.00 | 260.00 |
| ☐1880 | Rosecrans-Huston | Red Lg. | 45.00 | 100.00 | 400.00 | 1050.00 |
| ☐1880 | Rosecrans-Huston | Brown Lg. | 45.00 | 100.00 | 410.00 | 1050.00 |
| ☐1880 | Rosecrans-Nebeker | Brown Lg. | 45.00 | 100.00 | 410.00 | 1050.00 |
| ☐1880 | Rosecrans-Nebeker | Red Sm. | 18.00 | 30.00 | 65.00 | 220.00 |
| ☐1880 | Tillman-Morgan | Red Sm. | 18.00 | 30.00 | 65.00 | 210.00 |
| ☐1917 | Tehee-Burke | Red Sm. | 18.00 | 22.00 | 40.00 | 135.00 |

Sm.—Small Seal, Lg.—Large Seal

*This note with signatures of Burke and Elliott is an error issue. The regular procedure was to have the signature of the Register of the Treasury on the left, and that of the Treasurer to the right. The signatures were transposed in this instance.

| SERIES | SIGNATURES | SEAL | A.B.P. | GOOD | V. FINE | UNC. |
|--------|-----------|------|--------|------|---------|------|
| ☐1917 | Elliott-Burke | Red Sm. | 18.00 | 22.00 | 40.00 | 135.00 |
| ☐1917 | Burke-Elliott* | Red Sm. | 20.00 | 42.00 | 120.00 | 350.00 |
| ☐1917 | Elliott-White | Red Sm. | 18.00 | 21.00 | 40.00 | 120.00 |
| ☐1917 | Speelman-White | Red Sm. | 18.00 | 20.00 | 40.00 | 120.00 |

## ONE DOLLAR NOTES (1923) UNITED STATES NOTES
### (ALSO KNOWN AS LEGAL TENDER NOTES)
(Large Size)                                          **NOTE NO. 4**

**Face Design:** Portrait of President Washington in center. Red seal to left, red "1" to the right, red serial numbers.

**Back Design:** "United States of America" and "ONE DOL-LAR" in center. Figures "1" to right and left. This was the last issue of large-size "ONE DOLLAR" United States Notes. The last series of large-size notes was kept in use until 1929 when the first issue of small-size notes was released.

| SERIES | SIGNATURES | SEAL | A.B.P. | GOOD | V. FINE | UNC. |
|--------|-----------|------|--------|------|---------|------|
| ☐1923 | Speelman-White | Red | 18.00 | 25.00 | 65.00 | 240.00 |

**ONE DOLLAR NOTES (1928)** UNITED STATES NOTES
(ALSO KNOWN AS LEGAL TENDER NOTES)
(Small Size)                                     **NOTE NO. 5**

**Face Design:** Red seal to left—red serial numbers, large "ONE" to right. This is the only issue of the $1.00 United States Note, small size. At the present time only the $100.00 United States Note is current.

**Back Design:** Large "ONE" in center with "ONE DOLLAR" overprint, back printed in green.

| SERIES | SIGNATURES | SEAL | A.B.P. | GOOD | V. FINE | UNC. |
|--------|------------|------|--------|------|---------|------|
| ☐1928 | Woods-Woodin | Red | 9.00 | 12.00 | 25.00 | 75.00 |

## ONE DOLLAR NOTES (1863-1875)
### NATIONAL BANK NOTES
FIRST CHARTER PERIOD (Large Size)        **NOTE NO. 6**

**Face Design:** Name of National Bank top center, maidens at altar below.

**Back Design:** Landing of Pilgrims—center, state seal of state issuing bank to left, eagle and flag.

| SERIES | SIGNATURES | SEAL | A.B.P. | GOOD | V. FINE | UNC. |
|--------|-----------|------|--------|------|---------|------|
| ☐ Original* | Colby-Spinner | Red w/r | 40.00 | 65.00 | 190.00 | 950.00 |
| ☐ Original* | Jeffries-Spinner | Red w/r | 120.00 | 400.00 | 1200.00 | 2600.00 |
| ☐ Original* | Allison-Spinner | Red w/r | 30.00 | 60.00 | 190.00 | 950.00 |
| ☐ 1875 | Allison-New | Red w/s | 30.00 | 60.00 | 190.00 | 875.00 |
| ☐ 1875 | Allison-Wyman | Red w/s | 30.00 | 60.00 | 190.00 | 850.00 |
| ☐ 1875 | Allison-Gilfillan | Red w/s | 30.00 | 60.00 | 190.00 | 850.00 |
| ☐ 1875 | Scofield-Gilfillan | Red w/s | 30.00 | 60.00 | 195.00 | 850.00 |

w/r—with Rays, w/s—with Scallops
*Early notes of the First Charter Period did not have the series imprinted on them. They are known by the date on the bill which was usually the date of charter or organization, or as the Original Series. These notes had a seal with rays or small notches. In 1875 the series was imprinted in red, and the seal was changed to have scallops around the border. The charter number was added to later issues of notes of the original series and to all notes of the 1875 series.

## ONE DOLLAR NOTES (1886) SILVER CERTIFICATES
(Large Size)                                              NOTE NO. 7

| SERIES | SIGNATURES | SEAL | A.B.P. | GOOD | V. FINE | UNC. |
|---|---|---|---|---|---|---|
| ☐1886 | Rosecrans-Jordan | Red Sm | 23.00 | 50.00 | 200.00 | 700.00 |
| ☐1886 | Rosecrans-Hyatt | Red Sm | 23.00 | 50.00 | 200.00 | 850.00 |
| ☐1886 | Rosecrans-Hyatt | Red Lg | 23.00 | 50.00 | 200.00 | 700.00 |
| ☐1886 | Rosecrans-Huston | Red Lg | 23.00 | 50.00 | 190.00 | 750.00 |
| ☐1886 | Rosecrans-Huston | Brown Lg | 23.00 | 45.00 | 190.00 | 725.00 |
| ☐1886 | Rosecrans-Nebeker | Brown Lg | 24.00 | 45.00 | 200.00 | 750.00 |
| ☐1886 | Rosecrans-Nebeker | Red Sm | 25.00 | 46.00 | 240.00 | 750.00 |

## ONE DOLLAR NOTES (1891) SILVER CERTIFICATES
(Large Size)                                              NOTE NO. 8
**Back Design**
**Face Design:**
Same as Note
No. 7

| SERIES | SIGNATURES | SEAL | A.B.P. | GOOD | V. FINE | UNC. |
|---|---|---|---|---|---|---|
| ☐1891 | Rosecrans-Nebeker | Red Sm | 26.00 | 50.00 | 180.00 | 710.00 |
| ☐1891 | Tillman-Morgan | Red Sm | 35.00 | 61.00 | 185.00 | 750.00 |

**ONE DOLLAR NOTES** (1896) SILVER CERTIFICATES
(Large Size)                                          **NOTE NO. 9**

**Face Design:** History instructing youth. To the right, panoramic view of the Capitol and Washington Monument. Constitution on tablet, names of famous Americans on top and side borders.

**Back Design:** Portrait of Martha Washington to left and President Washington to right with large numeral "1" in center.

There is a story that when this note was issued people objected to it because they said No. "1" (ONE) should stand between George and Martha Washington. The set consists of $1.00, $2.00, and $5.00 denominations. They all have very beautiful engravings, and they are truly the most beautiful notes ever issued by our government. They were first released in 1896 and replaced by a new issue in 1899. They were short-lived because of objections to the unclad female on the $5.00 note.

| SERIES | SIGNATURES | SEAL | A.B.P. | GOOD | V. FINE | UNC. |
|--------|-----------|------|--------|------|---------|------|
| ☐1896 | Tillman-Morgan | Red | 30.00 | 60.00 | 280.00 | 700.00 |
| ☐1896 | Bruce-Roberts | Red | 30.00 | 60.00 | 250.00 | 750.00 |

**ONE DOLLAR NOTES** (1899) SILVER CERTIFICATES
(Large Size)                                    **NOTE NO. 10**

**Face Design:** Eagle on flag and Capitol background over portraits of Presidents Lincoln and Grant.

**Back Design**

| SERIES | SIGNATURES | SEAL | A.B.P. | GOOD | V. FINE | UNC. |
|---|---|---|---|---|---|---|
| | **SERIES OF 1899 is above upper right serial number.** | | | | | |
| ☐1899 | Lyons-Roberts | Blue | 15.00 | 40.00 | 75.00 | 180.00 |
| | **SERIES OF 1899 is below upper right serial number.** | | | | | |
| ☐1899 | Lyons-Roberts | Blue | 15.00 | 25.00 | 40.00 | 165.00 |
| ☐1899 | Lyons-Treat | Blue | 15.00 | 25.00 | 40.00 | 165.00 |
| ☐1899 | Vernon-Treat | Blue | 15.00 | 25.00 | 40.00 | 165.00 |
| ☐1899 | Vernon-McClung | Blue | 15.00 | 25.00 | 40.00 | 165.00 |
| | **SERIES OF 1899 is vertical to right of blue seal on the following notes:** | | | | | |
| ☐1899 | Napier-McClung | Blue | 15.00 | 25.00 | 40.00 | 170.00 |
| ☐1899 | Napier-Thompson | Blue | 20.00 | 40.00 | 100.00 | 475.00 |
| ☐1899 | Parker-Burke | Blue | 15.00 | 25.00 | 40.00 | 140.00 |
| ☐1899 | Teehee-Burke | Blue | 15.00 | 25.00 | 40.00 | 140.00 |
| SERIES | SIGNATURES | SEAL | A.B.P. | GOOD | V. FINE | UNC. |
| ☐1899 | Elliott-Burke | Blue | 15.00 | 22.00 | 50.00 | 160.00 |
| ☐1899 | Elliott-White | Blue | 15.00 | 22.00 | 50.00 | 160.00 |

| SERIES | SIGNATURES | SEAL | A.B.P. | GOOD | V. FINE | UNC. |
|--------|------------|------|--------|------|---------|------|
| ☐1899 | Speelman-White | Blue | 15.00 | 22.00 | 50.00 | 160.00 |

## ONE DOLLAR NOTES (1923) SILVER CERTIFICATES
(Large Size)                                                **NOTE NO. 11**

**Face Design:** Portrait of President Washington in center, blue seal left, blue "1 DOLLAR" right, blue numbers.

**Back Design:** Same as Note No. 4

| SERIES | SIGNATURES | SEAL | A.B.P. | GOOD | V. FINE | UNC. |
|--------|------------|------|--------|------|---------|------|
| ☐1923 | Speelman-White | Blue | 8.00 | 15.00 | 20.00 | 48.00 |
| ☐1923 | Woods-White | Blue | 8.00 | 16.00 | 22.00 | 62.00 |
| ☐1923 | Woods-Tate | Blue | 12.00 | 25.00 | 45.00 | 240.00 |

**ONE DOLLAR NOTES** (1928) SILVER CERTIFICATES
(Small Size) **NOTE NO. 12**

**Face Design:** Portrait of President Washington, blue seal to the left, "ONE" to right, blue seal and numbers. "ONE SILVER DOLLAR" under portrait.

**Back Design**

First issue series of 1928. United States paper money was reduced in 1928 from the old large size to the size presently in use. This was mostly an economy measure. Unlike large-size notes, the small notes have a letter designation after the date to denote a minor change in design or change of one or both signatures.

| SERIES | SIGNATURES | SEAL | A.B.P. | GOOD | V. FINE | UNC. |
|--------|-----------|------|--------|------|---------|------|
| ☐1928 | Tate-Mellon | Blue | 2.00 | 6.00 | 9.00 | 18.00 |
| ☐1928A | Woods-Mellon | Blue | 2.00 | 4.00 | 7.00 | 17.00 |
| ☐1928B | Woods-Mills | Blue | 2.00 | 5.00 | 9.00 | 19.00 |
| ☐1928C | Woods-Woodin | Blue | 15.00 | 32.00 | 91.00 | 410.00 |
| ☐1928D | Julian-Woodin | Blue | 15.00 | 30.00 | 80.00 | 310.00 |
| ☐1928E | Julian-Morgenthau | Blue | 65.00 | 125.00 | 310.00 | 1000.00 |

ONE DOLLAR NOTES / 81

## ONE DOLLAR NOTES (1934) SILVER CERTIFICATES
(Small Size) **NOTE NO. 13**

**Face Design:** Portrait of President Washington, blue "1" to left. "ONE" and blue seal to right. "ONE DOLLAR IN SILVER," under portrait.
**Back Design:** Same as Note No. 12.

| SERIES | SIGNATURES | SEAL | A.B.P. | GOOD | V. FINE | UNC. |
|--------|-----------|------|--------|------|---------|------|
| ☐1934 | Julian-Morgenthau | Blue | 1.75 | 3.00 | 6.00 | 26.00 |

## ONE DOLLAR NOTES (1935) SILVER CERTIFICATES
(Small Size) **NOTE NO. 14**

**Face Design:** Portrait of President Washington in center. Gray "1" to left, blue seal right, and blue numbers. "ONE DOLLAR IN SILVER," under portrait.
The following notes are without "IN GOD WE TRUST" on back.

| SERIES | SIGNATURES | SEAL | A.B.P. | GOOD | V. FINE | UNC. |
|--------|-----------|------|--------|------|---------|------|
| ☐1935 | Julian-Morgenthau | Blue | 1.50 | 3.00 | 4.00 | 11.00 |
| ☐1935A | Julian-Morgenthau | Blue | 1.50 | 2.50 | 3.50 | 5.00 |
| ☐1935A | Julian-Morgenthau | Brown | 2.50 | 5.00 | 8.50 | 23.00 |

This note was a special issue for use in war zones in the Pacific area during World War II. Brown serial numbers and HAWAII stamped on front and back.

## ONE DOLLAR NOTES (1935) SILVER CERTIFICATES
(Small Size)                                                    **NOTE NO. 14**

| SERIES SIGNATURES | SEAL | A.B.P. | GOOD | V. FINE | UNC. |
|---|---|---|---|---|---|
| ☐1935A Julian-Morgenthau | Yellow | 3.00 | 8.00 | 22.00 | 83.00 |

The above note was a special issue for use in war zones in the North African and European areas during World War II. Blue serial numbers and yellow seal.

| | | | | | |
|---|---|---|---|---|---|
| ☐1935A Julian-Morgenthau | Blue | 6.00 | 15.00 | 30.00 | 210.00 |

Red "R" between the Treasury Seal and signatures of Morgenthau. This was an experimental issue to test wearing qualities of differently treated paper.

| | | | | | |
|---|---|---|---|---|---|
| ☐1935A Julian-Morgenthau | Blue | 5.00 | 14.00 | 24.00 | 200.00 |

Above note with red "S" between Treasury Seal and signature of Morgenthau. Experimental issue "R" was for regular paper, "S" for special paper.

| | | | | | |
|---|---|---|---|---|---|
| ☐1935B Julian-Vinson | Blue | 1.50 | 2.10 | 5.00 | 6.50 |
| ☐1935C Julian-Snyder | Blue | 1.50 | 2.10 | 5.00 | 6.50 |
| ☐1935D Clark-Snyder | Blue | 1.50 | 2.00 | 3.00 | 4.50 |

Wide design on back. This and all notes of 1935 prior to this, have the wide design. See Fig I.

| | | | | | |
|---|---|---|---|---|---|
| ☐1935D Clark-Snyder | Blue | 1.50 | 2.10 | 3.00 | 5.00 |

Narrow design on back. This and all $1.00 notes following have narrow design. See Fig. II.

## ONE DOLLAR NOTES (1935) SILVER CERTIFICATES
(Small Size)                                                    **NOTE NO. 14**

| SERIES SIGNATURES | SEAL | A.B.P. | GOOD | V. FINE | UNC. |
|---|---|---|---|---|---|
| ☐1935E Priest-Humphrey | Blue | 1.50 | 2.00 | 2.75 | 3.50 |
| ☐1935F Priest-Anderson | Blue | 1.50 | 2.00 | 3.00 | 6.00 |
| ☐1935G Smith-Dillon | Blue | 1.50 | 2.00 | 3.00 | 4.00 |

"IN GOD WE TRUST" added. All notes following have the motto.

| | | | | | |
|---|---|---|---|---|---|
| ☐1935G Smith-Dillon | Blue | 1.50 | 2.00 | 3.00 | 4.50 |
| ☐1935H Granahan-Dillon | Blue | 1.50 | 2.00 | 3.00 | 6.00 |

## ONE DOLLAR NOTES (1957) SILVER CERTIFICATES
(Small Size)                                                    **NOTE NO. 14**

The following three notes are the last issue of the $1.00 Silver Certificates. The reason for the change in series from 1935H to 1957 was due to printing improvements. The 1935 series, up until the issue of Clark and Snyder, was printed in sheets of 12 subjects to a sheet. During the term of Clark and Snyder notes were printed 18 subjects to a sheet. Starting with the series of 1957, new high speed rotary presses were installed and notes were printed 32 subjects to a sheet.

| SERIES SIGNATURES | SEAL | A.B.P. | GOOD | V. FINE | UNC. |
|---|---|---|---|---|---|
| ☐1957 Priest-Anderson | Blue | 1.25 | 1.50 | 2.10 | 3.00 |
| ☐1957A Smith-Dillon | Blue | 1.25 | 1.50 | 2.10 | 2.75 |
| ☐1957B Granahan-Dillon | Blue | 1.25 | 1.50 | 2.10 | 3.00 |

The redemption of Silver Certificates by the U.S. Treasury Department ended on June 24, 1968. These notes are now worth only their face value, plus the numismatic value to collectors. Notes in used condition are not regarded as collectors' items.

## ONE DOLLAR NOTES (1890)
### TREASURY OR COIN NOTES

(Large Size)                                    **NOTE NO. 15**

**Face Design:** Portrait of Stanton, Secretary of War during the Civil War.

**Back Design:** Green large ornate "ONE." Entire back is beautifully engraved.

| SERIES | SIGNATURES | SEAL | A.B.P. | GOOD | V. FINE | UNC. |
|--------|-----------|------|--------|------|---------|------|
| ☐1890 | Rosecrans-Huston | Brown | 35.00 | 80.00 | 400.00 | 1365.00 |
| ☐1890 | Rosecrans-Nebeker | Brown | 35.00 | 80.00 | 370.00 | 1400.00 |
| ☐1890 | Rosecrans-Nebeker | Red | 35.00 | 80.00 | 360.00 | 1325.00 |

## ONE DOLLAR NOTES (1891)
### TREASURY OR COIN NOTES

(Large Size)                                          **NOTE NO. 16**

**Face Design:** Is similar to Note No. 15.

**Back Design:** More unengraved area, numerous "ONEs" and "1s."

| SERIES | SIGNATURES | SEAL | A.B.P. | GOOD | V. FINE | UNC. |
|---|---|---|---|---|---|---|
| ☐1891 | Rosecrans-Nebeker | Red | 25.00 | 50.00 | 115.00 | 450.00 |
| ☐1891 | Tillman-Morgan | Red | 25.00 | 50.00 | 115.00 | 380.00 |
| ☐1891 | Bruce-Roberts | Red | 25.00 | 50.00 | 115.00 | 380.00 |

## ONE DOLLAR NOTES (1918)
### FEDERAL RESERVE BANK NOTES
(Large Size)                                      **NOTE NO. 17**

**Face Design:** Portrait of President Washington, signature to left of center. Bank and city center, blue seal to right. Signatures of government officials above. Signatures of bank officials below. Federal Reserve district letter and numbers in four corners.

**Back Design:** Flying eagle and flag in center. All are series 1918, and have blue seals and blue numbers.

## ONE DOLLAR NOTES (1918)
### FEDERAL RESERVE BANK NOTES
(Large Size)                                      **NOTE NO. 17**

| BANK & CITY | GOV'T SIGNATURES | BANK SIGNATURES | A.B.P. | GOOD | V. FINE | UNC. |
|---|---|---|---|---|---|---|
| ☐ Boston | Teehee-Burke | Bullen-Morss | | | | |
| | | | 8.00 | 15.00 | 45. 00 | 155.00 |
| ☐ Boston | Teehee-Burke | Willet-Morss | | | | |
| | | | 20.00 | 30.00 | 60.00 | 360.00 |
| ☐ Boston | Elliot-Burke | Willet-Morss | | | | |
| | | | 8.00 | 15.00 | 45.00 | 160.00 |

| BANK & CITY | GOV'T SIGNATURES | BANK SIGNATURES | A.B.P. | GOOD | V. FINE | UNC. |
|---|---|---|---|---|---|---|
| ☐ New York | Teehee-Burke | Sailer-Strong | 8.00 | 15.00 | 45.00 | 160.00 |
| ☐ New York | Teehee-Burke | Hendricks-Strong | 8.00 | 15.00 | 45.00 | 160.00 |
| ☐ New York | Elliott-Burke | Hendricks-Strong | 8.00 | 15.00 | 45.00 | 160.00 |
| ☐ Philadelphia | Teehee-Burke | Hardt-Passmore | 8.00 | 15.00 | 45.00 | 160.00 |
| ☐ Philadelphia | Teehee-Burke | Dyer-Passmore | 8.00 | 15.00 | 45.00 | 160.00 |
| ☐ Philadelphia | Elliott-Burke | Dyer-Passmore | 8.00 | 15.00 | 45.00 | 160.00 |
| ☐ Philadelphia | Elliott-Burke | Dyer-Norris | 8.00 | 15.00 | 45.00 | 160.00 |
| ☐ Cleveland | Teehee-Burke | Baxter-Fancher | 8.00 | 15.00 | 45.00 | 160.00 |
| ☐ Cleveland | Teehee-Burke | Davis-Fancher | 8.00 | 15.00 | 45.00 | 160.00 |
| ☐ Cleveland | Elliott-Burke | Davis-Fancher | 8.00 | 15.00 | 45.00 | 160.00 |
| ☐ Richmond | Teehee-Burke | Keesee-Seay | 8.00 | 15.00 | 45.00 | 160.00 |
| ☐ Richmond | Elliott-Burke | Keesee-Seay | 8.00 | 15.00 | 45.00 | 160.00 |
| ☐ Atlanta | Teehee-Burke | Pike-McCord | 8.00 | 15.00 | 45.00 | 160.00 |
| ☐ Atlanta | Teehee-Burke | Bell-McCord | 8.00 | 15.00 | 45.00 | 160.00 |
| ☐ Atlanta | Teehee-Burke | Bell-Wellborn | 8.00 | 15.00 | 45.00 | 160.00 |
| ☐ Atlanta | Elliott-Burke | Bell-Wellborn | 8.00 | 15.00 | 45.00 | 160.00 |
| ☐ Chicago | Teehee-Burke | McCloud-McDougal | 8.00 | 15.00 | 45.00 | 160.00 |
| ☐ Chicago | Teehee-Burke | Cramer-McDougal | 8.00 | 15.00 | 45.00 | 160.00 |
| ☐ Chicago | Elliott-Burke | Cramer-McDougal | 8.00 | 15.00 | 45.00 | 160.00 |
| ☐ St. Louis | Teehee-Burke | Attebery-Wells | 8.00 | 15.00 | 45.00 | 160.00 |
| ☐ St. Louis | Teehee-Burke | Attebery-Biggs | 8.00 | 15.00 | 45.00 | 160.00 |

| BANK & CITY | GOV'T SIGNATURES | BANK SIGNATURES | A.B.P. | GOOD | V. FINE | UNC. |
|---|---|---|---|---|---|---|
| ☐ St. Louis | Elliott-Burke | Attebery-Biggs | 8.00 | 15.00 | 45.00 | 160.00 |
| ☐ St. Louis | Elliott-Burke | White-Biggs | 8.00 | 15.00 | 45.00 | 160.00 |
| ☐ Minneapolis | Teehee-Burke | Cook-Wold | 10.00 | 21.00 | 60.00 | 250.00 |
| ☐ Minneapolis | Teehee-Burke | Cook-Young | 100.00 | 200.00 | 450.00 | 1050.00 |
| ☐ Minneapolis | Elliott-Burke | Cook-Young | 11.00 | 25.00 | 60.00 | 250.00 |
| ☐ Kansas City | Teehee-Burke | Anderson-Miller | 8.00 | 15.00 | 45.00 | 160.00 |
| ☐ Kansas City | Elliott-Burke | Anderson-Miller | 8.00 | 15.00 | 45.00 | 160.00 |
| ☐ Kansas City | Elliott-Burke | Helm-Miller | 8.00 | 15.00 | 45.00 | 160.00 |
| ☐ Dallas | Teehee-Burke | Talley-VanZandt | 8.00 | 15.00 | 45.00 | 160.00 |
| ☐ Dallas | Elliott-Burke | Talley-VanZandt | 15.00 | 42.00 | 100.00 | 250.00 |
| ☐ Dallas | Elliott-Burke | Lawder-VanZandt | 8.00 | 15.00 | 45.00 | 160.00 |
| ☐ San Francisco | Teehee-Burke | Clerk-Lynch | 8.00 | 15.00 | 45.00 | 160.00 |
| ☐ San Francisco | Teehee-Burke | Clerk-Calkins | 8.00 | 15.00 | 45.00 | 160.00 |
| ☐ San Francisco | Elliott-Burke | Clerk-Calkins | 8.00 | 15.00 | 45.00 | 160.00 |
| ☐ San Francisco | Elliott-Burke | Ambrose-Calkins | 8.00 | 15.00 | 45.00 | 160.00 |

## ONE DOLLAR NOTES (1963)
### FEDERAL RESERVE NOTES

(Small Size) **NOTE NO. 18**

**Face Design:** Portrait of President Washington in center, black Federal Reserve seal with city and district letter to left, green Treasury Seal to right. Green serial numbers, Federal Reserve numbers in four corners.

**Back Design:** Same as all $1.00 Notes from 1935.

### SERIES OF 1963 GRANAHAN-DILLON—GREEN SEAL

| DISTRICT | A.B.P. | UNC. | DISTRICT | A.B.P. | UNC. |
|---|---|---|---|---|---|
| ☐1A Boston | 1.25 | 3.25 | ☐7G Chicago | 1.25 | 3.25 |
| ☐2B New York | 1.25 | 3.25 | ☐8H St. Louis | 1.25 | 3.25 |
| ☐3C Philadelphia | 1.25 | 3.25 | ☐9I Minneapolis | 1.25 | 3.25 |
| ☐4D Cleveland | 1.25 | 3.25 | ☐10J Kansas City | 1.25 | 3.25 |
| ☐5E Richmond | 1.25 | 3.25 | ☐11K Dallas | 1.25 | 3.25 |
| ☐6F Atlanta | 1.25 | 3.25 | ☐12L San Francisco | 1.25 | 3.25 |

The Dallas note of this series as shown, with the letter "K" in the black seal and the numbers "11" in the four corners, does not have any more significance or value than any other notes with their respective district letter and corresponding number.

A false rumor was circulated several years ago that the "K" was for Kennedy, the "11" was for November, the month in which he was assassinated, and that the note was issued by the Dallas bank to commemorate the occasion. The entire story is apocryphal.

This note is in no way associated with the late President Kennedy. The notes were authorized by the act of June 4, 1963. This was five months before Kennedy was assassinated. The Federal Reserve district for Dallas is K-11.

## SERIES OF 1963A GRANAHAN-FOWLER—GREEN SEAL

| DISTRICT | A.B.P. | UNC. | DISTRICT | A.B.P. | UNC. |
|---|---|---|---|---|---|
| ☐1A Boston | 1.25 | 3.50 | ☐7G Chicago | 1.25 | 3.50 |
| ☐2B New York | 1.25 | 3.50 | ☐8H St. Louis | 1.25 | 3.50 |
| ☐3C Philadelphia | 1.25 | 3.50 | ☐9I Minneapolis | 1.25 | 3.50 |
| ☐4D Cleveland | 1.25 | 3.50 | ☐10J Kansas City | 1.25 | 3.50 |
| ☐5E Richmond | 1.25 | 3.50 | ☐11K Dallas | 1.25 | 3.50 |
| ☐6F Atlanta | 1.25 | 3.50 | ☐12L San Francisco | 1.25 | 3.50 |

## ONE DOLLAR NOTES (1963-B) FEDERAL RESERVE (WITH SIGNATURE OF JOSEPH W. BARR)

(Small Size)                                                    **NOTE NO. 18**

Joseph W. Barr served as Secretary of the Treasury from December 20, 1968, to January 20, 1969, filling the unexpired term of Henry H. Fowler. His signature appears on the $1.00 Federal Reserve notes of the series of 1963-B only.

During the one-month term of Joseph W. Barr about 471 million notes were printed with his signature. These notes were for the following Federal Reserve Banks.

### NOTES ISSUED

| | REGULAR NUMBERS | A.B.P. | UNC. | STAR NUMBERS | A.B.P. | UNC. |
|---|---|---|---|---|---|---|
| ☐2B New York | 123,040,000 | 1.50 | 4.50 | 3,680,000 | 1.50 | 4.50 |
| ☐5E Richmond | 93,600,000 | 1.50 | 4.50 | 3,040,000 | 1.50 | 4.50 |
| ☐7G Chicago | 91,040,000 | 1.50 | 4.50 | 2,400,000 | 1.50 | 4.50 |
| ☐10J Kansas City | 44,800,000 | 1.50 | 4.50 | None Printed | 1.50 | 4.50 |
| ☐12L San Francisco | 106,400,000 | 1.50 | 4.50 | 3,040,000 | 1.50 | 4.50 |

## ONE DOLLAR NOTES (1969)
## FEDERAL RESERVE NOTES
## (WORDING IN GREEN, TREASURY SEAL
## CHANGED FROM LATIN TO ENGLISH)

**FORMER DESIGN:**
The former design had the Latin inscription: *"Thesaur. Amer. Septent. Sigil.,"* which has several translations. It was the Seal of the North American Treasury.

**NEW DESIGN:**
This new design drops the Latin and states *"The Department of The Treasury, 1789."* First used on the $100 Note of the Series of 1966.

## ONE DOLLAR NOTES (1969)
## FEDERAL RESERVE NOTES

(Small Size)                                                          **NOTE NO. 18A**

### SERIES OF 1969—ELSTON-KENNEDY, GREEN SEAL

| | | | | | | | |
|---|---|---|---|---|---|---|---|
| Boston | 2.60 | Cleveland | 2.60 | Chicago | 2.60 | Kansas City | 2.60 |
| New York | 2.60 | Richmond | 2.60 | St. Louis | 2.60 | Dallas | 2.60 |
| Philadelphia | 2.60 | Atlanta | 2.60 | Minneapolis | 2.60 | San Francisco | 2.60 |

### SERIES OF 1969A—KABIS-KENNEDY, GREEN SEAL

| | | | | | | | |
|---|---|---|---|---|---|---|---|
| Boston | 2.60 | Cleveland | 2.60 | Chicago | 2.60 | Kansas City | 2.60 |
| New York | 2.60 | Richmond | 2.60 | St. Louis | 2.60 | Dallas | 2.60 |
| Philadelphia | 2.60 | Atlanta | 2.60 | Minneapolis | 2.60 | San Francisco | 2.60 |

### SERIES OF 1969B—KABIS-CONNALLY, GREEN SEAL

| | | | | | | | |
|---|---|---|---|---|---|---|---|
| Boston | 2.60 | Cleveland | 2.60 | Chicago | 2.60 | Kansas City | 2.60 |
| New York | 2.60 | Richmond | 2.60 | St. Louis | 2.60 | Dallas | 2.60 |
| Philadelphia | 2.60 | Atlanta | 2.60 | Minneapolis | 2.60 | San Francisco | 2.60 |

### SERIES OF 1969C—BANUELOS-CONNALLY, GREEN SEAL

| | | | | | | | |
|---|---|---|---|---|---|---|---|
| Boston | 2.60 | Cleveland | 2.60 | Chicago | 2.60 | Kansas City | 2.60 |
| New York | 2.60 | Richmond | 2.60 | St. Louis | 2.60 | Dallas | 2.60 |
| Philadelphia | 2.60 | Atlanta | 2.60 | Minneapolis | 2.60 | San Francisco | 2.60 |

### SERIES OF 1969D—BANUELOS-CONNALLY, GREEN SEAL

| | | | | | | | |
|---|---|---|---|---|---|---|---|
| Boston | 2.60 | Cleveland | 2.60 | Chicago | 2.60 | Kansas City | 2.60 |
| New York | 2.60 | Richmond | 2.60 | St. Louis | 2.60 | Dallas | 2.60 |
| Philadelphia | 2.60 | Atlanta | 2.60 | Minneapolis | 2.60 | San Francisco | 2.60 |

### SERIES OF 1974—NEFF-SIMON, GREEN SEAL

| | | | | | | | |
|---|---|---|---|---|---|---|---|
| Boston | 2.10 | Cleveland | 2.10 | Chicago | 2.10 | Kansas City | 2.10 |
| New York | 2.10 | Richmond | 2.10 | St. Louis | 2.10 | Dallas | 2.10 |
| Philadelphia | 2.10 | Atlanta | 2.10 | Minneapolis | 2.10 | San Francisco | 2.10 |

### SERIES OF 1977—MORTON-BLUMENTHAL, GREEN SEAL

| | | | | | | | |
|---|---|---|---|---|---|---|---|
| Boston | 2.10 | Cleveland | 2.10 | Chicago | 2.10 | Kansas City | 2.10 |
| New York | 2.10 | Richmond | 2.10 | St. Louis | 2.10 | Dallas | 2.10 |
| Philadelphia | 2.10 | Atlanta | 2.10 | Minneapolis | 2.10 | San Francisco | 2.10 |

### SERIES OF 1977A—MORTON-MILLER, GREEN SEAL

| | | | | | | | |
|---|---|---|---|---|---|---|---|
| Boston | 2.10 | Cleveland | 2.10 | Chicago | 2.10 | Kansas City | 2.10 |
| New York | 2.10 | Richmond | 2.10 | St. Louis | 2.10 | Dallas | 2.10 |
| Philadelphia | 2.10 | Atlanta | 2.10 | Minneapolis | 2.10 | San Francisco | 2.10 |

### SERIES OF 1981—BUCHANAN-REGAN, GREEN SEAL

| | | | | | | | |
|---|---|---|---|---|---|---|---|
| Boston | 2.10 | Cleveland | 2.10 | Chicago | 2.10 | Kansas City | 2.10 |
| New York | 2.10 | Richmond | 2.10 | St. Louis | 2.10 | Dallas | 2.10 |
| Philadelphia | 2.10 | Atlanta | 2.10 | Minneapolis | 2.10 | San Francisco | 2.10 |

### SERIES OF 1981A—ORTEGA-REGAN, GREEN SEAL

| | | | | | | | |
|---|---|---|---|---|---|---|---|
| Boston | 2.10 | Cleveland | 2.10 | Chicago | 2.10 | Kansas City | 2.10 |
| New York | 2.10 | Richmond | 2.10 | St. Louis | 2.10 | Dallas | 2.10 |
| Philadelphia | 2.10 | Atlanta | 2.10 | Minneapolis | 2.10 | San Francisco | 2.10 |

### SERIES OF 1981-A—ORTEGA-REGAN-REVERSE #129 LEFT

| | | | | | | | |
|---|---|---|---|---|---|---|---|
| Boston | 7.00 | Cleveland | 7.00 | Chicago | 7.00 | Kansas City | 7.00 |
| New York | 7.00 | Richmond | 7.00 | St. Louis | 7.00 | Dallas | 7.00 |
| Philadelphia | 7.00 | Atlanta | 7.00 | Minneapolis | 7.00 | San Francisco | 7.00 |

### SERIES OF 1985—ORTEGA-BAKER, GREEN SEAL

| | | | | | | | |
|---|---|---|---|---|---|---|---|
| Boston | 2.10 | Cleveland | 2.10 | Chicago | 2.10 | Kansas City | 2.10 |
| New York | 2.10 | Richmond | 2.10 | St. Louis | 2.10 | Dallas | 2.10 |
| Philadelphia | 2.10 | Atlanta | 2.10 | Minneapolis | 2.10 | San Francisco | 2.10 |

### SERIES OF 1985—ORTEGA-BAKER-REVERSE #129 LEFT

| | | | | | | | |
|---|---|---|---|---|---|---|---|
| Boston | 7.00 | Cleveland | 7.00 | Chicago | 7.00 | Kansas City | 7.00 |
| New York | 7.00 | Richmond | 7.00 | St. Louis | 7.00 | Dallas | 7.00 |
| Philadelphia | 7.00 | Atlanta | 7.00 | Minneapolis | 7.00 | San Francisco | 7.00 |

### SERIES OF 1988—ORTEGA-BAKER, GREEN SEAL

| | | | | | | | |
|---|---|---|---|---|---|---|---|
| Boston | 1.90 | Cleveland | 1.90 | Chicago | 1.90 | Kansas City | 1.90 |
| New York | 1.90 | Richmond | 1.90 | St. Louis | 1.90 | Dallas | 1.90 |
| Philadelphia | 1.90 | Atlanta | 1.90 | Minneapolis | 1.90 | San Francisco | 1.90 |

### SERIES OF 1988-A—VILLAIPANDO-BRADY

| | | | | | | | |
|---|---|---|---|---|---|---|---|
| Boston | 1.50 | Cleveland | 1.50 | Chicago | 1.50 | Kansas City | 1.50 |
| New York | 1.50 | Richmond | 1.50 | St. Louis | 1.50 | Dallas | 1.50 |
| Philadelphia | 1.50 | Atlanta | 1.50 | Minneapolis | 1.50 | San Francisco | 1.50 |

# TWO DOLLAR NOTES

**TWO DOLLAR NOTES** (1862) UNITED STATES NOTES
(ALSO KNOWN AS LEGAL TENDER NOTES)
(Large Size) **NOTE NO. 19**

### ALEXANDER HAMILTON (1754-1804)

**Face Design:** Portrait of Hamilton, cloverleaf twos in upper corners, medallion with "11" in lower left, medallion with "1, 2, 3," right of portrait.

**Back Design:** "2" in each corner, with "2" motif repeated in scallop circles around obligation, back is printed green.

| SERIES | SIGNATURES | SEAL | A.B.P. | GOOD | V. FINE | UNC. |
|--------|------------|------|--------|------|---------|------|
| ☐1862 | Chittenden-Spinner | | | | | |
| | TYPE I: American Banknote Company vertical in left border | Red | 70.00 | 125.00 | 475.00 | 1550.00 |
| ☐1862 | Chittenden-Spinner | | | | | |
| | TYPE II: National Banknote Company vertical in left border | Red | 70.00 | 125.00 | 425.00 | 1450.00 |

# TWO DOLLAR NOTES (1869) UNITED STATES NOTES
## (ALSO KNOWN AS LEGAL TENDER NOTES)
(Large Size)                                    **NOTE NO. 20**

**Face Design:** Portrait of President Jefferson to left, Capitol in center, large red seal to right.

**Back Design:** Roman II left, Arabic "2" center, "TWO," right. This is the companion note to the $1.00 "RAINBOW NOTE" (see Note No. 2).

| SERIES | SIGNATURES | SEAL | A.B.P. | GOOD | V. FINE | UNC. |
|--------|-----------|------|--------|------|---------|------|
| ☐1869 | Allison-Spinner | Red | 75.00 | 140.00 | 550.00 | 1850.00 |

**TWO DOLLAR NOTES** (1874) UNITED STATES NOTES
(ALSO KNOWN AS LEGAL TENDER NOTES)
(Large Size)                                                    **NOTE NO. 21**

**Face Design:** Portrait of President Jefferson, same as previous Note No. 20.

**Back Design:** Completely revised.

| SERIES | SIGNATURES | SEAL | A.B.P. | GOOD | V. FINE | UNC. |
|--------|-----------|------|--------|------|---------|------|
| ☐1874 | Allison-Spinner | Red | 45.00 | 70.00 | 310.00 | 575.00 |
| ☐1875 | Allison-New | Red | 40.00 | 80.00 | 200.00 | 610.00 |
| ☐SERIES A Allison-New | | Red | 50.00 | 110.00 | 350.00 | 600.00 |
| ☐SERIES B Allison-New | | Red | 50.00 | 110.00 | 350.00 | 600.00 |
| ☐1875 | Allison-Wyman | Red | 28.00 | 80.00 | 200.00 | 500.00 |
| ☐1878 | Allison-Gilfillan | Red | 28.00 | 80.00 | 200.00 | 500.00 |
| ☐1878 | Scofield-Gilfillan | Red | 850.00 | 1000.00 | 2500.00 | 5000.00 |
| ☐1880 | Scofield-Gilfillan | Brown | 18.00 | 30.00 | 80.00 | 400.00 |
| ☐1880 | Bruce-Gilfillan | Brown | 18.00 | 30.00 | 70.00 | 380.00 |
| ☐1880 | Bruce-Wyman | Brown | 18.00 | 30.00 | 70.00 | 380.00 |
| ☐1880 | Rosecrans-Huston | Red | 50.00 | 100.00 | 500.00 | 1800.00 |
| ☐1880 | Rosecrans-Huston | Brown | 50.00 | 100.00 | 500.00 | 1800.00 |
| ☐1880 | Rosecrans-Nebeker | Red | 18.00 | 30.00 | 70.00 | 260.00 |
| ☐1880 | Tillman-Morgan | Red | 18.00 | 32.00 | 70.00 | 300.00 |

| SERIES | SIGNATURES | SEAL | A.B.P. | GOOD | V. FINE | UNC. |
|---|---|---|---|---|---|---|
| ☐1917 | Teehee-Burke | Red | 15.00 | 25.00 | 50.00 | 160.00 |
| ☐1917 | Elliott-Burke | Red | 15.00 | 25.00 | 50.00 | 160.00 |
| ☐1917 | Elliott-White | Red | 15.00 | 25.00 | 50.00 | 160.00 |
| ☐1917 | Speelman-White | Red | 15.00 | 25.00 | 50.00 | 160.00 |

## TWO DOLLAR NOTES (1928) UNITED STATES NOTES (ALSO KNOWN AS LEGAL TENDER NOTES)

(Small Size)                                          **NOTE NO. 22**

**Face Design:** Portrait of President Jefferson, red seal left, "TWO" right, red serial numbers.

**Back Design:** Jefferson Home—Monticello.

| SERIES | SIGNATURES | SEAL | A.B.P. | GOOD | V. FINE | UNC. |
|---|---|---|---|---|---|---|
| ☐1928 | Tate-Mellon | Red | 4.00 | 9.00 | 14.00 | 42.00 |
| ☐1928A | Woods-Mellon | Red | 6.00 | 15.00 | 26.00 | 170.00 |
| ☐1928B | Woods-Mills | Red | 25.00 | 50.00 | 90.00 | 510.00 |
| ☐1928C | Julian-Morgenthau | Red | 3.00 | 6.00 | 13.00 | 65.00 |
| ☐1928D | Julian-Morgenthau | Red | 3.00 | 5.00 | 10.00 | 18.00 |
| ☐1928E | Julian-Vinson | Red | 3.00 | 6.00 | 16.00 | 45.00 |
| ☐1928F | Julian-Snyder | Red | 3.00 | 4.00 | 9.00 | 20.00 |
| ☐1928G | Clark-Snyder | Red | 3.00 | 4.00 | 8.00 | 15.00 |

## TWO DOLLAR NOTES (1953) UNITED STATES NOTES
### (ALSO KNOWN AS LEGAL TENDER NOTES)
(Small Size)                                          **NOTE NO. 23**

**Face Design:** Portrait of President Jefferson, gray "2" to left, red seal to right over "TWO."
**Back Design:** Same as Note No. 22.

| SERIES | SIGNATURES | SEAL | A.B.P. | GOOD | V. FINE | UNC. |
|--------|-----------|------|--------|------|---------|------|
| ☐1953  Priest-Humphrey | | Red | 2.50 | 3.00 | 4.50 | 8.00 |
| ☐1953A Priest-Anderson | | Red | 2.50 | 3.00 | 4.50 | 7.00 |
| ☐1953B Smith-Dillon | | Red | 2.50 | 3.00 | 4.00 | 6.50 |
| ☐1953C Granahan-Dillon | | Red | 2.50 | 3.00 | 4.00 | 6.50 |

**Back Design:** "IN GOD WE TRUST" on back.
**Face Design:** Same as previous note.

| SERIES | SIGNATURES | SEAL | A.B.P. | GOOD | V. FINE | UNC. |
|--------|-----------|------|--------|------|---------|------|
| ☐1963  Granahan-Dillon | | Red | 2.50 | 3.00 | 5.00 | 7.00 |
| ☐1963A Granahan-Fowler | | Red | 2.50 | 3.00 | 5.00 | 7.00 |

Production of Two Dollar United States Notes was discontinued on August 10, 1966.

**TWO DOLLAR NOTES** (1875) NATIONAL BANK NOTES
FIRST CHARTER PERIOD (Large Size)                    **NOTE NO. 24**

**Face Design:** This note is known as "The Lazy Two Note" due to the unusual "lying down" shape of the "2" shown on the face. Liberty with flag and red seal.

**Back Design:** Sir Walter Raleigh in England, 1585, exhibiting corn and smoking tobacco from America, state seal and eagle.

| SERIES | SIGNATURES | SEAL | A.B.P. | GOOD | V. FINE | UNC. |
|---|---|---|---|---|---|---|
| ☐Original | Colby-Spinner | Red | 90.00 | 200.00 | 700.00 | 3150.00 |
| ☐Original | Jeffries-Spinner | Red | 225.00 | 800.00 | 1300.00 | 4200.00 |
| ☐Original | Allison-Spinner | Red | 90.00 | 210.00 | 700.00 | 3100.00 |
| ☐1875 | Allison-New | Red | 90.00 | 210.00 | 700.00 | 2400.00 |
| ☐1875 | Allison-Wyman | Red | 90.00 | 210.00 | 700.00 | 2400.00 |
| ☐1875 | Allison-Gilfillan | Red | 90.00 | 210.00 | 700.00 | 2400.00 |
| ☐1875 | Scofield-Gilfillan | Red | 90.00 | 210.00 | 700.00 | 2400.00 |

**TWO DOLLAR NOTES** (1886) SILVER CERTIFICATES
(Large Size)                                    **NOTE NO. 25**

**Face Design:** General Hancock portrait left. Treasury seal
to the right of center.

**Back Design:** "2" left and right, very ornate engraving,
obligation in center of note. Note is printed in green.

| SERIES | SIGNATURES | SEAL | A.B.P. | GOOD | V. FINE | UNC. |
|--------|------------|------|--------|------|---------|------|
| ☐1886 | Rosecrans-Jordan | Red | 50.00 | 100.00 | 500.00 | 1100.00 |
| ☐1886 | Rosecrans-Hyatt | Red Sm | 50.00 | 100.00 | 500.00 | 1100.00 |
| ☐1886 | Rosecrans-Hyatt | Red Lg | 50.00 | 100.00 | 500.00 | 1100.00 |
| ☐1886 | Rosecrans-Huston | Red | 50.00 | 100.00 | 500.00 | 1100.00 |
| ☐1886 | Rosecrans-Huston | Brown | 50.00 | 100.00 | 500.00 | 1100.00 |

**TWO DOLLAR NOTES** (1891) SILVER CERTIFICATES
(Large Size)                                    **NOTE NO. 26**

**Face Design:** Portrait of William Windom, Secretary of the
Treasury 1881-1884 and 1889-1891, red seal right.

**Back Design:** "2" left and right, scalloped design center
with obligation, printed in green.

| SERIES | SIGNATURES | SEAL | A.B.P. | GOOD | V. FINE | UNC. |
|--------|-----------|------|--------|------|---------|------|
| ☐1891 | Rosecrans-Nebeker | Red | 40.00 | 100.00 | 400.00 | 2600.00 |
| ☐1891 | Tillman-Morgan | Red | 40.00 | 100.00 | 400.00 | 1650.00 |

**TWO DOLLAR NOTES** (1896) SILVER CERTIFICATES
(Large Size) **NOTE NO. 27**

**Face Design:** Science presenting Steam and Electricity to Industry and Commerce.

**Back Design:** Portraits of Robert Fulton and Samuel F. B. Morse.

### THIS IS THE SECOND NOTE OF
### THE POPULAR EDUCATIONAL SERIES

| SERIES | SIGNATURES | SEAL | A.B.P. | GOOD | V. FINE | UNC. |
|--------|------------|------|--------|------|---------|------|
| ☐1896 | Tillman-Morgan | Red | 60.00 | 170.00 | 700.00 | 1900.00 |
| ☐1896 | Bruce-Roberts | Red | 60.00 | 150.00 | 700.00 | 1850.00 |

**TWO DOLLAR NOTES** (1899) SILVER CERTIFICATES
(Large Size)                                    **NOTE NO. 28**

**Face Design:** Portrait of President Washington between figures of Trade and Agriculture, blue "2" left, blue seal right.

**Back Design**

| SERIES | SIGNATURES | SEAL | A.B.P. | GOOD | V. FINE | UNC. |
|--------|-----------|------|--------|------|---------|------|
| ☐1899 | Lyons-Roberts | Blue | 13.00 | 30.00 | 110.00 | 325.00 |
| ☐1899 | Lyons-Treat | Blue | 13.00 | 30.00 | 110.00 | 325.00 |
| ☐1899 | Vernon-Treat | Blue | 13.00 | 30.00 | 110.00 | 325.00 |
| ☐1899 | Vernon-McClung | Blue | 13.00 | 30.00 | 110.00 | 325.00 |
| ☐1899 | Napier-McClung | Blue | 13.00 | 30.00 | 110.00 | 325.00 |
| ☐1899 | Napier-Thompson | Blue | 15.00 | 35.00 | 270.00 | 1050.00 |
| ☐1899 | Parker-Burke | Blue | 13.00 | 30.00 | 110.00 | 325.00 |
| ☐1899 | Teehee-Burke | Blue | 13.00 | 30.00 | 110.00 | 325.00 |
| ☐1899 | Elliott-Burke | Blue | 13.00 | 30.00 | 110.00 | 325.00 |
| ☐1899 | Speelman-White | Blue | 13.00 | 30.00 | 110.00 | 325.00 |

**TWO DOLLAR NOTES** (1890-1891)
TREASURY OR COIN NOTES

(Large Size)                                    **NOTE NO. 29**

**Face Design:** Portrait of General James McPherson.

**Back Design:** Large "TWO" center, over obligation. Large "2" on engraved background right. Intricate engraving, printed green.

| SERIES | SIGNATURES | SEAL | A.B.P. | GOOD | V. FINE | UNC. |
|--------|------------|------|--------|------|---------|------|
| ☐1890 | Rosecrans-Huston | Brown | 90.00 | 250.00 | 800.00 | 2800.00 |
| ☐1890 | Rosecrans-Nebeker | Brown | 90.00 | 250.00 | 800.00 | 2800.00 |
| ☐1890 | Rosecrans-Nebeker | Red | 90.00 | 250.00 | 800.00 | 2800.00 |

**TWO DOLLAR NOTES** (1890-1891)
TREASURY OR COIN NOTES

(Large Size)                                    **NOTE NO. 30**

**Face Design:** Similar to Note No. 29
**Back Design:** Revised.

| SERIES | SIGNATURES | SEAL | A.B.P. | GOOD | V. FINE | UNC. |
|--------|------------|------|--------|------|---------|------|
| ☐1891 | Rosecrans-Nebeker | Red | 40.00 | 90.00 | 250.00 | 800.00 |
| ☐1891 | Tillman-Morgan | Red | 40.00 | 90.00 | 250.00 | 800.00 |
| ☐1891 | Bruce-Roberts | Red | 40.00 | 90.00 | 250.00 | 800.00 |

**TWO DOLLAR NOTES** (1918)
FEDERAL RESERVE BANK NOTES

(Large Size) **NOTE NO. 31**

**Face Design:** Portrait of President Jefferson to left, name of bank in center, blue seal to the right, blue numbers, Federal Reserve district letter and number in four corners.

**Back Design:** American battleship of World War I.

## TWO DOLLAR NOTES (1918)
### FEDERAL RESERVE BANK NOTES
(Large Size)                                    **NOTE NO. 31**

| BANK & CITY | GOV'T SIGNATURES | BANK SIGNATURES | A.B.P. | GOOD | V. FINE | UNC. |
|---|---|---|---|---|---|---|
| ☐ Boston | Teehee-Burke | Bullen-Morss | 25.00 | 85.00 | 190.00 | 425.00 |
| ☐ Boston | Teehee-Burke | Willet-Morss | 25.00 | 85.00 | 190.00 | 425.00 |
| ☐ Boston | Elliot-Burke | Willet-Morss | 25.00 | 85.00 | 190.00 | 425.00 |
| ☐ New York | Teehee-Burke | Sailer-Strong | 25.00 | 85.00 | 190.00 | 425.00 |
| ☐ New York | Teehee-Burke | Hendricks-Strong | 25.00 | 85.00 | 190.00 | 425.00 |
| ☐ New York | Elliott-Burke | Hendricks-Strong | 25.00 | 85.00 | 190.00 | 425 00 |
| ☐ Philadelphia | Teehee-Burke | Hardt-Passmore | 25.00 | 85 00 | 190.00 | 425.00 |
| ☐ Philadelphia | Teehee-Burke | Dyer-Passmore | 25.00 | 85.00 | 190.00 | 425.00 |
| ☐ Philadelphia | Elliott-Burke | Dyer-Passmore | 25.00 | 85 00 | 190.00 | 425.00 |
| ☐ Philadelphia | Elliott-Burke | Dyer-Norris | 25.00 | 85.00 | 190.00 | 425.00 |
| ☐ Cleveland | Teehee-Burke | Baxter-Francher | 25.00 | 85.00 | 190.00 | 425.00 |
| ☐ Cleveland | Teehee-Burke | Davis-Francher | 25.00 | 85.00 | 190.00 | 425.00 |
| ☐ Cleveland | Elliott-Burke | Davis-Francher | 25.00 | 85.00 | 190.00 | 425.00 |
| ☐ Richmond | Teehee-Burke | Keesee-Seay | 25.00 | 85.00 | 190.00 | 425.00 |
| ☐ Richmond | Elliott-Burke | Keesee-Seay | 25.00 | 85.00 | 190.00 | 425.00 |
| ☐ Atlanta | Teehee-Burke | Pike-McCord | 25.00 | 85.00 | 190.00 | 425.00 |
| ☐ Atlanta | Teehee-Burke | Bell-McCord | 25.00 | 85.00 | 190.00 | 425.00 |
| ☐ Atlanta | Elliott-Burke | Bell-Wellborn | 25.00 | 85.00 | 190.00 | 425.00 |
| ☐ Chicago | Teehee-Burke | McCloud-McDougal | 25.00 | 85.00 | 190.00 | 425.00 |

| BANK & CITY | GOV'T SIGNATURES | BANK SIGNATURES | A.B.P. | GOOD | V. FINE | UNC. |
|---|---|---|---|---|---|---|
| ☐ Chicago | Teehee-Burke | Cramer-McDougal | 25.00 | 85.00 | 190.00 | 425.00 |
| ☐ Chicago | Elliott-Burke | Cramer-McDougal | 25.00 | 85.00 | 190.00 | 425.00 |
| ☐ St. Louis | Teehee-Burke | Attebery-Wells | 25.00 | 85.00 | 190.00 | 425.00 |
| ☐ St. Louis | Teehee-Burke | Attebery-Biggs | 25.00 | 85.00 | 190.00 | 425.00 |
| ☐ St. Louis | Elliott-Burke | Attebery-Biggs | 25.00 | 85.00 | 190.00 | 425.00 |
| ☐ St. Louis | Elliott-Burke | White-Biggs | 25.00 | 85.00 | 190.00 | 425.00 |
| ☐ Minneapolis | Teehee-Burke | Cook-Wold | 25.00 | 85.00 | 190.00 | 425.00 |
| ☐ Minneapolis | Elliott-Burke | Cook-Young | 25.00 | 85.00 | 190.00 | 425.00 |
| ☐ Kansas City | Teehee-Burke | Anderson-Miller | 25.00 | 85.00 | 190.00 | 425.00 |
| ☐ Kansas City | Elliott-Burke | Helm-Miller | 25.00 | 85.00 | 190.00 | 425.00 |
| ☐ Dallas | Teehee-Burke | Talley-VanZandt | 25.00 | 85.00 | 190.00 | 425.00 |
| ☐ Dallas | Elliott-Burke | Talley-VanZandt | 25.00 | 85.00 | 190.00 | 425.00 |
| ☐ San Francisco | Teehee-Burke | Clerk-Lynch | 25.00 | 85.00 | 190.00 | 425.00 |
| ☐ San Francisco | Elliott-Burke | Clerk-Calkins | 25.00 | 85.00 | 190.00 | 425.00 |
| ☐ San Francisco | Elliott-Burke | Ambrose-Calkins | 25.00 | 85.00 | 190.00 | 425.00 |

## TWO DOLLAR NOTES (1976)
### FEDERAL RESERVE NOTES

(Small Size)                                    **NOTE NO. 31A**

**Face Design:** Portrait of President Jefferson.

**Back Design:** Signing of The Declaration of Independence.

### SERIES OF 1976 NEFF-SIMON—GREEN SEAL

| DISTRICT | A.B.P. | UNC. | DISTRICT | A.B.P. | UNC. |
|---|---|---|---|---|---|
| ☐1A Boston | 2.50 | 4.50 | ☐7G Chicago | 2.50 | 4.50 |
| ☐2B New York | 2.50 | 4.50 | ☐8H St. Louis | 2.50 | 4.50 |
| ☐3C Philadelphia | 2.50 | 4.50 | ☐9I Minneapolis | 2.50 | 4.50 |
| ☐4D Cleveland | 2.50 | 4.50 | ☐10J Kansas City | 2.50 | 4.50 |
| ☐5E Richmond | 2.50 | 4.50 | ☐11K Dallas | 2.50 | 4.50 |
| ☐6F Atlanta | 2.50 | 4.50 | ☐12L San Francisco | 2.50 | 4.50 |

# FIVE DOLLAR NOTES

**FIVE DOLLAR NOTES** (1861) DEMAND NOTES
(Large Size)                                          **NOTE NO. 32**

**Face Design:** Left, Statue of America by Crawford atop
United States Capitol. Center, numeral "5" in green. Right,
portrait of Alexander Hamilton, statesman, first Secretary of
the Treasury.

**Back Design:** Numerous small "fives" in ovals. This note
has no Treasury Seal. The signatures are those of Treasury
Department employees who signed for officials.

| CITY | A.B.P. | GOOD | V. GOOD |
|------|--------|------|---------|
| ☐Boston (I) | 275.00 | 1500.00 | 2600.00 |
| ☐New York (I) | 275.00 | 1500.00 | 2600.00 |
| ☐Philadelphia (I) | 275.00 | 1500.00 | 2600.00 |
| ☐Cincinnati (I) | 500.00 | 8000.00 | 16,500.00 |
| ☐St. Louis (I) | 500.00 | 8000.00 | 16,500.00 |
| ☐Boston (II) | 275.00 | 350.00 | 900.00 |
| ☐New York (II) | 275.00 | 350.00 | 900.00 |
| ☐Philadelphia (II) | 275.00 | 350.00 | 900.00 |
| ☐Cincinnati (II) | 300.00 | 6000.00 | 12,000.00 |
| ☐St. Louis (II) | 300.00 | 6000.00 | 12,000.00 |

# FIVE DOLLAR NOTES (1875-1907)
## UNITED STATES NOTES
## (ALSO KNOWN AS LEGAL TENDER NOTES)
(Large Size)                                      **NOTE NO. 35**

**Back Design:** Note No. 33. First Obligation.

**Back Design:** Note No. 33A. Second Obligation

| SERIES | SIGNATURES | SEAL | A.B.P. | GOOD | V. FINE | UNC. |
|--------|------------|------|--------|------|---------|------|
| ☐1862 | Crittenden-Spinner* | Red | 40.00 | 85.00 | 320.00 | 650.00 |
| ☐1862 | Crittenden-Spinner** | Red | 40.00 | 80.00 | 320.00 | 600.00 |
| ☐1863 | Crittenden-Spinner** | Red | 40.00 | 85.00 | 320.00 | 650.00 |

*First Obligation
**Second Obligation

## FIVE DOLLAR NOTES (1869) UNITED STATES NOTES
### (ALSO KNOWN AS LEGAL TENDER NOTES)

(Large Size)                                        **NOTE NO. 34**

**Face Design:** Portrait of President Jackson on left. Pioneer and family in center.

**Back Design:** Color, green. This is a companion note to the $1.00 and $2.00 notes of 1869 Rainbow Notes.

| SERIES | SIGNATURES | SEAL | A.B.P. | GOOD | V. FINE | UNC. |
|--------|-----------|------|--------|------|---------|------|
| ☐1869 | Allison-Spinner | Red | 42.00 | 100.00 | 280.00 | 700.00 |

**FIVE DOLLAR NOTES** (1875-1907)
UNITED STATES NOTES
(ALSO KNOWN AS LEGAL TENDER NOTES)
(Large Size) **NOTE NO. 35**

**Back Design:** Revised.
**Face Design:** Similar to previous Note.

| SERIES | SIGNATURES | SEAL | A.B.P. | GOOD | V. FINE | UNC. |
|--------|------------|------|--------|------|---------|------|
| ☐1875 | Allison-New | Red | 17.00 | 50.00 | 100.00 | 410.00 |
| ☐1875A | Allison-New | Red | 18.00 | 50.00 | 120.00 | 600.00 |
| ☐1875B | Allison-New | Red | 18.00 | 50.00 | 120.00 | 600.00 |
| ☐1875 | Allison-Wyman | Red | 18.00 | 50.00 | 120.00 | 600.00 |
| ☐1878 | Allison-Gilfillan | Red | 25.00 | 60.00 | 150.00 | 600.00 |
| ☐1880 | Scofield-Gilfillan | Brown | 18.00 | 100.00 | 275.00 | 700.00 |
| ☐1880 | Bruce-Gilfillan | Brown | 15.00 | 40.00 | 100.00 | 350.00 |
| ☐1880 | Bruce-Wyman | Brown | 15.00 | 40.00 | 100.00 | 400.00 |
| ☐1880 | Bruce-Wyman | Red | 15.00 | 45.00 | 120.00 | 1350.00 |
| ☐1880 | Rosecrans-Jordan | Red | 15.00 | 42.00 | 100.00 | 650.00 |
| ☐1880 | Rosecrans-Hyatt | Red | 15.00 | 42.00 | 100.00 | 625.00 |
| ☐1880 | Rosecrans-Huston | Red | 22.00 | 50.00 | 115.00 | 650.00 |
| ☐1880 | Rosecrans-Huston | Brown | 18.00 | 50.00 | 120.00 | 750.00 |
| ☐1880 | Rosecrans-Nebeker | Brown | 20.00 | 50.00 | 120.00 | 700.00 |
| ☐1880 | Rosecrans-Nebeker | Red | 12.00 | 42.00 | 120.00 | 285.00 |
| ☐1880 | Tillman-Morgan | Red | 11.00 | 32.00 | 80.00 | 270.00 |
| ☐1880 | Bruce-Roberts | Red | 11.00 | 32.00 | 80.00 | 270.00 |
| ☐1880 | Lyons-Roberts | Red | 11.00 | 32.00 | 80.00 | 270.00 |
| ☐1907 | Vernon-Treat | Red | 11.00 | 30.00 | 60.00 | 200.00 |
| ☐1907 | Vernon-McClung | Red | 11.00 | 24.00 | 60.00 | 200.00 |
| ☐1907 | Napier-McClung | Red | 11.00 | 24.00 | 60.00 | 200.00 |
| ☐1907 | Napier-Thompson | Red | 40.00 | 90.00 | 280.00 | 675.00 |
| ☐1907 | Parker-Burke | Red | 10.00 | 24.00 | 60.00 | 190.00 |
| ☐1907 | Teehee-Burke | Red | 10.00 | 24.00 | 60.00 | 190.00 |
| ☐1907 | Elliott-Burke | Red | 10.00 | 24.00 | 60.00 | 190.00 |

| SERIES | SIGNATURES | SEAL | A.B.P. | GOOD | V. FINE | UNC. |
|--------|-----------|------|--------|------|---------|------|
| ☐1907 | Elliott-White | Red | 10.00 | 24.00 | 60.00 | 190.00 |
| ☐1907 | Speelman-White | Red | 10.00 | 24.00 | 60.00 | 190.00 |
| ☐1907 | Woods-White | Red | 10.00 | 24.00 | 60.00 | 210.00 |

## FIVE DOLLAR NOTES (1928) UNITED STATES NOTES
### (ALSO KNOWN AS LEGAL TENDER NOTES)
(Small Size)                                          **NOTE NO. 36**

**Face Design:** Portrait of President Lincoln center. Red seal to left, red serial numbers.

**Back Design:** Lincoln Memorial in Washington, D.C.

| SERIES | SIGNATURES | SEAL | A.B.P | GOOD | V. FINE | UNC. |
|--------|-----------|------|-------|------|---------|------|
| ☐1928 | Woods-Mellon | Red | 6.00 | 7.00 | 11.00 | 28.00 |
| ☐1928A | Woods-Mills | Red | 6.00 | 7.00 | 13.00 | 42.00 |
| ☐1928B | Julian-Morgenthau | Red | 6.00 | 7.00 | 11.00 | 22.00 |
| ☐1928C | Julian-Morgenthau | Red | 6.00 | 7.00 | 11.00 | 22.00 |
| ☐1928D | Julian-Vinson | Red | 6.00 | 7.00 | 18.00 | 140.00 |
| ☐1928E | Julian-Snyder | Red | 6.00 | 7.00 | 11.00 | 23.00 |
| ☐1928F | Clark-Snyder | Red | 6.00 | 7.00 | 11.00 | 23.00 |

## FIVE DOLLAR NOTES (1953-1963)
### UNITED STATES NOTES

(Small Size)                                    NOTE NO. 37

**Face Design:** Similar to previous note. Portrait of President Lincoln center. Red Seal is moved to the right, red numbers.
**Back Design:** Similar to previous note.

| SERIES | SIGNATURES | SEAL | A.B.P. | GOOD | V. FINE | UNC. |
|--------|-----------|------|--------|------|---------|------|
| ☐1953 | Priest-Humphrey | Red | 6.00 | 7.00 | 9.00 | 16.00 |
| ☐1953A | Priest-Anderson | Red | 6.00 | 7.00 | 11.00 | 16.00 |
| ☐1953B | Smith-Dillon | Red | 6.00 | 7.00 | 9.00 | 13.00 |
| ☐1953C | Granahan-Dillon | Red | 6.00 | 7.00 | 9.00 | 16.00 |

### FIVE DOLLAR NOTES (1953-1963)
### UNITED STATES NOTES
### (ALSO KNOWN AS LEGAL TENDER NOTES)

(Small Size)                                    NOTE NO. 37A

**Back Design:** The following notes have "IN GOD WE TRUST" on the back.
**Face Design:** Similar to previous note.

| SERIES | SIGNATURES | SEAL | A.B.P. | GOOD | V. FINE | UNC. |
|--------|-----------|------|--------|------|---------|------|
| ☐1963 | Granahan-Dillon | Red | 6.00 | 7.00 | 11.00 | 14.00 |

Production of Five Dollar United States Notes ended in 1967.

## FIVE DOLLAR NOTES (1863-1875)
### NATIONAL BANK NOTES
FIRST CHARTER PERIOD (Large Size)                    **NOTE NO. 38**

**Face Design:** The Columbus Note. The face shows Columbus in sight of land and Columbus with an Indian Princess.

**Back Design:** Christopher Columbus landing at San Salvador, 1492. Also the State seal left, and American Eagle right.

| SERIES | SIGNATURES | SEAL | A.B.P. | GOOD | V. FINE | UNC. |
|--------|-----------|------|--------|------|---------|------|
| ☐ Original | Chittenden-Spinner | Red | 25.00 | 80.00 | 250.00 | 1300.00 |
| ☐ Original | Colby-Spinner | Red | 25.00 | 80.00 | 250.00 | 1250.00 |
| ☐ Original | Jeffries-Spinner | Red | 180.00 | 500.00 | 1600.00 | 3600.00 |
| ☐ Original | Allison-Spinner | Red | 25.00 | 75.00 | 250.00 | 1300.00 |
| ☐ 1875 | Allison-New | Red | 25.00 | 75.00 | 250.00 | 1100.00 |
| ☐ 1875 | Allison-Wyman | Red | 25.00 | 75.00 | 250.00 | 1100.00 |
| ☐ 1875 | Allison-Gilfillan | Red | 25.00 | 75.00 | 250.00 | 1100.00 |
| ☐ 1875 | Scofield-Gilfillan | Red | 25.00 | 75.00 | 250.00 | 1100.00 |
| ☐ 1875 | Bruce-Gilfillan | Red | 25.00 | 75.00 | 250.00 | 1100.00 |
| ☐ 1875 | Bruce-Wyman | Red | 25.00 | 75.00 | 250.00 | 1100.00 |
| ☐ 1875 | Bruce-Jordan | Red | | EXTREMELY RARE | | |
| ☐ 1875 | Rosecrans-Huston | Red | 25.00 | 75.00 | 250.00 | 1100.00 |
| ☐ 1875 | Rosecrans-Jordan | Red | 25.00 | 75.00 | 250.00 | 1100.00 |

# FIVE DOLLAR NOTES (1882) NATIONAL BANK NOTES
## SECOND CHARTER PERIOD (Large Size)     NOTE NO. 39

**First Issue**—Brown seal and brown backs.
**Face Design:** Portrait of President Garfield left. Name of bank and city center, brown seal to right. Brown charter number.

**Back Design:** Brown border design similar to previous note. Center oval now has the bank's charter number in green. The top signatures are those of the treasury officials. Bottom signatures, usually hand written or probably rubber stamped, are bank officials.

| SERIES | SIGNATURES | SEAL | A.B.P. | GOOD | V. FINE | UNC. |
|--------|-----------|------|--------|------|---------|------|
| ☐1882 | Bruce-Gilfillan | Brown | 25.00 | 65.00 | 160.00 | 650.00 |
| ☐1882 | Bruce-Wyman | Brown | 25.00 | 65.00 | 160.00 | 650.00 |
| ☐1882 | Bruce-Jordan | Brown | 25.00 | 65.00 | 160.00 | 650.00 |
| ☐1882 | Rosecrans-Jordan | Brown | 25.00 | 65.00 | 160.00 | 650.00 |
| ☐1882 | Rosecrans-Hyatt | Brown | 25.00 | 65.00 | 160.00 | 650.00 |
| ☐1882 | Rosecrans-Huston | Brown | 25.00 | 65.00 | 160.00 | 650.00 |
| ☐1882 | Rosecrans-Nebeker | Brown | 25.00 | 65.00 | 160.00 | 650.00 |
| ☐1882 | Rosecrans-Morgan | Brown | 70.00 | 165.00 | 400.00 | 1100.00 |
| ☐1882 | Tillman-Morgan | Brown | 25.00 | 65.00 | 160.00 | 650.00 |
| ☐1882 | Tillman-Roberts | Brown | 25.00 | 65.00 | 160.00 | 650.00 |
| ☐1882 | Bruce-Roberts | Brown | 25.00 | 65.00 | 160.00 | 650.00 |
| ☐1882 | Lyons-Roberts | Brown | 25.00 | 65.00 | 160.00 | 650.00 |
| ☐1882 | Lyons-Treat | | | (Unknown in any collection) | | |
| ☐1882 | Vernon-Treat | Brown | 25.00 | 70.00 | 160.00 | 650.00 |

**FIVE DOLLAR NOTES** (1882) NATIONAL BANK NOTES
SECOND CHARTER PERIOD (Large Size)     **NOTE NO. 40**

**Face Design:** Similar to preceding portrait of President
Garfield.

**Back Design:** Back is now green with date 1882-1908 in
center.

| SERIES | SIGNATURES | SEAL | A.B.P. | GOOD | V. FINE | UNC. |
|--------|-----------|------|--------|------|---------|------|
| ☐1882 | Rosecrans-Huston | Blue | 20.00 | 50.00 | 115.00 | 550.00 |
| ☐1882 | Rosecrans-Nebeker | Blue | 20.00 | 50.00 | 115.00 | 550.00 |
| ☐1882 | Rosecrans-Morgan | Blue | 100.00 | 200.00 | 800.00 | 1850.00 |
| ☐1882 | Tillman-Morgan | Blue | 20.00 | 50.00 | 115.00 | 550.00 |
| ☐1882 | Tillman-Roberts | Blue | 20.00 | 50.00 | 115.00 | 550.00 |
| ☐1882 | Bruce-Roberts | Blue | 20.00 | 50.00 | 115.00 | 550.00 |
| ☐1882 | Lyons-Roberts | Blue | 20.00 | 50.00 | 115.00 | 550.00 |
| ☐1882 | Vernon-Treat | Blue | 20.00 | 50.00 | 115.00 | 550.00 |
| ☐1882 | Vernon-McClung | Blue | | | | RARE |
| ☐1882 | Napier-McClung | Blue | | | | RARE |

**FIVE DOLLAR NOTES** (1882) NATIONAL BANK NOTES
SECOND CHARTER PERIOD, Third Issue (Large Size)   **NOTE NO. 41**

**Face Design:** Same as Note No. 39. Blue Seal.

**Back Design:** Similar to Note No. 40, "FIVE DOLLARS"
replaces 1882-1908.

| SERIES | SIGNATURES | SEAL | A.B.P. | GOOD | V. FINE | UNC. |
|---|---|---|---|---|---|---|
| ☐1882 | Tillman-Morgan | Blue | 35.00 | 80.00 | 310.00 | 1250.00 |
| ☐1882 | Tillman-Roberts | Blue | 35.00 | 80.00 | 310.00 | 1250.00 |
| ☐1882 | Bruce-Roberts | Blue | 35.00 | 80.00 | 310.00 | 1250.00 |
| ☐1882 | Lyons-Roberts | Blue | 35.00 | 80.00 | 310.00 | 1250.00 |
| ☐1882 | Vernon-Treat | Blue | 35.00 | 80.00 | 310.00 | 1250.00 |
| ☐1882 | Napier-McClung | Blue | 35.00 | 80.00 | 310.00 | 1250.00 |
| ☐1882 | Teehee-Burke | Blue | | EXTREMELY RARE | | |

## FIVE DOLLAR NOTES (1902) NATIONAL BANK NOTES
THIRD CHARTER PERIOD (Large Size)     **NOTE NO. 42**

**First Issue**—Red seal and charter numbers.
**Face Design:** Portrait of President Harrison left, name of bank and city center, Treasury Seal to right, red seal and charter number.

**Back Design:** Landing of Pilgrims.

| SERIES | SIGNATURES | SEAL | A.B.P. | GOOD | V. FINE | UNC. |
|--------|------------|------|--------|------|---------|------|
| ☐1902 | Lyons-Roberts | Red | 24.00 | 60.00 | 165.00 | 750.00 |
| ☐1902 | Lyons-Treat | Red | 24.00 | 60.00 | 165.00 | 750.00 |
| ☐1902 | Vernon-Treat | Red | 24.00 | 60.00 | 165.00 | 750.00 |

## FIVE DOLLAR NOTES (1902) NATIONAL BANK NOTES
THIRD CHARTER PERIOD (Large Size)     **NOTE NO. 42A**

| SERIES | SIGNATURES | SEAL | A.B.P. | GOOD | V. FINE | UNC. |
|--------|------------|------|--------|------|---------|------|
| ☐1902 | Lyons-Roberts | Blue | 9.00 | 21.00 | 45.00 | 250.00 |
| ☐1902 | Lyons-Treat | Blue | 9.00 | 21.00 | 45.00 | 250.00 |
| ☐1902 | Vernon-Treat | Blue | 9.00 | 21.00 | 45.00 | 250.00 |
| ☐1902 | Vernon-McClung | Blue | 9.00 | 21.00 | 45.00 | 250.00 |
| ☐1902 | Napier-McClung | Blue | 9.00 | 21.00 | 45.00 | 250.00 |
| ☐1902 | Napier-Thompson | Blue | 15.00 | 32.00 | 65.00 | 450.00 |
| ☐1902 | Napier-Burke | Blue | 9.00 | 21.00 | 45.00 | 250.00 |
| ☐1902 | Parker-Burke | Blue | 9.00 | 21.00 | 45.00 | 250.00 |
| ☐1902 | Teehee-Burke | Blue | 9.00 | 21.00 | 80.00 | 325.00 |

**FIVE DOLLAR NOTES** (1902) NATIONAL BANK NOTES
THIRD CHARTER PERIOD (Large Size)          **NOTE NO. 42B**
**Third Issue**—Blue seal and numbers. The following notes
do not have date of 1902-1908 on the back.

| SERIES | SIGNATURES | SEAL | A.B.P. | GOOD | V. FINE | UNC. |
|--------|-----------|------|--------|------|---------|------|
| ☐1902 | Lyons-Roberts | Blue | 8.50 | 18.00 | 40.00 | 185.00 |
| ☐1902 | Lyons-Treat | Blue | 8.50 | 18.00 | 40.00 | 185.00 |
| ☐1902 | Vernon-Treat | Blue | 8.50 | 18.00 | 40.00 | 185.00 |
| ☐1902 | Vernon-McClung | Blue | 8.50 | 18.00 | 40.00 | 185.00 |
| ☐1902 | Napier-McClung | Blue | 8.50 | 18.00 | 40.00 | 185.00 |
| ☐1902 | Napier-Thompson | Blue | 8.50 | 18.00 | 60.00 | 210.00 |
| ☐1902 | Napier-Burke | Blue | 8.50 | 18.00 | 40.00 | 185.00 |
| ☐1902 | Parker-Burke | Blue | 8.50 | 18.00 | 40.00 | 185.00 |
| ☐1902 | Teehee-Burke | Blue | 8.50 | 18.00 | 40.00 | 185.00 |
| ☐1902 | Elliott-Burke | Blue | 8.50 | 18.00 | 40.00 | 185.00 |
| ☐1902 | Elliott-White | Blue | 8.50 | 18.00 | 40.00 | 185.00 |
| ☐1902 | Speelman-White | Blue | 8.50 | 18.00 | 40.00 | 185.00 |
| ☐1902 | Woods-White | Blue | 8.50 | 18.00 | 40.00 | 185.00 |
| ☐1902 | Woods-Tate | Blue | 8.50 | 18.00 | 40.00 | 185.00 |
| ☐1902 | Jones-Woods | Blue | 25.00 | 85.00 | 180.00 | 420.00 |

FIVE DOLLAR NOTES (1929) NATIONAL BANK NOTES
(Small Size)                              **NOTE NO. 43**

**TYPE I**

**TYPE II**

**Face Design:** Portrait of President Lincoln in center, name of
bank to left, brown seal to the right. TYPE I—Charter number
in black. TYPE II—Similar, charter number added in brown.

**Back Design:** Lincoln Memorial

| SERIES | SIGNATURES | SEAL | A.B.P. | GOOD | V. FINE | UNC. |
|--------|-----------|------|--------|------|---------|------|
| ☐1929 | TYPE I Jones-Woods | Brown | 6.50 | 9.00 | 18.00 | 60.00 |
| ☐1929 | TYPE II Jones-Woods | Brown | 6.50 | 12.00 | 25.00 | 65.00 |

## FIVE DOLLAR NOTES (1870)
### NATIONAL GOLD BANK NOTES

(Large Size) **NOTE NO. 44**

**Face Design:** Vignettes of Columbus sighting land. Presentation of an Indian Princess. Red seal. Signatures, Allison-Spinner.

**Back Design:** California State Seal left, gold coins center, American Eagle right.

| DATE | BANK | CITY | A.B.P. | GOOD | V. GOOD |
|------|------|------|--------|------|---------|
| ☐1870 First National Gold Bank | | San Francisco | 200.00 | 600.00 | 1300.00 |
| ☐1872 National Gold Bank and Trust Company | | | | | |
| | | San Francisco | 200.00 | 600.00 | 1300.00 |
| ☐1872 National Gold Bank of D.O. Mills and Company | | | | | |
| | | Sacramento | 200.00 | 800.00 | 1600.00 |
| ☐1873 First National Gold Bank | | Santa Barbara | 200.00 | 800.00 | 1600.00 |
| ☐1873 First National Gold Bank | | Stockton | 200.00 | 800.00 | 2000.00 |
| ☐1874 Farmers National Gold Bank | | San Jose | 200.00 | 800.00 | 2000.00 |

## FIVE DOLLAR NOTES (1886-1891)
### SILVER CERTIFICATES

(Large Size) **NOTE NO. 45**

**Face Design:** Portrait of President Grant.

**Back Design:** Five silver dollars.

| SERIES | SIGNATURES | SEAL | A.B.P. | GOOD | V. FINE | UNC. |
|--------|-----------|------|--------|------|---------|------|
| ☐1886 | Rosecrans-Jordan | Red | 75.00 | 200.00 | 900.00 | 3100.00 |
| ☐1886 | Rosecrans-Hyatt | Red Sm | 75.00 | 200.00 | 800.00 | 2400.00 |
| ☐1886 | Rosecrans-Hyatt | Red Lg | 75.00 | 200.00 | 870.00 | 2900.00 |
| ☐1886 | Rosecrans-Huston | Red Lg | 75.00 | 200.00 | 870.00 | 2800.00 |
| ☐1886 | Rosecrans-Huston | Brown | 75.00 | 200.00 | 800.00 | 2800.00 |
| ☐1886 | Rosecrans-Nebeker | Brown | 75.00 | 200.00 | 900.00 | 2600.00 |
| ☐1886 | Rosecrans-Nebeker | Red Sm | 100.00 | 250.00 | 1300.00 | 4100.00 |

**FIVE DOLLAR NOTES** (1891) SILVER CERTIFICATES
(Large Size)                                    **NOTE NO. 46**

**Face Design:** Similar to previous note.

**Back Design:** Revised.

| SERIES | SIGNATURES | SEAL | A.B.P. | GOOD | V. FINE | UNC. |
|--------|-----------|------|--------|------|---------|------|
| ☐1891 | Rosecrans-Nebeker | Red | 50.00 | 100.00 | 600.00 | 2600.00 |
| ☐1891 | Tillman-Morgan | Red | 50.00 | 100.00 | 600.00 | 1800.00 |

# FIVE DOLLAR NOTES (1896) SILVER CERTIFICATES
(Large Size) **NOTE NO. 47**

**Face Design:** Portrait of General Grant and General Sheridan.

## LAST NOTE OF THE POPULAR EDUCATIONAL SERIES

**Back Design**: Five females representing electricity as the dominant force in the world.

| SERIES | SIGNATURES | SEAL | A.B.P. | GOOD | V. FINE | UNC. |
|--------|-----------|------|--------|------|---------|------|
| ☐1896 | Tillman-Morgan | Red | 130.00 | 260.00 | 1200.00 | 3400.00 |
| ☐1896 | Bruce-Roberts | Red | 130.00 | 260.00 | 1200.00 | 3400.00 |
| ☐1896 | Lyons-Roberts | Red | 130.00 | 260.00 | 1200.00 | 3400.00 |

## FIVE DOLLAR NOTES (1899) SILVER CERTIFICATES
(Large Size)                                    **NOTE NO. 48**

**Face Design:** Portrait of Indian Chief.

**Back Design:** Green "V" and "5."

| SERIES | SIGNATURES | SEAL | A.B.P. | GOOD | V. FINE | UNC. |
|--------|-----------|------|--------|------|---------|------|
| ☐1899 | Lyons-Roberts | Blue | 25.00 | 80.00 | 350.00 | 950.00 |
| ☐1899 | Lyons-Treat | Blue | 25.00 | 80.00 | 350.00 | 850.00 |
| ☐1899 | Vernon-Treat | Blue | 25.00 | 80.00 | 350.00 | 850.00 |
| ☐1899 | Vernon-McClung | Blue | 25.00 | 80.00 | 350.00 | 850.00 |
| ☐1899 | Napier-McClung | Blue | 25.00 | 80.00 | 350.00 | 850.00 |
| ☐1899 | Napier-Thompson | Blue | 40.00 | 80.00 | 400.00 | 2300.00 |
| ☐1899 | Parker-Burke | Blue | 25.00 | 80.00 | 350.00 | 850.00 |
| ☐1899 | Teehee-Burke | Blue | 25.00 | 80.00 | 350.00 | 850.00 |
| ☐1899 | Elliott-Burke | Blue | 25.00 | 80.00 | 350.00 | 850.00 |
| ☐1899 | Elliott-White | Blue | 25.00 | 80.00 | 350.00 | 850.00 |
| ☐1899 | Speelman-White | Blue | 25.00 | 80.00 | 350.00 | 1000.00 |

**FIVE DOLLAR NOTES** (1923) SILVER CERTIFICATES
(Large Size)                                                  **NOTE NO. 49**

**Face Design:** Portrait of President Lincoln in oval, nickname "Porthole Note," blue seal left, blue "5" right.

**Back Design:** Obverse of Great Seal of the United States.

| SERIES | SIGNATURES | SEAL | A.B.P. | GOOD | V. FINE | UNC. |
|--------|-----------|------|--------|------|---------|------|
| ☐1923 | Speelman-White | Blue | 35.00 | 80.00 | 400.00 | 1200.00 |

**FIVE DOLLAR NOTES** (1934) SILVER CERTIFICATES
(Small Size)                                    **NOTE NO. 50**

**First Issue**—Small size of $5.00 Silver Certificates 1934.
**Face Design:** Portrait of President Lincoln, blue "5" to left,
blue seal to right.

**Back Design:** All small-size $5.00 notes have the same
back design.

| SERIES | SIGNATURES | SEAL | A.B.P. | GOOD | V. FINE | UNC. |
|--------|-----------|------|--------|------|---------|------|
| ☐1934 | Julian-Morgenthau | Blue | 6.00 | 7.00 | 9.00 | 22.00 |
| ☐1934A | Julian-Morgenthau | Blue | 6.00 | 7.00 | 9.00 | 20.00 |
| ☐1934A | Julian-Morgenthau | Yellow | 6.50 | 8.00 | 11.00 | 46.00 |

This note, with Yellow Treasury Seal, was a Special Issue during World War
II for military use in combat areas of North Africa and Europe.

| SERIES | SIGNATURES | SEAL | A.B.P. | GOOD | V. FINE | UNC. |
|--------|-----------|------|--------|------|---------|------|
| ☐1934B | Julian-Vinson | Blue | 6.00 | 7.50 | 9.00 | 36.00 |
| ☐1934C | Julian-Synder | Blue | 6.00 | 7.50 | 9.00 | 20.00 |
| ☐1934C | Clark-Snyder | Blue | 6.00 | 7.50 | 10.00 | 16.00 |

## FIVE DOLLAR NOTES (1953) SILVER CERTIFICATES
(Small Size) **NOTE NO. 51**

**Face Design:** The following notes are similar to the previous note. The face design has been revised. Gray "5" replaces blue "5" to left of Lincoln. Blue seal is slightly smaller.

**Back Design:** Same as previous note.

| SERIES | SIGNATURES | SEAL | A.B.P. | GOOD | V. FINE | UNC. |
|--------|-----------|------|--------|------|---------|------|
| ☐1953 | Priest-Humphrey | Blue | 6.00 | 7.00 | 8.00 | 13.50 |
| ☐1953A | Priest-Anderson | Blue | 6.00 | 7.00 | 8.00 | 13.00 |
| ☐1953B | Smith-Dillon | Blue | 6.00 | 7.00 | 8.00 | 13.00 |

Production of Five Dollar Silver Certificates ended in 1962.

## FIVE DOLLAR NOTES (1890) TREASURY NOTES
(Large Size) **NOTE NO. 52**

**Face Design:** Portrait of General George Henry Thomas (1816-1870), the "Rock of Chickamaugua."

**Back Design:** Note No. 52.

| SERIES | SIGNATURES | SEAL | A.B.P. | GOOD | V. FINE | UNC. |
|--------|-----------|------|--------|------|---------|------|
| ☐1890 | Rosecrans-Huston | Brown | 40.00 | 150.00 | 475.00 | 1750.00 |
| ☐1890 | Rosecrans-Nebeker | Brown | 40.00 | 110.00 | 450.00 | 1650.00 |
| ☐1890 | Rosecrans-Nebeker | Red | 40.00 | 110.00 | 450.00 | 1650.00 |

**Back Design:** Note No. 53
**Face Design:** Same as previous note.

| SERIES | SIGNATURES | SEAL | A.B.P. | GOOD | V.FINE | UNC. |
|--------|-----------|------|--------|------|--------|------|
| ☐1891 | Rosecrans-Nebeker | Red | 36.00 | 90.00 | 200.00 | 750.00 |
| ☐1891 | Tillman-Morgan | Red | 36.00 | 90.00 | 200.00 | 925.00 |
| ☐1891 | Bruce-Roberts | Red | 36.00 | 90.00 | 200.00 | 925.00 |
| ☐1891 | Lyons-Roberts | Red | 36.00 | 90.00 | 200.00 | 925.00 |

## FIVE DOLLAR NOTES (1914)
### FEDERAL RESERVE NOTES

(Large Size)                                      **NOTE NO. 54**

**Face Design:** Portrait of President Lincoln center, Federal Reserve Seal left, Treasury Seal right.

**Back Design:** Scene of Columbus in sight of land left, Landing of Pilgrims right.

### SERIES OF 1914—RED TREASURY SEAL AND RED NUMBERS

| SERIES | CITY | SIGNATURES | SEAL | A.B.P. | GOOD | V. FINE | UNC. |
|---|---|---|---|---|---|---|---|
| ☐1914 | Boston | Burke-McAdoo | Red | 15.00 | 30.00 | 80.00 | 315.00 |
| ☐1914 | New York | Burke-McAdoo | Red | 15.00 | 30.00 | 80.00 | 315.00 |
| ☐1914 | Philadelphia | Burke-McAdoo | Red | 15.00 | 30.00 | 80.00 | 315.00 |
| ☐1914 | Cleveland | Burke-McAdoo | Red | 15.00 | 30.00 | 80.00 | 315.00 |
| ☐1914 | Richmond | Burke-McAdoo | Red | 15.00 | 30.00 | 80.00 | 315.00 |
| ☐1914 | Atlanta | Burke-McAdoo | Red | 15.00 | 30.00 | 80.00 | 315.00 |
| ☐1914 | Chicago | Burke-McAdoo | Red | 15.00 | 30.00 | 80.00 | 315.00 |
| ☐1914 | St. Louis | Burke-McAdoo | Red | 15.00 | 30.00 | 80.00 | 315.00 |
| ☐1914 | Minneapolis | Burke-McAdoo | Red | 15.00 | 30.00 | 80.00 | 315.00 |
| ☐1914 | Kansas City | Burke-McAdoo | Red | 15.00 | 30.00 | 80.00 | 315.00 |
| ☐1914 | Dallas | Burke-McAdoo | Red | 15.00 | 30.00 | 80.00 | 315.00 |
| ☐1914 | San Francisco | Burke-McAdoo | Red | 15.00 | 30.00 | 80.00 | 315.00 |

### FIVE DOLLAR NOTES (1914)
FEDERAL RESERVE NOTES

**NOTE NO. 54A**

### SERIES OF 1914—BLUE TREASURY SEAL AND BLUE NUMBERS

| SERIES | CITY | SIGNATURES | SEAL | A.B.P. | GOOD | V. FINE | UNC. |
|---|---|---|---|---|---|---|---|
| ☐1914 | Boston | Burke-McAdoo | Blue | 7.50 | 12.00 | 26.00 | 135.00 |
| ☐1914 | Boston | Burke-Glass | Blue | 7.50 | 12.00 | 26.00 | 135.00 |
| ☐1914 | Boston | Burke-Huston | Blue | 7.50 | 12.00 | 26.00 | 135.00 |
| ☐1914 | Boston | White-Mellon | Blue | 7.50 | 12.00 | 26.00 | 135.00 |
| ☐1914 | New York | Burke-McAdoo | Blue | 7.50 | 12.00 | 26.00 | 135.00 |
| ☐1914 | New York | Burke-Glass | Blue | 7.50 | 12.00 | 26.00 | 135.00 |
| ☐1914 | New York | Burke-Huston | Blue | 7.50 | 12.00 | 26.00 | 135.00 |
| ☐1914 | New York | White-Mellon | Blue | 7.50 | 12.00 | 26.00 | 135.00 |
| ☐1914 | Philadelphia | Burke-McAdoo | Blue | 7.50 | 12.00 | 26.00 | 135.00 |
| ☐1914 | Philadelphia | Burke-Glass | Blue | 7.50 | 12.00 | 26.00 | 135.00 |
| ☐1914 | Philadelphia | Burke-Huston | Blue | 7.50 | 12.00 | 26.00 | 135.00 |

| SERIES | CITY | SIGNATURES | SEAL | A.B.P. | GOOD | V. FINE | UNC. |
|---|---|---|---|---|---|---|---|
| ☐1914 | Philadelphia | White-Mellon | Blue | 7.50 | 12.00 | 26.00 | 135.00 |
| ☐1914 | Cleveland | Burke-McAdoo | Blue | 7.50 | 12.00 | 26.00 | 135.00 |
| ☐1914 | Cleveland | Burke-Glass | Blue | 7.50 | 12.00 | 26.00 | 135.00 |
| ☐1914 | Cleveland | Burke-Huston | Blue | 7.50 | 12.00 | 26.00 | 135.00 |
| ☐1914 | Cleveland | White-Mellon | Blue | 7.50 | 12.00 | 26.00 | 135.00 |
| ☐1914 | Richmond | Burke-McAdoo | Blue | 7.50 | 12.00 | 26.00 | 135.00 |
| ☐1914 | Richmond | Burke-Glass | Blue | 7.50 | 12.00 | 26.00 | 135.00 |
| ☐1914 | Richmond | Burke-Huston | Blue | 7.50 | 12.00 | 26.00 | 135.00 |
| ☐1914 | Richmond | White-Mellon | Blue | 7.50 | 12.00 | 26.00 | 135.00 |
| ☐1914 | Atlanta | Burke-McAdoo | Blue | 7.50 | 12.00 | 26.00 | 135.00 |
| ☐1914 | Atlanta | Burke-Glass | Blue | 7.50 | 12.00 | 26.00 | 135.00 |
| ☐1914 | Atlanta | Burke-Huston | Blue | 7.50 | 12.00 | 26.00 | 135.00 |
| ☐1914 | Atlanta | White-Mellon | Blue | 7.50 | 12.00 | 26.00 | 135.00 |
| ☐1914 | Chicago | Burke-McAdoo | Blue | 7.50 | 12.00 | 26.00 | 135.00 |
| ☐1914 | Chicago | Burke-Glass | Blue | 7.50 | 12.00 | 26.00 | 135.00 |
| ☐1914 | Chicago | Burke-Huston | Blue | 7.50 | 12.00 | 26.00 | 135.00 |
| ☐1914 | Chicago | White-Mellon | Blue | 7.50 | 12.00 | 26.00 | 135.00 |
| ☐1914 | St. Louis | Burke-McAdoo | Blue | 7.50 | 12.00 | 26.00 | 135.00 |
| ☐1914 | St. Louis | Burke-Glass | Blue | 7.50 | 14.00 | 30.00 | 135.00 |
| ☐1914 | St. Louis | Burke-Huston | Blue | 7.50 | 12.00 | 26.00 | 135.00 |
| ☐1914 | St. Louis | White-Mellon | Blue | 7.50 | 12.00 | 28.00 | 135.00 |
| ☐1914 | Minneapolis | Burke-McAdoo | Blue | 7.50 | 14.00 | 31.00 | 135.00 |
| ☐1914 | Minneapolis | Burke-Glass | Blue | 7.50 | 14.00 | 31.00 | 135.00 |
| ☐1914 | Minneapolis | Burke-Huston | Blue | 7.50 | 12.00 | 28.00 | 135.00 |
| ☐1914 | Minneapolis | White-Mellon | Blue | 7.50 | 12.00 | 28.00 | 135.00 |
| ☐1914 | Kansas City | Burke-McAdoo | Blue | 7.50 | 12.00 | 29.00 | 135.00 |
| ☐1914 | Kansas City | Burke-Glass | Blue | 7.50 | 14.00 | 32.00 | 135.00 |
| ☐1914 | Kansas City | Burke-Huston | Blue | 7.50 | 12.00 | 28.00 | 135.00 |
| ☐1914 | Kansas City | White-Mellon | Blue | 7.50 | 12.00 | 28.00 | 135.00 |
| ☐1914 | Dallas | Burke-McAdoo | Blue | 7.50 | 13.00 | 31.00 | 135.00 |
| ☐1914 | Dallas | Burke-Glass | Blue | 7.50 | 15.00 | 36.00 | 135.00 |
| ☐1914 | Dallas | Burke-Huston | Blue | 7.50 | 12.00 | 28.00 | 135.00 |
| ☐1914 | Dallas | White-Mellon | Blue | 7.50 | 12.00 | 28.00 | 135.00 |
| ☐1914 | San Francisco | Burke-McAdoo | Blue | 7.50 | 12.00 | 28.00 | 135.00 |
| ☐1914 | San Francisco | Burke-Glass | Blue | 7.50 | 14.00 | 31.00 | 135.00 |
| ☐1914 | San Francisco | Burke-Huston | Blue | 7.50 | 12.00 | 28.00 | 135.00 |
| ☐1914 | San Francisco | White-Mellon | Blue | 7.50 | 12.00 | 28.00 | 135.00 |

## FIVE DOLLAR NOTES (1928)
### FEDERAL RESERVE NOTES

(Small Size) **NOTE NO. 55**

**Face Design:** Portrait of Present Lincoln center, black Federal Reserve Seal with numeral for district in center. City of issuing bank in seal circle. Green Treasury Seal to right.
**Back Design:** Similar to Note No. 50, Lincoln Memorial in Washington, D.C.

### SERIES OF 1928—
### SIGNATURES OF TATE AND MELLON, GREEN SEAL

| BANK | A.B.P. | GOOD | V.FINE | UNC. | BANK | A.B.P. | GOOD | V.FINE | UNC. |
|---|---|---|---|---|---|---|---|---|---|
| ☐Boston | 6.50 | 8.00 | 12.00 | 42.00 | ☐Chicago | 6.50 | 8.00 | 12.00 | 42.00 |
| ☐New York | 6.50 | 8.00 | 12.00 | 42.00 | ☐St. Louis | 6.50 | 8.00 | 12.00 | 42.00 |
| ☐Philadelphia | 6.50 | 8.00 | 12.00 | 42.00 | ☐Minneapolis | 6.50 | 8.00 | 12.00 | 42.00 |
| ☐Cleveland | 6.50 | 8.00 | 12.00 | 42.00 | ☐Kansas City | 6.50 | 8.00 | 12.00 | 42.00 |
| ☐Richmond | 6.50 | 8.00 | 12.00 | 42.00 | ☐Dallas | 6.50 | 8.00 | 12.00 | 42.00 |
| ☐Atlanta | 6.50 | 8.00 | 12.00 | 42.00 | ☐San Francisco | 6.50 | 8.00 | 12.00 | 42.00 |

### SERIES OF 1928A—
### SIGNATURES OF WOODS-MELLON, GREEN SEAL

| BANK | A.B.P. | GOOD | V.FINE | UNC. | BANK | A.B.P. | GOOD | V.FINE | UNC. |
|---|---|---|---|---|---|---|---|---|---|
| ☐Boston | 6.50 | 8.00 | 12.00 | 42.00 | ☐Chicago | 6.50 | 8.00 | 12.00 | 42.00 |
| ☐New York | 6.50 | 8.00 | 12.00 | 42.00 | ☐St. Louis | 6.50 | 8.00 | 12.00 | 42.00 |
| ☐Philadelphia | 6.50 | 8.00 | 12.00 | 42.00 | ☐Minneapolis | 6.50 | 8.00 | 12.00 | 42.00 |
| ☐Cleveland | 6.50 | 8.00 | 12.00 | 42.00 | ☐Kansas City | 6.50 | 8.00 | 12.00 | 42.00 |
| ☐Richmond | 6.50 | 8.00 | 12.00 | 42.00 | ☐Dallas | 6.50 | 8.00 | 12.00 | 42.00 |
| ☐Atlanta | 6.50 | 8.00 | 12.00 | 42.00 | ☐San Francisco | 6.50 | 8.00 | 12.00 | 42.00 |

## SERIES OF 1928B—
### SIGNATURES OF WOODS-MELLON, GREEN SEAL
**Black Federal Reserve Seal now has a Letter
for District in place of the Numeral.**

(Small Size)

| BANK | A.B.P. | GOOD | V. FINE | UNC. | BANK | A.B.P. | GOOD | V.FINE | UNC. |
|---|---|---|---|---|---|---|---|---|---|
| ☐Boston | 6.50 | 9.00 | 18.00 | 52.00 | ☐Chicago | 6.50 | 9.00 | 18.00 | 52.00 |
| ☐New York | 6.50 | 9.00 | 18.00 | 52.00 | ☐St. Louis | 6.50 | 9.00 | 18.00 | 52.00 |
| ☐Philadelphia | 6.50 | 9.00 | 18.00 | 52.00 | ☐Minneapolis | 6.50 | 9.00 | 18.00 | 52.00 |
| ☐Cleveland | 6.50 | 9.00 | 18.00 | 52.00 | ☐Kansas City | 6.50 | 9.00 | 18.00 | 52.00 |
| ☐Richmond | 6.50 | 9.00 | 18.00 | 52.00 | ☐Dallas | 6.50 | 9.00 | 18.00 | 52.00 |
| ☐Atlanta | 6.50 | 9.00 | 18.00 | 52.00 | ☐San Francisco | 6.50 | 9.00 | 18.00 | 52.00 |

## FIVE DOLLAR NOTES (1928)
### FEDERAL RESERVE NOTES
## SERIES OF 1928C—
### SIGNATURES OF WOODS-WOODIN, GREEN SEAL

| BANK | A.B.P. | GOOD | V. FINE | UNC. | BANK | A.B.P. | GOOD | V.FINE | UNC. |
|---|---|---|---|---|---|---|---|---|---|
| ☐Cleveland | 38.00 | 80.00 | 190.00 | 800.00 | ☐ San | | | | |
| ☐Atlanta | 38.00 | 80.00 | 190.00 | 400.00 | Francisco | 38.00 | 80.00 | 190.00 | 800.00 |

This series not issued by other banks.

## SERIES OF 1928D—
### SIGNATURES OF WOODS-MILLS, GREEN SEAL

| BANK | A.B.P. | GOOD | V. FINE | UNC. |
|---|---|---|---|---|
| ☐Atlanta | 48.00 | 100.00 | 200.00 | 800.00 |

This series not issued by other banks.

## SERIES OF 1934—JULIAN-MORGENTHAU, GREEN SEAL
**"Redeemable in Gold" removed from obligation
over Federal Reserve Seal.**

Note: The Green Treasury Seal on this note is known in a light and dark color. The light seal is worth about 10% to 20% more in most cases.

| BANK | A.B.P. | V. FINE | UNC. | BANK | A.B.P. | V.FINE | UNC. |
|---|---|---|---|---|---|---|---|
| ☐Boston | 6.00 | 9.00 | 23.00 | ☐St. Louis | 6.00 | 9.00 | 23.00 |
| ☐New York | 6.00 | 9.00 | 23.00 | ☐Minneapolis | 6.00 | 9.00 | 23.00 |
| ☐Philadelphia | 6.00 | 9.00 | 23.00 | ☐Kansas City | 6.00 | 9.00 | 23.00 |
| ☐Cleveland | 6.00 | 9.00 | 23.00 | ☐Dallas | 6.00 | 9.00 | 23.00 |
| ☐Richmond | 6.00 | 9.00 | 23.00 | ☐San Francisco | 6.00 | 9.00 | 23.00 |
| ☐Atlanta | 6.00 | 9.00 | 23.00 | ☐San Francisco* | 17.00 | 45.00 | 190.00 |
| ☐Chicago | 6.00 | 9.00 | 23.00 | | | | |

*This note with BROWN Treasury Seal and surprinted HAWAII. For use in Pacific area of operations during World War II.

(Small Size)                                           **NOTE NO. 56**

**SERIES OF 1934-1934A**—1934A—JULIAN-MORGEN-
THAU, Surprinted HAWAII, used in Pacific area during
World War II. Used with Brown Treasury Seal.

### SERIES OF 1934A—JULIAN-MORGENTHAU, GREEN SEAL

| BANK | A.B.P. | V.FINE | UNC. | BANK | A.B.P. | V.FINE | UNC. |
|------|--------|--------|------|------|--------|--------|------|
| ☐Boston | 6.00 | 10.00 | 23.00 | ☐Atlanta | 6.00 | 10 00 | 23.00 |
| ☐New York | 6.00 | 10.00 | 23.00 | ☐Chicago | 6.00 | 10 00 | 23.00 |
| ☐Philadelphia | 6.00 | 10.00 | 23.00 | ☐St. Louis | 6.00 | 10.00 | 23.00 |
| ☐Cleveland | 6.00 | 10.00 | 23.00 | ☐San Francisco | 6.00 | 10.00 | 23.00 |
| ☐Richmond | 6.00 | 10.00 | 23.00 | ☐San Francisco* | 15.00 | 35.00 | 140.00 |

*This note with BROWN Treasury Seal and surprinted HAWAII. For use in
Pacific area of operations during World War II.

### FIVE DOLLAR NOTES (1934)
### FEDERAL RESERVE NOTES

(Small Size)                                           **NOTE NO. 56**
**Face Design:** Same as Note No. 55.
**Back Design:** Same as Note No. 50.

### SERIES OF 1934B—
### SIGNATURES OF JULIAN-VINSON, GREEN SEAL

| BANK & CITY | A.B.P. | V.FINE | UNC. | BANK & CITY | A.B.P. | V.FINE | UNC. |
|-------------|--------|--------|------|-------------|--------|--------|------|
| ☐Boston | 6.00 | 11.00 | 24.00 | ☐Chicago | 6.00 | 11 00 | 24.00 |
| ☐New York | 6.00 | 11.00 | 24.00 | ☐St. Louis | 6.00 | 11.00 | 24.00 |
| ☐Philadelphia | 6.00 | 11.00 | 24.00 | ☐Minneapolis | 6.00 | 11.00 | 24.00 |
| ☐Cleveland | 6.00 | 11.00 | 24.00 | ☐Kansas City | 6.00 | 11.00 | 24.00 |
| ☐Richmond | 6.00 | 11.00 | 24.00 | ☐Dallas | | NOT ISSUED | |
| ☐Atlanta | 6.00 | 11.00 | 24.00 | ☐San Francisco | 6.00 | 11.00 | 24.00 |

### SERIES OF 1934C—
### SIGNATURES OF JULIAN-SNYDER, GREEN SEAL

| BANK & CITY | A.B.P. | V.FINE | UNC. | BANK & CITY | A.B.P. | V.FINE | UNC. |
|-------------|--------|--------|------|-------------|--------|--------|------|
| ☐Boston | 6.00 | 9.00 | 23.00 | ☐Chicago | 6.00 | 9.00 | 23.00 |
| ☐New York | 6.00 | 9.00 | 23.00 | ☐St. Louis | 6.00 | 9.00 | 23.00 |

| BANK & CITY | A.B.P. | V.FINE | UNC. | BANK & CITY | A.B.P. | V.FINE | UNC. |
|---|---|---|---|---|---|---|---|
| ☐Philadelphia | 6.00 | 9.00 | 23.00 | ☐Minneapolis | 6.00 | 9.00 | 23.00 |
| ☐Cleveland | 6.00 | 9.00 | 23.00 | ☐Kansas City | 6.00 | 9.00 | 23.00 |
| ☐Richmond | 6.00 | 9.00 | 23.00 | ☐Dallas | 6.00 | 9.00 | 23.00 |
| ☐Atlanta | 6.00 | 9.00 | 23.00 | ☐San Francisco | 6.00 | 9.00 | 23.00 |

## SERIES OF 1934D—
## SIGNATURES OF CLARK-SNYDER, GREEN SEAL

| BANK & CITY | A.B.P. | V.FINE | UNC. | BANK & CITY | A.B.P. | V.FINE | UNC. |
|---|---|---|---|---|---|---|---|
| ☐Boston | 5.50 | 8.00 | 20.00 | ☐Chicago | 5.50 | 8.00 | 20.00 |
| ☐New York | 5.50 | 8.00 | 20.00 | ☐St. Louis | 5.50 | 8.00 | 20.00 |
| ☐Philadelphia | 5.50 | 8.00 | 20.00 | ☐Minneapolis | 5.50 | 8.00 | 20.00 |
| ☐Cleveland | 5.50 | 8.00 | 20.00 | ☐Kansas City | 5.50 | 8.00 | 20.00 |
| ☐Richmond | 5.50 | 8.00 | 20.00 | ☐Dallas | 5.50 | 8.00 | 20.00 |
| ☐Atlanta | 5.50 | 8.00 | 20.00 | ☐San Francisco | 5.50 | 8.00 | 20.00 |

## FIVE DOLLAR NOTES (1950)
## FEDERAL RESERVE NOTES
## BLACK FEDERAL RESERVE SEAL AND
## GREEN TREASURY SEALS ARE NOW SMALLER

(Small Size) **NOTE NO. 57**

**Face Design:** Similar to Note No. 55.
**Back Design:** Similar to Note No. 50.

## FIVE DOLLAR NOTES (1950-1963)
## FEDERAL RESERVE NOTES

(Small Size) **NOTE NO. 57**

## SERIES OF 1950—
## SIGNATURES OF CLARK-SNYDER, GREEN SEAL

| BANK & CITY | A.B.P. | V.FINE | UNC. | BANK & CITY | A.B.P. | V.FINE | UNC. |
|---|---|---|---|---|---|---|---|
| ☐Boston | 5.50 | 7.50 | 21.00 | ☐Chicago | 5.50 | 7.50 | 21.00 |
| ☐New York | 5.50 | 7.50 | 21.00 | ☐St. Louis | 5.50 | 7.50 | 21.00 |
| ☐Philadelphia | 5.50 | 7.50 | 21.00 | ☐Minneapolis | 5.50 | 7.50 | 21.00 |
| ☐Cleveland | 5.50 | 7.50 | 21.00 | ☐Kansas City | 5.50 | 7.50 | 21.00 |
| ☐Richmond | 5.50 | 7.50 | 21.00 | ☐Dallas | 5.50 | 7.50 | 21.00 |
| ☐Atlanta | 5.50 | 7.50 | 21.00 | ☐San Francisco | 5.50 | 7.50 | 21.00 |

## SERIES OF 1950A—PRIEST-HUMPHREY, GREEN SEAL

| | UNC. | | UNC. | | UNC. | | UNC. |
|---|---|---|---|---|---|---|---|
| Boston | 18.00 | Cleveland | 18.00 | Chicago | 18.00 | Kansas City | 18.00 |
| New York | 18.00 | Richmond | 18.00 | St. Louis | 18.00 | Dallas | 18.00 |
| Philadelphia | 18.00 | Atlanta | 18.00 | Minneapolis | 18.00 | San Francisco | 18.00 |

## SERIES OF 1950B—PRIEST-ANDERSON, GREEN SEAL

| Boston | 18.00 | Cleveland | 18.00 | Chicago | 18.00 | Kansas City | 18.00 |
|---|---|---|---|---|---|---|---|

| | UNC. | | UNC. | | UNC. | | UNC. |
|---|---|---|---|---|---|---|---|
| New York | 18.00 | Richmond | 18.00 | St. Louis | 18.00 | Dallas | 18.00 |
| Philadelphia | 18.00 | Atlanta | 18.00 | Minneapolis | 18.00 | San Francisco | 18.00 |

### SERIES OF 1950C—SMITH-DILLON, GREEN SEAL

| | | | | | | | |
|---|---|---|---|---|---|---|---|
| Boston | 16.00 | Cleveland | 16.00 | Chicago | 16.00 | Kansas City | 16.00 |
| New York | 16.00 | Richmond | 16.00 | St. Louis | 16.00 | Dallas | 16.00 |
| Philadelphia | 16.00 | Atlanta | 16.00 | Minneapolis | 16.00 | San Francisco | 16.00 |

### SERIES OF 1950D—GRANAHAN-DILLON, GREEN SEAL

| | | | | | | | |
|---|---|---|---|---|---|---|---|
| Boston | 17.00 | Cleveland | 17.00 | Chicago | 17.00 | Kansas City | 17.00 |
| New York | 17.00 | Richmond | 17.00 | St. Louis | 17.00 | Dallas | 17.00 |
| Philadelphia | 17.00 | Atlanta | 17.00 | Minneapolis | 17.00 | San Francisco | 17.00 |

### SERIES OF 1950E—GRANAHAN-FOWLER, GREEN SEAL

| | | | | | |
|---|---|---|---|---|---|
| New York | 21.00 | Chicago | 21.00 | San Francisco | 21.00 |

This note was issued by only three banks.

## FIVE DOLLAR NOTES (1963)
## FEDERAL RESERVE NOTES
## ("IN GOD WE TRUST" IS ADDED ON THE BACK)

(Small Size)                                              **NOTE NO. 57A**

### SERIES OF 1963—GRANAHAN-DILLON, GREEN SEAL

| | UNC. | | UNC. | | UNC. | | UNC. |
|---|---|---|---|---|---|---|---|
| Boston | 15.00 | Cleveland | 15.00 | Chicago | 15.00 | Kansas City | 15.00 |
| New York | 15.00 | Richmond | NONE | St. Louis | 15.00 | Dallas | 15.00 |
| Philadelphia | 15.00 | Atlanta | 15.00 | Minneapolis | NONE | San Francisco | 15.00 |

### SERIES OF 1963A—GRANAHAN-FOWLER, GREEN SEAL

| | | | | | | | |
|---|---|---|---|---|---|---|---|
| Boston | 14.00 | Cleveland | 14.00 | Chicago | 14.00 | Kansas City | 14.00 |
| New York | 14.00 | Richmond | NONE | St. Louis | 14.00 | Dallas | 14.00 |
| Philadelphia | 14.00 | Atlanta | 14.00 | Minneapolis | 14.00 | San Francisco | 14.00 |

## FIVE DOLLAR NOTES (1969)
## FEDERAL RESERVE NOTES
## (WORDING IN GREEN TREASURY SEAL
## CHANGED FROM LATIN TO ENGLISH)

(Small Size)                                              **NOTE NO. 57B**

### SERIES OF 1969—ELSTON-KENNEDY, GREEN SEAL

| | | | | | | | |
|---|---|---|---|---|---|---|---|
| Boston | 12.00 | Cleveland | 12.00 | Chicago | 12.00 | Kansas City | 12.00 |
| New York | 12.00 | Richmond | 12.00 | St. Louis | 12.00 | Dallas | 12.00 |
| Philadelphia | 12.00 | Atlanta | 12.00 | Minneapolis | 12.00 | San Francisco | 12.00 |

### SERIES OF 1969A—KABIS-CONNALLY, GREEN SEAL

| | | | | | | | |
|---|---|---|---|---|---|---|---|
| Boston | 11.00 | Cleveland | 11.00 | Chicago | 11.00 | Kansas City | 11.00 |
| New York | 11.00 | Richmond | 11.00 | St. Louis | 11.00 | Dallas | 11.00 |
| Philadelphia | 11.00 | Atlanta | 11.00 | Minneapolis | 11.00 | San Francisco | 11.00 |

## FIVE DOLLAR NOTES (1969)
## FEDERAL RESERVE NOTES
## (WORDING IN GREEN TREASURY SEAL
## CHANGED FROM LATIN TO ENGLISH)

(Small Size)                                        NOTE NO. 57B

### SERIES OF 1969B—BANUELOS-CONNALLY, GREEN SEAL

|  | UNC. |  | UNC. |  | UNC. |  | UNC. |
|---|---|---|---|---|---|---|---|
| Boston | 10.00 | Cleveland | 10.00 | Chicago | 10.00 | Kansas City | 10.00 |
| New York | 10.00 | Richmond | 10.00 | St. Louis | 10.00 | Dallas | 10.00 |
| Philadelphia | 10.00 | Atlanta | 10.00 | Minneapolis | 10.00 | San Francisco | 10.00 |

### SERIES OF 1969C—BANUELOS-SHULTZ, GREEN SEAL

| Boston | 10.00 | Cleveland | 10.00 | Chicago | 10.00 | Kansas City | 10.00 |
|---|---|---|---|---|---|---|---|
| New York | 10.00 | Richmond | 10.00 | St. Louis | 10.00 | Dallas | 10.00 |
| Philadelphia | 10.00 | Atlanta | 10.00 | Minneapolis | 10.00 | San Francisco | 10.00 |

### SERIES OF 1974—NEFF-SIMON, GREEN SEAL

| Boston | 9.50 | Cleveland | 9.50 | Chicago | 9.50 | Kansas City | 9.50 |
|---|---|---|---|---|---|---|---|
| New York | 9.50 | Richmond | 9.50 | St. Louis | 9.50 | Dallas | 9.50 |
| Philadelphia | 9.50 | Atlanta | 9.50 | Minneapolis | 9.50 | San Francisco | 9.50 |

### SERIES OF 1977—MORTON-BLUMENTHAL, GREEN SEAL

| Boston | 8.00 | Cleveland | 8.00 | Chicago | 8.00 | Kansas City | 8.00 |
|---|---|---|---|---|---|---|---|
| New York | 8.00 | Richmond | 8.00 | St. Louis | 8.00 | Dallas | 8.00 |
| Philadelphia | 8.00 | Atlanta | 8.00 | Minneapolis | 8.00 | San Francisco | 8.00 |

### SERIES OF 1977A—MORTON-MILLER, GREEN SEAL

| Boston | 8.00 | Cleveland | 8.00 | Chicago | 8.00 | Kansas City | 8.00 |
|---|---|---|---|---|---|---|---|
| New York | 8.00 | Richmond | 8.00 | St. Louis | 8.00 | Dallas | 8.00 |
| Philadelphia | 8.00 | Atlanta | 8.00 | Minneapolis | 8.00 | San Francisco | 8.00 |

### SERIES OF 1981—BUCHANAN-REGAN, GREEN SEAL

| Boston | 7.00 | Cleveland | 7.00 | Chicago | 7.00 | Kansas City | 7.00 |
|---|---|---|---|---|---|---|---|
| New York | 7.00 | Richmond | 7.00 | St. Louis | 7.00 | Dallas | 7.00 |
| Philadelphia | 7.00 | Atlanta | 7.00 | Minneapolis | 7.00 | San Francisco | 7.00 |

### SERIES OF 1981A—ORTEGA-REGAN, GREEN SEAL

| Boston | 7.00 | Cleveland | 7.00 | Chicago | 7.00 | Kansas City | 7.00 |
|---|---|---|---|---|---|---|---|
| New York | 7.00 | Richmond | 7.00 | St. Louis | 7.00 | Dallas | 7.00 |
| Philadelphia | 7.00 | Atlanta | 7.00 | Minneapolis | 7.00 | San Francisco | 7.00 |

### SERIES OF 1985—ORTEGA-BAKER, GREEN SEAL

| Boston | 7.00 | Cleveland | 7.00 | Chicago | 7.00 | Kansas City | 7.00 |
|---|---|---|---|---|---|---|---|
| New York | 7.00 | Richmond | 7.00 | St. Louis | 7.00 | Dallas | 7.00 |
| Philadelphia | 7.00 | Atlanta | 7.00 | Minneapolis | 7.00 | San Francisco | 7.00 |

### SERIES OF 1988—ORTEGA-BAKER, GREEN SEAL

| Boston | 6.50 | Cleveland | 6.50 | Chicago | 6.50 | Kansas City | 6.50 |
|---|---|---|---|---|---|---|---|
| New York | 6.50 | Richmond | 6.50 | St. Louis | 6.50 | Dallas | 6.50 |
| Philadelphia | 6.50 | Atlanta | 6.50 | Minneapolis | 6.50 | San Francisco | 6.50 |

## FIVE DOLLAR NOTES (1918)
### FEDERAL RESERVE BANK NOTES
### (ALL WITH BLUE SEAL AND BLUE SERIAL NUMBERS)

(Large Size)                                          **NOTE NO. 58**

**Face Design:** Portrait of President Lincoln with Reserve City in center.

**Back Design:** Same as Note No. 54.

| BANK & CITY | SERIES | GOV'T SIGNATURES | BANK SIGNATURES | A.B.P. | GOOD | V. FINE | UNC. |
|---|---|---|---|---|---|---|---|
| ☐Boston | 1918 | Teehee-Burke | Bullen-Morse | 250.00 | 600.00 | 1000.00 | 1900.00 |
| ☐New York | 1918 | Teehee-Burke | Hendricks-Strong | 17.00 | 40.00 | 90.00 | 375.00 |
| ☐Phila. | 1918 | Teehee-Burke | Hardt-Passmore | 17.00 | 40.00 | 90.00 | 375.00 |
| ☐Phila. | 1918 | Teehee-Burke | Dyer-Passmore | 17.00 | 40.00 | 90.00 | 375.00 |
| ☐Cleveland | 1918 | Teehee-Burke | Dyer-Fancher | 17.00 | 40.00 | 90.00 | 375.00 |
| ☐Cleveland | 1918 | Teehee-Burke | Davis-Fancher | 17.00 | 40.00 | 90.00 | 375.00 |
| ☐Cleveland | 1918 | Elliott-Burke | Davis-Fancher | 17.00 | 40.00 | 90.00 | 375.00 |
| ☐Atlanta | 1915 | Teehee-Burke | Bell-Wellborn | 18.00 | 40.00 | 110.00 | 450.00 |
| ☐Atlanta | 1915 | Teehee-Burke | Pike-McCord | 18.00 | 40.00 | 110.00 | 450.00 |
| ☐Atlanta | 1918 | Teehee-Burke | Pike-McCord | 17.00 | 40.00 | 90.00 | 375.00 |
| ☐Atlanta | 1918 | Teehee-Burke | Bell-Wellborn | 17.00 | 40.00 | 90.00 | 375.00 |
| ☐Atlanta | 1918 | Elliott-Burke | Bell-Wellborn | 17.00 | 40.00 | 90.00 | 375.00 |
| ☐Chicago | 1915 | Teehee-Burke | McLallen-McDougal | 17.00 | 40.00 | 110.00 | 450.00 |
| ☐Chicago | 1918 | Teehee-Burke | McCloud-McDougal | 17.00 | 38.00 | 90.00 | 375.00 |
| ☐Chicago | 1918 | Teehee-Burke | Cramer-McDougal | 17.00 | 38.00 | 90.00 | 375.00 |
| ☐St. Louis | 1918 | Teehee-Burke | Attebery-Wells | 17.00 | 38.00 | 90.00 | 375.00 |
| ☐St. Louis | 1918 | Teehee-Burke | Attebery-Biggs | 17.00 | 38.00 | 90.00 | 375.00 |

| BANK & CITY | SERIES | GOV'T SIGNATURES | BANK SIGNATURES | A.B.P. | GOOD | V. FINE | UNC. |
|---|---|---|---|---|---|---|---|
| ☐St. Louis | 1918 | Elliott-Burke | White-Biggs | | | | |
| | | | | 17.00 | 38.00 | 90.00 | 375.00 |
| ☐Minn. | 1918 | Teehee-Burke | Cook-Wold | | | | |
| | | | | 17.00 | 38.00 | 90.00 | 375.00 |
| ☐Kan. City | 1915 | Teehee-Burke | Anderson-Miller | | | | |
| | | | | 17.00 | 40.00 | 110.00 | 450.00 |
| ☐Kan. City | 1915 | Teehee-Burke | Cross-Miller | | | | |
| | | | | 17.00 | 40.00 | 110.00 | 450.00 |
| ☐Kan. City | 1915 | Teehee-Burke | Helm-Miller | | | | |
| | | | | 17.00 | 40.00 | 110.00 | 450.00 |
| ☐Kan. City | 1918 | Teehee-Burke | Anderson-Miller | | | | |
| | | | | 17.00 | 38.00 | 90.00 | 375.00 |
| ☐Kan. City | 1918 | Elliott-Burke | Helm-Miller | | | | |
| | | | | 17.00 | 38.00 | 90.00 | 375.00 |
| ☐Dallas | 1915 | Teehee-Burke | Hoopes-VanZandt | | | | |
| | | | | 17.00 | 40.00 | 125.00 | 450.00 |
| ☐Dallas | 1915 | Teehee-Burke | Talley-VanZandt | | | | |
| | | | | 17.00 | 40.00 | 110.00 | 450.00 |
| ☐Dallas | 1918 | Teehee-Burke | Talley-VanZandt | | | | |
| | | | | 17.00 | 38.00 | 90.00 | 375.00 |
| ☐San Fran. | 1915 | Teehee-Burke | Clerk-Lynch | | | | |
| | | | | 17.00 | 40.00 | 125.00 | 450.00 |
| ☐San Fran. | 1918 | Teehee-Burke | Clerk-Lynch | | | | |
| | | | | 17.00 | 38.00 | 90.00 | 375.00 |

## FIVE DOLLAR NOTES (1929)
### FEDERAL RESERVE BANK NOTES

(Small Size)                                          **NOTE NO. 59**

**Face Design:** Portrait of President Lincoln.

## SERIES 1929—Brown seal.

| BANK & CITY | SIGNATURES | A.B.P. | GOOD | V.FINE | UNC. |
|---|---|---|---|---|---|
| ☐Boston | Jones-Woods | 6.50 | 9.00 | 16.00 | 88.00 |
| ☐New York | Jones-Woods | 6.50 | 9.00 | 15.00 | 70.00 |
| ☐Philadelphia | Jones-Woods | 6.50 | 9.00 | 16.00 | 70.00 |
| ☐Cleveland | Jones-Woods | 6.50 | 9.00 | 16.00 | 70.00 |
| ☐Richmond | Jones-Woods | 6.50 | 9.00 | 14.00 | 120.00 |
| ☐Atlanta | Jones-Woods | 6.50 | 9.00 | 14.00 | 65.00 |
| ☐Chicago | Jones-Woods | 6.50 | 9.00 | 14.00 | 65.00 |
| ☐St. Louis | Jones-Woods | 6.50 | 9.00 | 150.00 | 350.00 |
| ☐Minneapolis | Jones-Woods | 6.50 | 9.00 | 40.00 | 135.00 |
| ☐Kansas City | Jones-Woods | 6.50 | 9.00 | 15.00 | 72.00 |
| ☐Dallas | Jones-Woods | 75.00 | 180.00 | 750.00 | 2100.00 |
| ☐San Francisco | Jones-Woods | 75.00 | 350.00 | 725.00 | 2000.00 |

# TEN DOLLAR NOTES

## TEN DOLLAR NOTES (1861) DEMAND NOTES
## NO TREASURY SEAL

(Large Size)                                        **NOTE NO. 60**

**Face Design:** Portrait of President Lincoln left, female figure with sword and shield.

**Back Design:** Ornate designs of "TEN."

| CITY | A.B.P. | GOOD | V. GOOD |
|---|---|---|---|
| ☐Boston (I) | 350.00 | 1600.00 | 7600.00 |
| ☐New York (I) | 350.00 | 1600.00 | 7600.00 |
| ☐Philadelphia (I) | 350.00 | 1600.00 | 7600.00 |
| ☐Cincinnati (I) | 700.00 | 2500.00 | RARE |
| ☐St. Louis (I) | 700.00 | 2500.00 | RARE |
| ☐Boston (II) | 300.00 | 600.00 | 1250.00 |
| ☐New York (II) | 300.00 | 550.00 | 1250.00 |
| ☐Philadelphia (II) | 300.00 | 550.00 | 1250.00 |
| ☐Cincinnati (II) | 450.00 | 7800.00 | 18,000.00 |
| ☐St. Louis (II) | 500.00 | 8200.00 | 25,000.00 |

## TEN DOLLAR NOTES (1862-1863)
### UNITED STATES NOTES
### (ALSO KNOWN AS LEGAL TENDER NOTES)
(Large Size)                                      **NOTE NO. 61**

**Back Design**
**Face Design:** Similar to previous note.

| SERIES | SIGNATURES | SEAL | A.B.P. | GOOD | V.FINE | UNC. |
|---|---|---|---|---|---|---|
| ☐1862 | Chittenden-Spinner* | Red | 70.00 | 175.00 | 600.00 | 1700.00 |
| ☐1862 | Chittenden-Spinner** | Red | 70.00 | 175.00 | 600.00 | 1700.00 |
| ☐1863 | Chittenden-Spinner** | Red | 70.00 | 175.00 | 600.00 | 1700.00 |

\* First Obligation: Similar to Note No. 33.
\*\* Second Obligation: Shown above.

## TEN DOLLAR NOTES (1869) UNITED STATES NOTES
(Large Size)          .                       **NOTE NO. 62**

**Face Design:** Portrait of Daniel Webster left, presentation of Indian Princess right. (This note is nicknamed "Jackass Note," because the EAGLE between the signatures resembles a donkey when it is held upside down.)

| SERIES | SIGNATURES | SEAL | A.B.P. | GOOD | V.FINE | UNC. |
|---|---|---|---|---|---|---|
| ☐1869 | Allison-Spinner | Red | 80.00 | 175.00 | 650.00 | 1500.00 |

## TEN DOLLAR NOTES (1875-1880)
### UNITED STATES NOTES

(Large Size) **NOTE NO. 63**

**Face Design:** Similar to previous note.

**Back Design:** Revised.

| SERIES | SIGNATURES | SEAL | A.B.P. | GOOD | V.FINE | UNC. |
|---|---|---|---|---|---|---|
| ☐1875 | Allison-New | Red | 45.00 | 125.00 | 450.00 | 1400.00 |
| ☐Same as above—SERIES A | | Red | 45.00 | 100.00 | 400.00 | 1000.00 |
| ☐1878 | Allison-Gilfillan | Red | 45.00 | 100.00 | 400.00 | 1550.00 |
| ☐1880 | Scofield-Gilfillan | Brown | 40.00 | 90.00 | 300.00 | 1100.00 |
| ☐1880 | Bruce-Gilfillan | Brown | 30.00 | 75.00 | 200.00 | 900.00 |
| ☐1880 | Bruce-Wyman | Brown | 30.00 | 75.00 | 200.00 | 900.00 |
| ☐1880 | Bruce-Wyman | Red Plain | 30.00 | 75.00 | 200.00 | 850.00 |
| ☐1880 | Rosecrans-Jordan | Red Plain | 30.00 | 75.00 | 300.00 | 950.00 |
| ☐1880 | Rosecrans-Hyatt | Red Plain | 30.00 | 75.00 | 300.00 | 950.00 |
| ☐1880 | Rosecrans-Hyatt | Red Spikes | 30.00 | 75.00 | 300.00 | 850.00 |
| ☐1880 | Rosecrans-Huston | Red Spikes | 30.00 | 75.00 | 200.00 | 950.00 |
| ☐1880 | Rosecrans-Huston | Brown | 30.00 | 75.00 | 200.00 | 1000.00 |
| ☐1880 | Rosecrans-Nebeker | Brown | 30.00 | 65.00 | 160.00 | 950.00 |
| ☐1880 | Rosecrans-Nebeker | Red | 30.00 | 65.00 | 160.00 | 650.00 |
| ☐1880 | Tillman-Morgan | Red | 30.00 | 65.00 | 160.00 | 650.00 |

| SERIES | SIGNATURES | SEAL | A.B.P. | GOOD | V.FINE | UNC. |
|--------|-----------|------|--------|------|--------|------|
| ☐1880 | Bruce-Roberts | Red | 30.00 | 65.00 | 200.00 | 650.00 |
| ☐1880 | Lyons-Roberts | Red | 30.00 | 65.00 | 200.00 | 650.00 |

## TEN DOLLAR NOTES (1901) UNITED STATES NOTES
LEGAL TENDER (Large Size)                          **NOTE NO. 64**

**Face Design:** American Bison (buffalo) center, portrait of Lewis left, portrait of Clark right.

**Back Design:** Female allegorical figure in arch.

| SERIES | SIGNATURES | SEAL | A.B.P. | GOOD | V.FINE | UNC. |
|--------|-----------|------|--------|------|--------|------|
| ☐1901 | Lyons-Roberts | Red | 40.00 | 125.00 | 450.00 | 1150.00 |
| ☐1901 | Lyons-Treat | Red | 40.00 | 125.00 | 450.00 | 1150.00 |
| ☐1901 | Vernon-Treat | Red | 40.00 | 125.00 | 450.00 | 1150.00 |
| ☐1901 | Vernon-McClung | Red | 40.00 | 125.00 | 450.00 | 1150.00 |
| ☐1901 | Napier-McClung | Red | 40.00 | 125.00 | 450.00 | 1150.00 |
| ☐1901 | Parker-Burke | Red | 40.00 | 125.00 | 450.00 | 1150.00 |
| ☐1901 | Teehee-Burke | Red | 40.00 | 125.00 | 450.00 | 1150.00 |
| ☐1901 | Elliott-White | Red | 40.00 | 125.00 | 450.00 | 1150.00 |
| ☐1901 | Speelman-White | Red | 40.00 | 125.00 | 450.00 | 1150.00 |

## TEN DOLLAR NOTES (1923) UNITED STATES NOTES
(Large Size)                                                    **NOTE NO. 65**

**Face Design:** Portrait of President Jackson center, red seal left, red "X" to right.

**Back Design**

| SERIES | SIGNATURES | SEAL | A.B.P. | GOOD | V.FINE | UNC. |
|--------|-----------|------|--------|------|--------|------|
| ☐1923 | Speelman-White | Red | 70.00 | 200.00 | 1000.00 | 2800.00 |

## TEN DOLLAR NOTES (1863-1875)
### NATIONAL BANK NOTES
FIRST CHARTER PERIOD (Large Size)                    **NOTE NO. 66**

**Face Design:** Benjamin Franklin and kite left, name of bank and city center. Effigy of Liberty and Eagle right.

☐1882 ～～～～～～～～ ～～～ 28.00 65.00 180.00 700.00
☐1882 Tillman-Roberts Brown 28.00 65.00 180.00 700.00

**Back Design:** Border green, center black. DeSoto on horseback at Mississippi River.

| SERIES | SIGNATURES | SEAL | A.B.P. | GOOD | V.FINE | UNC. |
|--------|-----------|------|--------|------|--------|------|
| ☐Original Chittenden-Spinner | | Red | 35.00 | 100.00 | 350.00 | 1900.00 |
| ☐Original Colby-Spinner | | Red | 35.00 | 100.00 | 375.00 | 1900.00 |
| ☐Original Jeffries-Spinner | | Red | 180.00 | 500.00 | 2000.00 | RARE |
| ☐Original Allison-Spinner | | Red | 35.00 | 100.00 | 375.00 | 1900.00 |
| ☐1875 | Allison-New | Red | 42.00 | 95.00 | 375.00 | 1500.00 |
| ☐1875 | Allison-Wyman | Red | 32.00 | 95.00 | 375.00 | 1500.00 |
| ☐1875 | Allison-Gilfillan | Red | 32.00 | 95.00 | 375.00 | 1500.00 |
| ☐1875 | Scofield-Gilfillan | Red | 32.00 | 95.00 | 375.00 | 1500.00 |
| ☐1875 | Bruce-Gilfillan | Red | 32.00 | 95.00 | 375.00 | 1500.00 |
| ☐1875 | Bruce-Wyman | Red | 32.00 | 95.00 | 375.00 | 1500.00 |
| ☐1875 | Rosecrans-Huston | Red | 32.00 | 95.00 | 375.00 | 1500.00 |
| ☐1875 | Rosecrans-Nebeker | Red | 32.00 | 95.00 | 375.00 | 1500.00 |

**TEN DOLLAR NOTES** (1882) NATIONAL BANK NOTES
SECOND CHARTER PERIOD (Large Size) **NOTE NO. 68**

**First Issue**—Brown seal and brown backs.
**Face Design:** Similar to previous Notes Nos. 66-67.
**Back Design:** Similar to Note No. 39, but border in brown with green Charter Number.

| SERIES | SIGNATURES | SEAL | A.B.P. | GOOD | V.FINE | UNC. |
|--------|-----------|------|--------|------|--------|------|
| ☐1882 | Bruce-Gilfillan | Brown | 28.00 | 65.00 | 160.00 | 700.00 |
| ☐1882 | Bruce-Wyman | Brown | 28.00 | 65.00 | 160.00 | 700.00 |
| ☐1882 | Bruce-Jordan | Brown | 28.00 | 65.00 | 160.00 | 700.00 |
| ☐1882 | Rosecrans-Jordan | Brown | 28.00 | 65.00 | 160.00 | 700.00 |
| ☐1882 | Rosecrans-Hyatt | Brown | 28.00 | 65.00 | 160.00 | 700.00 |
| ☐1882 | Rosecrans-Huston | Brown | 28.00 | 65.00 | 160.00 | 700.00 |
| ☐1882 | Rosecrans-Nebeker | Brown | 28.00 | 65.00 | 160.00 | 700.00 |
| ☐1882 | Rosecrans-Morgan | Brown | 150.00 | 250.00 | 750.00 | 1100.00 |
| ☐1882 | Tillman-Morgan | Brown | 28.00 | 65.00 | 160.00 | 700.00 |
| ☐1882 | Tillman-Roberts | Brown | 28.00 | 65.00 | 160.00 | 700.00 |

| SERIES | SIGNATURES | SEAL | A.B.P. | GOOD | V.FINE | UNC. |
|--------|------------|------|--------|------|--------|------|
| ☐1882 | Bruce-Roberts | Brown | 28.00 | 65.00 | 160.00 | 700.00 |
| ☐1882 | Lyons-Roberts | Brown | 28.00 | 65.00 | 160.00 | 700.00 |
| ☐1882 | Lyons-Treat | Brown | 28.00 | 65.00 | 160.00 | 700.00 |
| ☐1882 | Vernon-Treat | Brown | 28.00 | 65.00 | 160.00 | 700.00 |

**Second Issue**—Blue seal, green back with date 1882-1908.
**Face Design:** Similar to Note No. 66.
**Back Design:** Similar to Note No. 40.
(Large Size)                                      **NOTE NO. 69**

| SERIES | SIGNATURES | SEAL | A.B.P. | GOOD | V.FINE | UNC. |
|--------|------------|------|--------|------|--------|------|
| ☐1882 | Rosecrans-Huston | Blue | 24.00 | 50.00 | 150.00 | 600.00 |
| ☐1882 | Rosecrans-Nebeker | Blue | 24.00 | 50.00 | 150.00 | 600.00 |
| ☐1882 | Rosecrans-Morgan | Blue | 100.00 | 180.00 | 500.00 | 1150.00 |
| ☐1882 | Tillman-Morgan | Blue | 24.00 | 50.00 | 150.00 | 600.00 |
| ☐1882 | Tillman-Roberts | Blue | 24.00 | 50.00 | 150.00 | 600.00 |
| ☐1882 | Bruce-Roberts | Blue | 24.00 | 50.00 | 150.00 | 600.00 |
| ☐1882 | Lyons-Roberts | Blue | 24.00 | 50.00 | 150.00 | 600.00 |
| ☐1882 | Vernon-Treat | Blue | 24.00 | 50.00 | 150.00 | 600.00 |
| ☐1882 | Vernon-McClung | Blue | 24.00 | 50.00 | 150.00 | 600.00 |
| ☐1882 | Napier-McClung | Blue | 24.00 | 50.00 | 150.00 | 600.00 |

## TEN DOLLAR NOTES (1882) NATIONAL BANK NOTES
**NOTE NO. 70**

**Third Issue**—Blue seal, green back with value in block letters.
**Face Design:** Similar to previous notes (see Note No. 66).
**Back Design:** Similar to Note No. 41.

| SERIES | SIGNATURES | SEAL | A.B.P. | GOOD | V. FINE | UNC. |
|--------|------------|------|--------|------|---------|------|
| ☐1882 | Tillman-Roberts | Blue | 32.00 | 85.00 | 325.00 | 2200.00 |
| ☐1882 | Lyons-Roberts | Blue | 32.00 | 100.00 | 310.00 | 2600.00 |
| ☐1882 | Vernon-Treat | Blue | 32.00 | 85.00 | 360.00 | 2200.00 |
| ☐1882 | Napier-McClung | Blue | 32.00 | 80.00 | 310.00 | 2200.00 |

These notes may exist with other signatures, but are very rare.

**TEN DOLLAR NOTES** (1902) NATIONAL BANK NOTES
THIRD CHARTER PERIOD (Large Size) **NOTE NO. 71**

**First Issue**—Red seal and red Charter numbers.
**Face Design:** Portrait of President McKinley left, name of bank and city in center.

| SERIES | SIGNATURES | SEAL | A.B.P. | GOOD | V.FINE | UNC. |
|--------|-----------|------|--------|------|--------|------|
| ☐1902 | Lyons-Roberts | Red | 30.00 | 60.00 | 180.00 | 775.00 |
| ☐1902 | Lyons-Treat | Red | 30.00 | 60.00 | 180.00 | 775.00 |
| ☐1902 | Vernon-Treat | Red | 30.00 | 60.00 | 210.00 | 850.00 |

**TEN DOLLAR NOTES** (1902) NATIONAL BANK NOTES
THIRD CHARTER PERIOD (Large Size) **NOTE NO. 71A**

**Second Issue**—Blue seal and numbers, 1902-1908 on the back.
**Back Design:** Same as Note No. 70, date 1902-1908.
**Face Design:** Same as Note No. 71.

| SERIES | SIGNATURES | SEAL | A.B.P. | GOOD | V.FINE | UNC. |
|--------|-----------|------|--------|------|--------|------|
| ☐1902 | Lyons-Roberts | Blue | 14.00 | 23.00 | 48.00 | 210.00 |
| ☐1902 | Lyons-Treat | Blue | 14.00 | 23.00 | 48.00 | 210.00 |
| ☐1902 | Vernon-Treat | Blue | 14.00 | 23.00 | 48.00 | 210.00 |
| ☐1902 | Vernon-McClung | Blue | 14.00 | 23.00 | 48.00 | 210.00 |
| ☐1902 | Napier-McClung | Blue | 14.00 | 23.00 | 48.00 | 210.00 |

| SERIES | SIGNATURES | SEAL | A.B.P. | GOOD | V.FINE | UNC. |
|---|---|---|---|---|---|---|
| ☐1902 | Napier-Thompson | Blue | 15.00 | 30.00 | 75.00 | 650.00 |
| ☐1902 | Napier-Burke | Blue | 14.00 | 23.00 | 48.00 | 210.00 |
| ☐1902 | Parker-Burke | Blue | 14.00 | 23.00 | 48.00 | 210.00 |
| ☐1902 | Teehee-Burke | Blue | 15.00 | 25.00 | 65.00 | 240.00 |

**Third Issue**—Blue seal and numbers, without date on back.

| SERIES | SIGNATURES | SEAL | A.B.P. | GOOD | V.FINE | UNC. |
|---|---|---|---|---|---|---|
| ☐1902 | Lyons-Roberts | Blue | 13.00 | 20.00 | 48.00 | 210.00 |
| ☐1902 | Lyons-Treat | Blue | 13.00 | 20.00 | 48.00 | 210.00 |
| ☐1902 | Vernon-Treat | Blue | 13.00 | 20.00 | 48.00 | 210.00 |
| ☐1902 | Vernon-McClung | Blue | 13.00 | 20.00 | 48.00 | 210.00 |
| ☐1902 | Napier-McClung | Blue | 13.00 | 20.00 | 48.00 | 210.00 |
| ☐1902 | Napier-Thompson | Blue | 13.00 | 24.00 | 85.00 | 650.00 |
| ☐1902 | Napier-Burke | Blue | 13.00 | 20.00 | 48.00 | 210.00 |
| ☐1902 | Parker-Burke | Blue | 13.00 | 20.00 | 48.00 | 210.00 |
| ☐1902 | Teehee-Burke | Blue | 13.00 | 20.00 | 48.00 | 210.00 |
| ☐1902 | Elliott-Burke | Blue | 13.00 | 20.00 | 48.00 | 210.00 |
| ☐1902 | Elliott-White | Blue | 13.00 | 20.00 | 48.00 | 210.00 |
| ☐1902 | Speelman-White | Blue | 13.00 | 20.00 | 48.00 | 210.00 |
| ☐1902 | Woods-White | Blue | 13.00 | 20.00 | 48.00 | 210.00 |
| ☐1902 | Woods-Tate | Blue | 13.00 | 20.00 | 48.00 | 210.00 |
| ☐1902 | Jones-Woods | Blue | 40.00 | 82.00 | 280.00 | 1100.00 |

**TEN DOLLAR NOTES** (1929) NATIONAL BANK NOTES
(Small Size)                                      **NOTE NO. 72**

**Face Design—TYPE I:** Portrait of Hamilton center, name of
bank left, brown seal right, Charter number black.

**Face Design—TYPE II:** Charter number added in brown.

**Back Design:** United States Treasury Building.

| SERIES | SIGNATURES | SEAL | A.B.P. | GOOD | V.FINE | UNC. |
|---|---|---|---|---|---|---|
| ☐ 1929—TYPE I Jones-Woods | | Brown | 11.00 | 14.00 | 24.00 | 58.00 |
| ☐ 1929—TYPE II Jones-Woods | | Brown | 11.00 | 14.00 | 24.00 | 68.00 |

## TEN DOLLAR NOTES (1870-1875)
### NATIONAL GOLD BANK NOTES
(Large Size)                                    **NOTE NO. 67**

**Face Design:** Similar to Note No. 66.

**Back Design:** State Seal left, gold coins center, American Eagle right.

### SIGNATURES OF ALLISON-SPINNER, RED TREASURY SEAL

| DATE | BANK | CITY | A.B.P. | GOOD | V. GOOD |
|------|------|------|--------|------|---------|
| ☐1870 | First National Gold Bank | San Francisco | 250.00 | 650.00 | 2300.00 |
| ☐1872 | National Gold Bank and Trust Company | San Francisco | 250.00 | 650.00 | 2300.00 |
| ☐1872 | National Gold Bank of D. O. Mills and Company | Sacramento | 300.00 | 900.00 | 2800.00 |
| ☐1873 | First National Gold Bank | Santa Barbara | 300.00 | 1000.00 | 2800.00 |
| ☐1873 | First National Gold Bank | Stockton | 300.00 | 900.00 | 2800.00 |
| ☐1874 | Farmers Nat'l Gold Bank | San Jose | 300.00 | 900.00 | 2800.00 |
| ☐1874 | First National Gold Bank | Petaluma | 300.00 | 900.00 | 2800.00 |
| ☐1875 | First National Gold Bank | Oakland | 300.00 | 900.00 | 2800.00 |

**TEN DOLLAR NOTES** (1880) SILVER CERTIFICATES
(Large Size)                                              **NOTE NO. 73**

**Face Design:** Portrait of Robert Morris left.

**Back Design:** Printed in black ink, large letters "SILVER."

| SERIES | SIGNATURES | SEAL | A.B.P. | GOOD | V.FINE | UNC. |
|--------|------------|------|--------|------|--------|------|
| ☐1880 | Scofield-Gilfillan | Brown | 70.00 | 300.00 | 900.00 | 3200.00 |
| ☐1880 | Bruce-Gilfillan | Brown | 70.00 | 300.00 | 900.00 | 3100.00 |
| ☐1880 | Bruce-Wyman | Brown | 70.00 | 300.00 | 900.00 | 3100.00 |
| ☐1880 | Bruce-Wyman | Red | 72.00 | 300.00 | 900.00 | 2700.00 |

## TEN DOLLAR NOTES (1886) SILVER CERTIFICATES
(Large Size)                                    **NOTE NO. 74**

| SERIES | SIGNATURES | SEAL | A.B.P. | GOOD | V.FINE | UNC. |
|--------|------------|------|--------|------|--------|------|
| ☐1886 | Rosencrans-Jordan | Small Red | 80.00 | 400.00 | 1000.00 | 3100.00 |
| ☐1886 | Rosecrans-Hyatt | Small Red | 80.00 | 400.00 | 1000.00 | 3100.00 |
| ☐1886 | Rosecrans-Hyatt | Large Red | 80.00 | 400.00 | 1000.00 | 3100.00 |
| ☐1886 | Rosecrans-Huston | Large Red | 80.00 | 400.00 | 1000.00 | 3100.00 |
| ☐1886 | Rosecrans-Huston | Large Brown | 80.00 | 400.00 | 1000.00 | 3100.00 |
| ☐1886 | Rosecrans-Nebeker | Large Brown | 85.00 | 400.00 | 1000.00 | 3200.00 |
| ☐1886 | Rosecrans-Nebeker | Small Red | 85.00 | 400.00 | 1000.00 | 3200.00 |

## TEN DOLLAR NOTES (1891-1908)
### SILVER CERTIFICATES
(Large Size)                                    **NOTE NO. 75**

**Face Design:**
Same as
Note No. 74.
**Back Design**

| SERIES | SIGNATURES | SEAL | A.B.P. | GOOD | V.FINE | UNC. |
|--------|------------|------|--------|------|--------|------|
| ☐1891 | Rosecrans-Nebeker | Red | 60.00 | 110.00 | 350.00 | 1750.00 |
| ☐1891 | Tillman-Morgan | Red | 60.00 | 110.00 | 350.00 | 1750.00 |
| ☐1891 | Bruce-Roberts | Red | 60.00 | 110.00 | 350.00 | 1750.00 |
| ☐1891 | Lyons-Roberts | Red | 60.00 | 110.00 | 350.00 | 1750.00 |
| ☐1891 | Vernon-Treat | Blue | 50.00 | 100.00 | 350.00 | 1600.00 |
| ☐1891 | Vernon-McClung | Blue | 50.00 | 100.00 | 350.00 | 1600.00 |
| ☐1891 | Parker-Burke | Blue | 50.00 | 100.00 | 350.00 | 1600.00 |

## TEN DOLLAR NOTES (1933) SILVER CERTIFICATES
(Small Size)                                   **NOTE NO. 76**

**Face Design:** Portrait of Alexander Hamilton, center. Blue
seal to left, blue numbers.

**Back Design:** Green United States Treasury Building.

| SERIES | SIGNATURES | SEAL | A.B.P. | GOOD | V.FINE | UNC. |
|--------|-----------|------|--------|------|--------|------|
| ☐1933 | Julian-Woodin | Blue | 200.00 | 850.00 | 2400.00 | 7000.00 |

## TEN DOLLAR NOTES (1934) SILVER CERTIFICATES
(Small Size)                                   **NOTE NO. 77**

**Face Design:** Blue "10" to left of portrait, Treasury Seal is
now to right.
**Back Design:** Similar to previous issue.

## TEN DOLLAR NOTES (1934) SILVER CERTIFICATES
(Small Size)                                     NOTE NO. 77

| SERIES | SIGNATURES | SEAL | A.B.P. | GOOD | V.FINE | UNC. |
|---|---|---|---|---|---|---|
| ☐1934 Julian-Morgenthau | Blue | 12.00 | 14.00 | 21.00 | 52.00 |
| ☐1934 Julian-Morgenthau* | Yellow | 175.00 | 415.00 | 1200.00 | 7000.00 |
| ☐1934A Julian-Morgenthau | Blue | 12.00 | 16.00 | 21.00 | 45.00 |
| ☐1934A Julian-Morgenthau* | Yellow | 13.00 | 18.00 | 21.00 | 165.00 |
| ☐1934B Julian-Vinson | Blue | 12.00 | 25.00 | 87.00 | 900.00 |
| ☐1934C Julian-Snyder | Blue | 12.00 | 15.00 | 25.00 | 50.00 |
| ☐1934D Clark-Snyder | Blue | 12.00 | 15.00 | 25.00 | 45.00 |

* Silver Certificates with a yellow seal were a special issue for use in combat areas of North Africa and Europe during World War II.

## TEN DOLLAR NOTES (1953) SILVER CERTIFICATES
(Small Size)                                     NOTE NO. 78

**Face Design:** Gray "10" to left of portrait. Treasury Seal is smaller.
**Back Design:** Back similar to previous note.

| SERIES | SIGNATURES | SEAL | A.B.P. | GOOD | V.FINE | UNC. |
|---|---|---|---|---|---|---|
| ☐1953 Priest-Humphrey | Blue | 13.00 | 12.00 | 18.00 | 55.00 |
| ☐1953A Priest-Anderson | Blue | 35.00 | 15.00 | 21.00 | 110.00 |
| ☐1953B Smith-Dillon | Blue | 13.00 | 14.00 | 18.00 | 52.00 |

ABOVE NOTE ONLY—720,000 ISSUED.
NOTE: Last issue of $10.00 Silver Certificates. These were not issued with "In God We Trust" on the back. Production ended in 1962.

# TEN DOLLAR (1879) REFUNDING CERTIFICATES
## NOTE NO. 78A

**Face Design:** Portrait of Benjamin Franklin.

**Back Design:** Large "TEN," ornate cornucopia border.

| SERIES | SIGNATURES | SEAL | A.B.P. | GOOD | V.FINE | UNC. |
|---|---|---|---|---|---|---|
| ☐1879 | Scofield-Gilfillan | PAY TO ORDER | Red | | | VERY RARE |
| ☐1879 | Scofield-Gilfillan | PAY TO BEARER | Red | 200.00 | 1000.00 | 2100.00 |

## TEN DOLLAR NOTES (1907) GOLD CERTIFICATES
(Large Size)                                    **NOTE NO. 79**

**Face Design:** Portrait of Hillegas center, yellow "X" left, yellow seal right, yellow numbers.

**Back Design:** The backs are a bright yellow color.

| SERIES | SIGNATURES | SEAL | A.B.P. | GOOD | V.FINE | UNC. |
|--------|------------|------|--------|------|--------|------|
| ☐1907 | Vernon-Treat | Gold | 12.00 | 24.00 | 100.00 | 375.00 |
| ☐1907 | Vernon-McClung | Gold | 12.00 | 24.00 | 100.00 | 375.00 |
| ☐1907 | Napier-McClung | Gold | 12.00 | 24.00 | 100.00 | 375.00 |
| ☐1907 | Napier-Thompson | Gold | 20.00 | 48.00 | 140.00 | 1100.00 |
| ☐1907 | Parker-Burke | Gold | 12.00 | 24.00 | 100.00 | 375.00 |
| ☐1907 | Teehee-Burke | Gold | 12.00 | 24.00 | 100.00 | 375.00 |
| ☐1922 | Speelman-White | Gold | 12.00 | 24.00 | 100.00 | 375.00 |

**TEN DOLLAR NOTES** (1928) GOLD CERTIFICATES
(Small Size)                                          **NOTE NO. 80**

**Face Design:** Portrait of Alexander Hamilton center, yellow
seal to left, yellow numbers.

**Back Design:** Printed in green ink.

| SERIES | SIGNATURES | SEAL | A.B.P. | GOOD | V.FINE | UNC. |
|--------|-----------|------|--------|------|--------|------|
| ☐1928 | Woods-Mellon | Gold | 14.00 | 20.00 | 45.00 | 400.00 |

## TEN DOLLAR NOTES (1890) TREASURY NOTES

(Large Size)                                    **NOTE NO. 81**

**Face Design:** Portrait of General Philip Sheridan.

**Back Design:**
Very ornate
large "TEN."

| SERIES | SIGNATURES | SEAL | A.B.P. | GOOD | V.FINE | UNC. |
|--------|------------|------|--------|------|--------|------|
| ☐1890 | Rosecrans-Huston | Lg. Brown | 65.00 | 180.00 | 600.00 | 2600.00 |
| ☐1890 | Rosecrans-Nebeker | Lg. Brown | 65.00 | 190.00 | 600.00 | 2600.00 |
| ☐1890 | Rosecrans-Nebeker | Sm. Red | 65.00 | 180.00 | 600.00 | 2600.00 |

## TEN DOLLAR NOTES (1891) TREASURY NOTES

(Large Size)                                    **NOTE NO. 81A**

**Face Design:**
Same as No. 81.
**Back Design:**
Ornate small
"TEN."

| SERIES | SIGNATURES | SEAL | A.B.P. | GOOD | V.FINE | UNC. |
|--------|------------|------|--------|------|--------|------|
| ☐1891 | Rosecrans-Nebeker | Sm. Red | 40.00 | 100.00 | 600.00 | 1500.00 |

| SERIES | SIGNATURES | SEAL | A.B.P. | GOOD | V.FINE | UNC. |
|--------|------------|------|--------|------|--------|------|
| ☐1891 | Tillman-Morgan | Sm. Red | 39.00 | 90.00 | 600.00 | 1500.00 |
| ☐1891 | Bruce-Roberts | Sm. Red | 39.00 | 90.00 | 600.00 | 1500.00 |

**TEN DOLLAR NOTES** (1914)
FEDERAL RESERVE NOTES

(Large Size)                                         **NOTE NO. 82**

**Face Design:** Portrait of President Jackson center, Federal Reserve Seal left, Treasury Seal right.

**Back Design:** Scenes of farming and industry.

### SIGNATURES OF BURKE-McADOO, RED SEALS AND RED SERIAL NUMBERS

| SERIES | CITY | SEAL | A.B.P. | GOOD | V.FINE | UNC. |
|--------|------|------|--------|------|--------|------|
| ☐1914 | Boston | Red | 14.00 | 30.00 | 90.00 | 400.00 |
| ☐1914 | New York | Red | 14.00 | 30.00 | 90.00 | 400.00 |
| ☐1914 | Philadelphia | Red | 14.00 | 30.00 | 95.00 | 400.00 |
| ☐1914 | Cleveland | Red | 14.00 | 30.00 | 95.00 | 400.00 |
| ☐1914 | Richmond | Red | 14.00 | 30.00 | 95.00 | 400.00 |
| ☐1914 | Atlanta | Red | 14.00 | 30.00 | 95.00 | 400.00 |
| ☐1914 | Chicago | Red | 14.00 | 30.00 | 95.00 | 400.00 |
| ☐1914 | St. Louis | Red | 14.00 | 30.00 | 95.00 | 400.00 |
| ☐1914 | Minneapolis | Red | 14.00 | 30.00 | 95.00 | 400.00 |
| ☐1914 | Kansas City | Red | 14.00 | 30.00 | 95.00 | 400.00 |
| ☐1914 | Dallas | Red | 14.00 | 30.00 | 95.00 | 400.00 |
| ☐1914 | San Francisco | Red | 14.00 | 30.00 | 95.00 | 400.00 |

## TEN DOLLAR NOTES (1914)
### FEDERAL RESERVE NOTES

(Large Size)

NOTE NO. 82A

| BANK & CITY | SIGNATURES | SEAL | A.B.P. | V.FINE | UNC. |
|---|---|---|---|---|---|
| ☐ Boston | Burke-McAdoo | Blue | 15.00 | 36.00 | 150.00 |
| ☐ Boston | Burke-Glass | Blue | 15.00 | 36.00 | 150.00 |
| ☐ Boston | Burke-Huston | Blue | 15.00 | 36.00 | 150.00 |
| ☐ Boston | White-Mellon | Blue | 15.00 | 36.00 | 150.00 |
| ☐ New York | Burke-McAdoo | Blue | 15.00 | 34.00 | 150.00 |
| ☐ New York | Burke-Glass | Blue | 15.00 | 34.00 | 150.00 |
| ☐ New York | Burke-Huston | Blue | 15.00 | 36.00 | 150.00 |
| ☐ New York | White-Mellon | Blue | 15.00 | 36.00 | 150.00 |
| ☐ Philadelphia | Burke-McAdoo | Blue | 15.00 | 36.00 | 150.00 |
| ☐ Philadelphia | Burke-Glass | Blue | 15.00 | 36.00 | 150.00 |
| ☐ Philadelphia | Burke-Huston | Blue | 15.00 | 36.00 | 150.00 |
| ☐ Philadelphia | White-Mellon | Blue | 15.00 | 36.00 | 150.00 |
| ☐ Cleveland | Burke-McAdoo | Blue | 15.00 | 34.00 | 150.00 |
| ☐ Cleveland | Burke-Glass | Blue | 15.00 | 34.00 | 150.00 |
| ☐ Cleveland | Burke-Huston | Blue | 15.00 | 34.00 | 150.00 |
| ☐ Cleveland | White-Mellon | Blue | 15.00 | 34.00 | 150.00 |
| ☐ Richmond | Burke-McAdoo | Blue | 15.00 | 36.00 | 150.00 |
| ☐ Richmond | Burke-Glass | Blue | 15.00 | 36.00 | 150.00 |
| ☐ Richmond | Burke-Huston | Blue | 15.00 | 36.00 | 150.00 |
| ☐ Richmond | White-Mellon | Blue | 15.00 | 36.00 | 150.00 |
| ☐ Atlanta | Burke-McAdoo | Blue | 15.00 | 36.00 | 150.00 |
| ☐ Atlanta | Burke-Glass | Blue | 15.00 | 36.00 | 150.00 |
| ☐ Atlanta | Burke-Huston | Blue | 15.00 | 36.00 | 150.00 |
| ☐ Atlanta | White-Mellon | Blue | 15.00 | 36.00 | 150.00 |
| ☐ Chicago | Burke-McAdoo | Blue | 15.00 | 36.00 | 150.00 |
| ☐ Chicago | Burke-Glass | Blue | 15.00 | 34.00 | 150.00 |
| ☐ Chicago | Burke-Huston | Blue | 15.00 | 34.00 | 150.00 |
| ☐ Chicago | White-Mellon | Blue | 15.00 | 34.00 | 150.00 |
| ☐ St. Louis | Burke-McAdoo | Blue | 15.00 | 36.00 | 150.00 |
| ☐ St. Louis | Burke-Glass | Blue | 15.00 | 36.00 | 150.00 |
| ☐ St. Louis | Burke-Huston | Blue | 15.00 | 36.00 | 150.00 |
| ☐ St. Louis | White-Mellon | Blue | 15.00 | 36.00 | 150.00 |
| ☐ Minneapolis | Burke-McAdoo | Blue | 15.00 | 36.00 | 150.00 |
| ☐ Minneapolis | Burke-Glass | Blue | 15.00 | 36.00 | 150.00 |
| ☐ Minneapolis | Burke-Huston | Blue | 15.00 | 36.00 | 150.00 |
| ☐ Minneapolis | White-Mellon | Blue | 15.00 | 36.00 | 150.00 |
| ☐ Kansas City | Burke-McAdoo | Blue | 15.00 | 36.00 | 150.00 |
| ☐ Kansas City | Burke-Glass | Blue | 15.00 | 36.00 | 150.00 |

| BANK & CITY | SIGNATURES | SEAL | A.B.P. | V.FINE | UNC. |
|---|---|---|---|---|---|
| ☐Kansas City | Burke-Huston | Blue | 15.00 | 36.00 | 150.00 |
| ☐Kansas City | White-Mellon | Blue | 15.00 | 36.00 | 150.00 |
| ☐Dallas | Burke-McAdoo | Blue | 15.00 | 36.00 | 150.00 |
| ☐Dallas | Burke-Glass | Blue | 15.00 | 36.00 | 150.00 |
| ☐Dallas | Burke-Huston | Blue | 15.00 | 36.00 | 150.00 |
| ☐Dallas | White-Mellon | Blue | 15.00 | 36.00 | 150.00 |
| ☐San Francisco | Burke-McAdoo | Blue | 15.00 | 36.00 | 150.00 |
| ☐San Francisco | Burke-Glass | Blue | 15.00 | 40.00 | 170.00 |
| ☐San Francisco | Burke-Huston | Blue | 15.00 | 36.00 | 150.00 |
| ☐San Francisco | White Mellon | Blue | 15.00 | 36.00 | 150.00 |

## TEN DOLLAR NOTES (1928-1928A)
### FEDERAL RESERVE NOTES

(Small Size) **NOTE NO. 83**

**Face Design:** Portrait of Alexander Hamilton center, black Federal Reserve Seal left, with number green Treasury Seal to the right.

**Back Design:** United States Treasury Building.

### SERIES OF 1928—SIGNATURES OF TATE-MELLON, GREEN SEAL

| BANK & CITY | A.B.P. | V.FINE | UNC. | BANK & CITY | A.B.P. | V.FINE | UNC. |
|---|---|---|---|---|---|---|---|
| ☐Boston | 12.00 | 22.00 | 45.00 | ☐Chicago | 12.00 | 24.00 | 45.00 |
| ☐New York | 12.00 | 22.00 | 45.00 | ☐St. Louis | 12.00 | 24.00 | 45.00 |
| ☐Philadelphia | 12.00 | 22.00 | 45.00 | ☐Minneapolis | 12.00 | 24.00 | 45.00 |
| ☐Cleveland | 12.00 | 22.00 | 45.00 | ☐Kansas City | 12.00 | 24.00 | 45.00 |

| BANK & CITY | A.B.P. | V.FINE | UNC. | BANK & CITY | A.B.P. | V.FINE | UNC. |
|---|---|---|---|---|---|---|---|
| ☐Richmond | 12.00 | 24.00 | 45.00 | ☐Dallas | 12.00 | 24.00 | 45.00 |
| ☐Atlanta | 12.00 | 24.00 | 45.00 | ☐San Francisco | 12.00 | 24.00 | 45.00 |

## SERIES OF 1928A—
## SIGNATURES OF WOODS-MELLON, GREEN SEAL

| BANK & CITY | A.B.P. | V.FINE | UNC. | BANK & CITY | A.B.P. | V.FINE | UNC. |
|---|---|---|---|---|---|---|---|
| ☐Boston | 12.00 | 18.00 | 50.00 | ☐Chicago | 12.00 | 18.00 | 50.00 |
| ☐New York | 12.00 | 18.00 | 50.00 | ☐St. Louis | 12.00 | 18.00 | 50.00 |
| ☐Philadelphia | 12.00 | 18.00 | 50.00 | ☐Minneapolis | 12.00 | 18.00 | 50.00 |
| ☐Cleveland | 12.00 | 18.00 | 50.00 | ☐Kansas City | 12.00 | 18.00 | 50.00 |
| ☐Richmond | 12.00 | 18.00 | 50.00 | ☐Dallas | 12.00 | 18.00 | 50.00 |
| ☐Atlanta | 12.00 | 18.00 | 50.00 | ☐San Francisco | 12.00 | 18.00 | 50.00 |

## TEN DOLLAR NOTES (1928B-1928C)
### FEDERAL RESERVE NOTES
(Small Issue)                                    **NOTE NO. 83A**

**Face Design:** Alexander Hamilton; Black Federal Reserve Seal, left, has letter instead of number.
**Back Design:** Same as Note No. 83.

## SERIES OF 1928B—
## SIGNATURES OF WOODS-MELLON, GREEN SEAL

| BANK & CITY | A.B.P. | V.FINE | UNC. | BANK & CITY | A.B.P. | V.FINE | UNC. |
|---|---|---|---|---|---|---|---|
| ☐Boston | 12.00 | 18.00 | 42.00 | ☐Chicago | 12.00 | 16.00 | 34.00 |
| ☐New York | 12.00 | 16.00 | 34.00 | ☐St. Louis | 12.00 | 16.00 | 34.00 |
| ☐Philadelphia | 12.00 | 16.00 | 34.00 | ☐Minneapolis | 12.00 | 18.00 | 42.00 |
| ☐Cleveland | 12.00 | 16.00 | 34.00 | ☐Kansas City | 12.00 | 16.00 | 34.00 |
| ☐Richmond | 12.00 | 18.00 | 42.00 | ☐Dallas | 12.00 | 16.00 | 34.00 |
| ☐Atlanta | 12.00 | 16.00 | 34.00 | ☐San Francisco | 12.00 | 18.00 | 42.00 |

## SERIES OF 1928C—
## SIGNATURES OF WOOD-MILLS, GREEN SEAL

| BANK & CITY | A.B.P. | V.FINE | UNC. | BANK & CITY | A.B.P. | V.FINE | UNC. |
|---|---|---|---|---|---|---|---|
| ☐New York | 20.00 | 30.00 | 95.00 | ☐Atlanta | 20.00 | 30.00 | 95.00 |
| ☐Cleveland | 20.00 | 30.00 | 95.00 | ☐Chicago | 20.00 | 30.00 | 95.00 |
| ☐Richmond | 20.00 | 30.00 | 95.00 | | | | |

## TEN DOLLAR NOTES (1934)
## FEDERAL RESERVE NOTES

(Small Size)                                    **NOTE NO. 83B**

## SERIES OF 1934—
## SIGNATURES OF JULIAN-MORGENTHAU, GREEN SEAL

| BANK & CITY | A.B.P. | V.FINE | UNC. | BANK & CITY | A.B.P. | V.FINE | UNC. |
|---|---|---|---|---|---|---|---|
| ☐Boston | 12.00 | 15.00 | 30.00 | ☐Chicago | 12.00 | 15.00 | 30.00 |
| ☐New York | 12.00 | 15.00 | 30.00 | ☐St. Louis | 12.00 | 15.00 | 30.00 |
| ☐Philadelphia | 12.00 | 15.00 | 30.00 | ☐Minneapolis | 12.00 | 15.00 | 30.00 |
| ☐Cleveland | 12.00 | 15.00 | 30.00 | ☐Kansas City | 12.00 | 15.00 | 30.00 |
| ☐Richmond | 12.00 | 15.00 | 30.00 | ☐Dallas | 12.00 | 15.00 | 30.00 |
| ☐Atlanta | 12.00 | 15.00 | 30.00 | ☐San Francisco | 12.00 | 15.00 | 30.00 |

NOTE: The green Treasury Seal on this note is known in a light and dark color. The light seal is worth about 10% to 20% more in most cases. "Redeemable in Gold" removed from obligation over Federal Reserve Seal.

## TEN DOLLAR NOTES (1934)
## FEDERAL RESERVE NOTES

(Small Size)                                    **NOTE NO. 83B**

## SERIES OF 1934A—
## SIGNATURES OF JULIAN-MORGENTHAU, GREEN SEAL

| BANK & CITY | A.B.P. | V.FINE | UNC. | BANK & CITY | A.B.P. | V.FINE | UNC. |
|---|---|---|---|---|---|---|---|
| ☐Boston | 12.00 | 15.00 | 25.00 | ☐Chicago | 12.00 | 15.00 | 25.00 |
| ☐New York | 12.00 | 15.00 | 25.00 | ☐St. Louis | 12.00 | 15.00 | 25.00 |
| ☐Philadelphia | 12.00 | 15.00 | 25.00 | ☐Minneapolis | 12.00 | 15.00 | 25.00 |
| ☐Cleveland | 12.00 | 15.00 | 25.00 | ☐Kansas City | 12.00 | 15.00 | 25.00 |
| ☐Richmond | 12.00 | 15.00 | 25.00 | ☐Dallas | 12.00 | 15.00 | 25.00 |
| ☐Atlanta | 12.00 | 15.00 | 25.00 | ☐San Francisco* | 12.00 | 15.00 | 25.00 |

* San Francisco—1934A with brown seal and overprinted HAWAII on face and back. Special issue for use in combat areas during World War II. Value in V.FINE $35.00, Value in UNC. $250.00

## SERIES OF 1934B—
## SIGNATURES OF JULIAN-VINSON, GREEN SEAL

| BANK & CITY | A.B.P. | V.FINE | UNC. | BANK & CITY | A.B.P. | V.FINE | UNC. |
|---|---|---|---|---|---|---|---|
| ☐Boston | 12.00 | 16.00 | 28.00 | ☐Chicago | 12.00 | 16.00 | 28.00 |
| ☐New York | 12.00 | 16.00 | 28.00 | ☐St. Louis | 12.00 | 16.00 | 28.00 |
| ☐Philadelphia | 12.00 | 16.00 | 28.00 | ☐Minneapolis | 12.00 | 16.00 | 28.00 |
| ☐Cleveland | 12.00 | 16.00 | 28.00 | ☐Kansas City | 12.00 | 16.00 | 28.00 |
| ☐Richmond | 12.00 | 16.00 | 28.00 | ☐Dallas | 12.00 | 16.00 | 28.00 |
| ☐Atlanta | 12.00 | 16.00 | 28.00 | ☐San Francisco | 12.00 | 16.00 | 28.00 |

## SERIES OF 1934C—
## SIGNATURES OF JULIAN-SNYDER, GREEN SEAL

| BANK & CITY | A.B.P. | V.FINE | UNC. | BANK & CITY | A.B.P. | V.FINE | UNC. |
|---|---|---|---|---|---|---|---|
| ☐Boston | 12.00 | 15.00 | 23.00 | ☐Chicago | 12.00 | 15.00 | 23.00 |
| ☐New York | 12.00 | 15.00 | 23.00 | ☐St. Louis | 12.00 | 15.00 | 23.00 |
| ☐Philadelphia | 12.00 | 15.00 | 23.00 | ☐Minneapolis | 12.00 | 15.00 | 23.00 |
| ☐Cleveland | 12.00 | 15.00 | 23.00 | ☐Kansas City | 12.00 | 15.00 | 23.00 |
| ☐Richmond | 12.00 | 15.00 | 23.00 | ☐Dallas | 12.00 | 15.00 | 23.00 |
| ☐Atlanta | 12.00 | 15.00 | 23.00 | ☐San Francisco | 12.00 | 15.00 | 23.00 |

## SERIES OF 1934D—
## SIGNATURES OF CLARK-SNYDER, GREEN SEAL

| BANK & CITY | A.B.P. | V.FINE | UNC. | BANK & CITY | A.B.P. | V.FINE | UNC. |
|---|---|---|---|---|---|---|---|
| ☐Boston | 12.00 | 15.00 | 23.00 | ☐Chicago | 12.00 | 15.00 | 23.00 |
| ☐New York | 12.00 | 15.00 | 23.00 | ☐St. Louis | 12.00 | 15.00 | 23.00 |
| ☐Philadelphia | 12.00 | 15.00 | 23.00 | ☐Minneapolis | 12.00 | 15.00 | 23.00 |
| ☐Cleveland | 12.00 | 15.00 | 23.00 | ☐Kansas City | 12.00 | 15.00 | 23.00 |
| ☐Richmond | 12.00 | 15.00 | 23.00 | ☐Dallas | 12.00 | 15.00 | 23.00 |
| ☐Atlanta | 12.00 | 15.00 | 23.00 | ☐San Francisco | 12.00 | 15.00 | 23.00 |

## TEN DOLLAR NOTES (1950)
### FEDERAL RESERVE NOTES

(Small Size) **NOTE NO. 83C**
## SERIES OF 1950—CLARK-SNYDER SIGNATURES, GREEN SEAL

| | UNC. |
|---|---|
| Issued for all Federal Reserve Banks | 28.00 |

## TEN DOLLAR NOTES (1950)
### FEDERAL RESERVE NOTES

(Small Size) **NOTE NO. 83C**
## SERIES OF 1950A—
## SIGNATURES OF PRIEST-HUMPHREY, GREEN SEAL

| Issued for all Federal Reserve Banks | 22.00 |
|---|---|

## SERIES OF 1950B—
## SIGNATURES OF PRIEST-ANDERSON, GREEN SEAL

| Issued for all Federal Reserve Banks | 23.00 |
|---|---|

## SERIES OF 1950C—
## SIGNATURES OF SMITH-DILLON, GREEN SEAL

| Issued for all Federal Reserve Banks | 21.00 |
|---|---|

## SERIES OF 1950D—
## SIGNATURES OF GRANAHAN-DILLON, GREEN SEAL

| Issued for all Federal Reserve Banks | 21.00 |
|---|---|

## SERIES OF 1950E—
## SIGNATURES OF GRANAHAN-FOWLER, GREEN SEAL

| BANK | UNC. | BANK | UNC. |
|------|------|------|------|
| ☐New York | 22.00 | ☐San Francisco | 22.00 |
| ☐Chicago | 22.00 | ..ONLY DISTRICTS USED | |

## TEN DOLLAR NOTES (1963)
## FEDERAL RESERVE NOTES
## ("IN GOD WE TRUST" ADDED ON BACK)
(Small Size)                                    NOTE NO. 83D

## SERIES OF 1963—
## SIGNATURES OF GRANAHAN-DILLON, GREEN SEAL
Issued for all banks except Minneapolis                 20.00

## SERIES OF 1963A—
## SIGNATURES OF GRANAHAN-FOWLER, GREEN SEAL
Issued for all Federal Reserve Banks                    20.00

## TEN DOLLAR NOTES (1969)
## FEDERAL RESERVE NOTES
## (WORDING IN GREEN TREASURY SEAL
## CHANGED FROM LATIN TO ENGLISH)
(Small Size)                                    NOTE NO. 83E

## SERIES OF 1969—SIGNATURES OF ELSTON-KENNEDY
Issued for all Federal Reserve Banks                    21.00

## SERIES OF 1969A—SIGNATURES OF KABIS-CONNALLY
Issued for all Federal Reserve Banks                    21.00

## SERIES OF 1969B—SIGNATURES OF BANUELOS-CONNALLY
Issued for all Federal Reserve Banks                    18.00

## SERIES OF 1969C—SIGNATURES OF BANUELOS-SHULTZ
Issued for all Federal Reserve Banks                    18.00

## SERIES OF 1974—SIGNATURES OF NEFF-SIMON
Issued for all Federal Reserve Banks                    16.00

## SERIES OF 1977—SIGNATURES OF MORTON-BLUMENTHAL
Issued for all Federal Reserve Banks                    16.00

## SERIES OF 1977A—SIGNATURES OF MORTON-MILLER
Issued for all Federal Reserve Banks                    16.00

## SERIES OF 1981—
## SIGNATURES OF BUCHANAN-REGAN, GREEN SEAL
Issued for all Federal Reserve Banks                    14.00

## SERIES OF 1981A—
## SIGNATURES OF ORTEGA-REGAN, GREEN SEAL
Issued for all Federal Reserve Banks                    14.00

## SERIES OF 1985—
## SIGNATURES OF ORTEGA-BAKER, GREEN SEAL
Issued for all Federal Reserve Banks

14.00

## TEN DOLLAR NOTES (1915-1918)
### FEDERAL RESERVE BANK NOTES
(Large Size)                                          **NOTE NO. 84**

**Face Design:** Portrait of President Jackson to left, bank and city in center, blue seal to the right.

**Back Design:** Similar to Note No. 82.

| BANK & CITY | SERIES | GOV'T SIGNATURES | BANK SIGNATURES | A.B.P. | GOOD | V.FINE | UNC. |
|---|---|---|---|---|---|---|---|
| ☐New York | 1918 | Teehee-Burke | Hendricks-Strong | | | | |
| | | | | 40.00 | 100.00 | 500.00 | 2100.00 |
| ☐Atlanta | 1915 | Teehee-Burke | Bell-Wellborn | | | | |
| | | | | 50.00 | 100.00 | 500.00 | 1700.00 |
| ☐Atlanta | 1918 | Elliott-Burke | Bell-Wellborn | | | | |
| | | | | 40.00 | 100.00 | 500.00 | 1600.00 |
| ☐Chicago | 1915 | Teehee-Burke | McLallen-McDougal | | | | |
| | | | | 40.00 | 100.00 | 500.00 | 1600.00 |
| ☐Chicago | 1918 | Teehee-Burke | McCloud-McDougal | | | | |
| | | | | 40.00 | 100.00 | 500.00 | 1600.00 |

| BANK & CITY | SERIES | GOV'T SIGNATURES | BANK SIGNATURES | A.B.P. | GOOD | V.FINE | UNC. |
|---|---|---|---|---|---|---|---|
| ☐St. Louis | 1918 | Teehee-Burke | Attebery-Wells | | | | |
| | | | | 40.00 | 100.00 | 500.00 | 1600.00 |
| ☐Kan. City | 1915 | Teehee-Burke | Anderson-Miller | | | | |
| | | | | 40.00 | 100.00 | 500.00 | 1600.00 |
| ☐Kan. City | 1915 | Teehee-Burke | Cross-Miller | | | | |
| | | | | 40.00 | 100.00 | 500.00 | 1600.00 |
| ☐Kan. City | 1915 | Teehee-Burke | Helm-Miller | | | | |
| | | | | 40.00 | 100.00 | 500.00 | 1600.00 |
| ☐Dallas | 1915 | Teehee-Burke | Hoopes-Van Zandt | | | | |
| | | | | 40.00 | 100 00 | 500.00 | 1600.00 |
| ☐Dallas | 1915 | Teehee-Burke | Gilbert-Van Zandt | | | | |
| | | | | 50.00 | 100.00 | 710.00 | 2100.00 |
| ☐Dallas | 1915 | Teehee-Burke | Talley-Van Zandt | | | | |
| | | | | 40.00 | 100.00 | 500.00 | 1600.00 |

## TEN DOLLAR NOTES (1929)
### FEDERAL RESERVE BANK NOTES

(Small Size)                                    **NOTE NO. 85**

**Face Design:** Portrait of Alexander Hamilton.

**Back Design:** Same as all small size $10.00 notes.

## SIGNATURES OF JONES-WOODS, BROWN SEAL

| BANK | SEAL | A.B.P. | GOOD | V.FINE | UNC. |
|------|------|--------|------|--------|------|
| ☐ Boston | Brown | 11.00 | 12.00 | 23.00 | 85.00 |
| ☐ New York | Brown | 11.00 | 12.00 | 20.00 | 70.00 |
| ☐ Philadelphia | Brown | 11.00 | 12.00 | 20.00 | 70.00 |
| ☐ Cleveland | Brown | 11.00 | 12.00 | 20.00 | 70.00 |
| ☐ Richmond | Brown | 11.00 | 12.00 | 22.00 | 98.00 |
| ☐ Atlanta | Brown | 11.00 | 12.00 | 22.00 | 98.00 |
| ☐ Chicago | Brown | 11.00 | 12.00 | 20.00 | 70.00 |
| ☐ St. Louis | Brown | 11.00 | 12.00 | 20.00 | 70.00 |
| ☐ Minneapolis | Brown | 11.00 | 12.00 | 22.00 | 90.00 |
| ☐ Kansas City | Brown | 11.00 | 12.00 | 21.00 | 75.00 |
| ☐ Dallas | Brown | 100.00 | 210.00 | 40.00 | 1100.00 |
| ☐ San Francisco | Brown | 11.00 | 12.00 | 24.00 | 115.00 |

# TWENTY DOLLAR NOTES

ORDER OF ISSUE

**TWENTY DOLLAR NOTES** (1861) DEMAND NOTES
(Large Size)                                                **NOTE NO. 86**

**Face Design:** Liberty with sword and shield.

**Back Design:** Intricate design of numerals, "20." Demand Notes have no Treasury Seal.

| SERIES | PAYABLE AT | A.B.P. | GOOD | V.GOOD |
|--------|-----------|--------|------|--------|
| ☐1861 | Boston (I) | RARE | RARE | RARE |
| ☐1861 | New York (I) | 1600.00 | 4800.00 | 10,000.00 |
| ☐1861 | Philadelphia (I) | 1600.00 | 4800.00 | 10,000.00 |
| ☐1861 | Cincinnati (I) | RARE | RARE | RARE |
| ☐1861 | St. Louis (I) | (Unknown in any collection) | | |
| ☐1861 | Boston (II) | RARE | RARE | RARE |
| ☐1861 | New York (II) | 1600.00 | 4800.00 | 10,000.00 |
| ☐1861 | Philadelphia (II) | 1600.00 | 4800.00 | 10,000.00 |
| ☐1861 | Cincinnati (II) | RARE | RARE | RARE |
| ☐1861 | St. Louis (II) | (Unknown in any collection) | | |

NOTE: Counterfeits and expertly repaired specimens exist. Use caution in buying.

**TWENTY DOLLAR NOTES** (1862-1863)
UNITED STATES NOTES
(ALSO KNOWN AS LEGAL TENDER NOTES)

(Large Size)                                    **NOTE NO. 86A**

**Face Design:** Liberty with sword and shield.

**Back Design:** Second obligation. This note was also issued with first obligation on the back. See Notes Nos. 33 and 33A.

| SERIES | SIGNATURES | SEAL | A.B.P. | GOOD | V.FINE | UNC. |
|--------|-----------|------|--------|------|--------|------|
| ☐1862 | Chittenden-Spinner* | Red | 95.00 | 400.00 | 1100.00 | 3100.00 |
| ☐1862 | Chittenden-Spinner** | Red | 95.00 | 400.00 | 1100.00 | 3100.00 |
| ☐1863 | Chittenden-Spinner** | Red | 95.00 | 400.00 | 1100.00 | 3100.00 |

\* First Obligation: Similar to Note No. 33.
\*\* Second Obligation: Shown above.

## TWENTY DOLLAR NOTES (1869)
### UNITED STATES NOTES
### (ALSO KNOWN AS LEGAL TENDER NOTES)
(Large Size)                                    NOTE NOS. 87-87A

| SERIES | SIGNATURES | SEAL | A.B.P. | GOOD | V.FINE | UNC. |
|--------|-----------|------|--------|------|--------|------|
| ☐1869 | Allison-Spinner | Red | 125.00 | 210.00 | 1400.00 | 4600.00 |
| **87A SERIES Back Design: Revised** | | | | | | |
| ☐1875 | Allison-New | Red | 42.00 | 95.00 | 600.00 | 2300.00 |
| ☐1878 | Allison-Gilfillan | Red | 42.00 | 85.00 | 600.00 | 1800.00 |
| ☐1880 | Scofield-Gilfillan | Brown Lg | 42.00 | 85.00 | 500.00 | 1350.00 |
| ☐1880 | Bruce-Gilfillan | Brown Lg | 42.00 | 95.00 | 500.00 | 1350.00 |
| ☐1880 | Bruce-Wyman | Brown Lg | 42.00 | 86.00 | 500.00 | 1350.00 |
| ☐1880 | Bruce-Wyman | Red Lg | 42.00 | 85.00 | 400.00 | 1350.00 |
| ☐1880 | Rosecrans-Jordan | Red Lg | 42.00 | 85.00 | 400.00 | 1350.00 |
| ☐1880 | Rosecrans-Hyatt | Red Plain | 42.00 | 85.00 | 400.00 | 1350.00 |
| ☐1880 | Rosecrans-Hyatt | Red Spikes | 42.00 | 85.00 | 500.00 | 1500.00 |
| ☐1880 | Rosecrans-Huston | Red Lg | 42.00 | 85.00 | 500.00 | 1500.00 |
| ☐1880 | Rosecrans-Huston | Brown Lg | 42.00 | 85.00 | 400.00 | 1500.00 |
| ☐1880 | Rosecrans-Nebeker | Brown Lg | 42.00 | 80.00 | 500.00 | 950.00 |
| ☐1800 | Rosecrans-Nebeker | Red Sm | 42.00 | 80.00 | 350.00 | 950.00 |
| ☐1880 | Tillman-Morgan | Red Sm | 35.00 | 70.00 | 350.00 | 925.00 |
| ☐1880 | Bruce-Roberts | Red Sm | 35.00 | 70.00 | 350.00 | 975.00 |
| ☐1880 | Lyons-Roberts | Red Sm | 35.00 | 70.00 | 350.00 | 975.00 |
| ☐1880 | Vernon-Treat | Red Sm | 35.00 | 70.00 | 350.00 | 975.00 |
| ☐1880 | Vernon-McClung | Red Sm | 35.00 | 70.00 | 300.00 | 975.00 |
| ☐1880 | Teehee-Burke | Red Sm | 35.00 | 70.00 | 300.00 | 975.00 |
| ☐1880 | Elliott-White | Red Sm | 35.00 | 70.00 | 300.00 | 975.00 |

**TWENTY DOLLAR NOTES** (1863-1875)
NATIONAL BANK NOTES
FIRST CHARTER PERIOD (Large Size)          **NOTE NO. 88**

**Face Design:** Battle of Lexington left, name of bank in center. Columbia with flag right.

**Back Design:** Green border, black center picture of baptism of Pocahontas.

| SERIES | SIGNATURES | SEAL | A.B.P. | GOOD | V.FINE | UNC. |
|---|---|---|---|---|---|---|
| ☐Original | Chittenden-Spinner | Red | 100.00 | 200.00 | 700.00 | 3200.00 |
| ☐Original | Colby-Spinner | Red | 100.00 | 210.00 | 500.00 | 3100.00 |
| ☐Original | Jeffries-Spinner | Red | 150.00 | 600.00 | 2100.00 | 4600.00 |
| ☐Original | Allison-Spinner | Red | 85.00 | 240.00 | 600.00 | 3000.00 |
| ☐1875 | Allison-New | Red | 85.00 | 200.00 | 550.00 | 2800.00 |
| ☐1875 | Allison-Wyman | Red | 90.00 | 200.00 | 550.00 | 2900.00 |
| ☐1875 | Allison-Gilfillan | Red | 85.00 | 200.00 | 550.00 | 2800.00 |
| ☐1875 | Scofield-Gilfillan | Red | 85.00 | 200.00 | 550.00 | 2800.00 |
| ☐1875 | Bruce-Gilfillan | Red | 85.00 | 200.00 | 550.00 | 2800.00 |
| ☐1875 | Bruce-Wyman | Red | 100.00 | 240.00 | 550.00 | 3850.00 |
| ☐1875 | Rosecrans-Huston | Red | 85.00 | 200.00 | 600.00 | 2800.00 |
| ☐1875 | Rosecrans-Nebeker | Red | 100.00 | 450.00 | 750.00 | 4300.00 |
| ☐1875 | Tillman-Morgan | Red | 100.00 | 450.00 | 800.00 | 4400.00 |

## TWENTY DOLLAR NOTES (1882)
### NATIONAL BANK NOTES
SECOND CHARTER PERIOD (Large Size)          **NOTE NO. 88A**

**First Issue**—Brown seal and brown backs.
**Face Design:** Similar to Note No. 88.
**Back Design:** Similar to Note No. 39, border is brown, green Charter number in center.

| SERIES | SIGNATURES | SEAL | A.B.P. | GOOD | V.FINE | UNC. |
|--------|------------|------|--------|------|--------|------|
| ☐1882 | Bruce-Gilfillan | Brown | 30.00 | 75.00 | 250.00 | 1000.00 |
| ☐1882 | Bruce-Wyman | Brown | 30.00 | 75.00 | 250.00 | 1000.00 |
| ☐1882 | Bruce-Jordan | Brown | 30.00 | 75.00 | 250.00 | 1000.00 |
| ☐1882 | Rosecrans-Jordan | Brown | 30.00 | 75.00 | 250.00 | 1000.00 |
| ☐1882 | Rosecrans-Hyatt | Brown | 30.00 | 75.00 | 250.00 | 1000.00 |
| ☐1882 | Rosecrans-Huston | Brown | 30.00 | 75.00 | 250.00 | 1000.00 |
| ☐1882 | Rosecrans-Nebeker | Brown | 30.00 | 75.00 | 250.00 | 1000.00 |
| ☐1882 | Rosecrans-Morgan | Brown | 130.00 | 280.00 | 800.00 | 2100.00 |
| ☐1882 | Tillman-Morgan | Brown | 30.00 | 75.00 | 250.00 | 1000.00 |
| ☐1882 | Tillman-Roberts | Brown | 30.00 | 75.00 | 250.00 | 1000.00 |
| ☐1882 | Bruce-Roberts | Brown | 30.00 | 75.00 | 250.00 | 1000.00 |
| ☐1882 | Lyons-Roberts | Brown | 30.00 | 75.00 | 250.00 | 1000.00 |
| ☐1882 | Lyons-Treat | Brown | 30.00 | 75.00 | 250.00 | 1100.00 |
| ☐1882 | Vernon-Treat | Brown | 30.00 | 75.00 | 250.00 | 1100.00 |

SECOND CHARTER PERIOD, Second Issue          **NOTE NO. 88B**

**Face Design:** Similar to Note No. 88.
**Back Design:** Similar to Note No. 40.

| SERIES | SIGNATURES | SEAL | A.B.P. | GOOD | V.FINE | UNC. |
|--------|------------|------|--------|------|--------|------|
| ☐1882 | Rosecrans-Huston | Blue | 26.00 | 70.00 | 250.00 | 850.00 |
| ☐1882 | Rosecrans-Nebeker | Blue | 26.00 | 70.00 | 250.00 | 850.00 |
| ☐1882 | Rosecrans-Morgan | Blue | 120.00 | 300.00 | 800.00 | 1600.00 |
| ☐1882 | Tillman-Morgan | Blue | 26.00 | 70.00 | 250.00 | 850.00 |
| ☐1882 | Tillman-Roberts | Blue | 26.00 | 70.00 | 250.00 | 850.00 |
| ☐1882 | Bruce-Roberts | Blue | 26.00 | 70.00 | 250.00 | 850.00 |
| ☐1882 | Lyons-Roberts | Blue | 26.00 | 70.00 | 250.00 | 850.00 |
| ☐1882 | Vernon-Treat | Blue | 26.00 | 70.00 | 250.00 | 850.00 |
| ☐1882 | Napier-McClung | Blue | 26.00 | 70.00 | 250.00 | 850.00 |

SECOND CHARTER PERIOD, Third Issue (Large Size)  **NOTE NO. 88C**

**Face Design:** Similar to Note No. 88 with blue seal.
**Back Design:** Similar to Note No. 41, green back, value in block letters.

| SERIES | SIGNATURES | SEAL | A.B.P. | GOOD | V.FINE | UNC. |
|--------|-----------|------|--------|------|--------|------|
| ☐1882 | Tillman-Morgan | Blue | 40.00 | 80.00 | 450.00 | 1800.00 |
| ☐1882 | Lyons-Roberts | Blue | 40.00 | 80.00 | 500.00 | 2200.00 |
| ☐1882 | Lyons-Treat | Blue | 40.00 | 80.00 | 450.00 | 2200 00 |
| ☐1882 | Vernon-Treat | Blue | 40.00 | 80.00 | 450.00 | 1800.00 |
| ☐1882 | Napier-McClung | Blue | 40.00 | 80.00 | 450.00 | 1800.00 |
| ☐1882 | Teehee-Burke | Blue | 40.00 | 80.00 | 550.00 | 2300.00 |

## TWENTY DOLLAR NOTES (1902)
### NATIONAL BANK NOTES
THIRD CHARTER PERIOD, First Issue (Large Size)          **NOTE NO. 89**

**Face Design:** Portrait of McCulloch left, name of bank center, Treasury Seal right.

| SERIES | SIGNATURES | SEAL | A.B.P. | GOOD | V.FINE | UNC. |
|--------|-----------|------|--------|------|--------|------|
| ☐1902 | Lyons-Roberts | Red | 30.00 | 75.00 | 210.00 | 1000.00 |
| ☐1902 | Lyons-Treat | Red | 30.00 | 75.00 | 210.00 | 1000.00 |
| ☐1902 | Vernon-Treat | Red | 30.00 | 75.00 | 240.00 | 1650.00 |

### Second Issue—Date 1902-1908 added on back,
### Treasury seal and serial numbers blue.

| SERIES | SIGNATURES | SEAL | A.B.P. | GOOD | V.FINE | UNC. |
|--------|-----------|------|--------|------|--------|------|
| ☐1902 | Lyons-Roberts | Blue | 22.00 | 30.00 | 80.00 | 310.00 |
| ☐1902 | Lyons-Treat | Blue | 22.00 | 30.00 | 80.00 | 310.00 |
| ☐1902 | Vernon-Treat | Blue | 22.00 | 30.00 | 80.00 | 310.00 |
| ☐1902 | Vernon-McClung | Blue | 22.00 | 30.00 | 80.00 | 310.00 |
| ☐1902 | Napier-McClung | Blue | 22.00 | 30.00 | 80.00 | 310.00 |
| ☐1902 | Napier-Thompson | Blue | 22.00 | 34.00 | 90.00 | 600.00 |
| ☐1902 | Napier-Burke | Blue | 22.00 | 30.00 | 80.00 | 310.00 |
| ☐1902 | Parker-Burke | Blue | 22.00 | 30.00 | 80.00 | 310.00 |

### Third Issue—Date 1902-1908 removed from back,
### seal and serial numbers are blue.

| SERIES | SIGNATURES | SEAL | A.B.P. | GOOD | V.FINE | UNC. |
|--------|-----------|------|--------|------|--------|------|
| ☐1902 | Lyons-Roberts | Blue | 22.00 | 30.00 | 70.00 | 290.00 |
| ☐1902 | Lyons-Treat | Blue | 22.00 | 30.00 | 70.00 | 290.00 |
| ☐1902 | Vernon-Treat | Blue | 22.00 | 30.00 | 70.00 | 290.00 |
| ☐1902 | Vernon-McClung | Blue | 22.00 | 30.00 | 70.00 | 290.00 |

| SERIES | SIGNATURES | SEAL | A.B.P. | GOOD | V.FINE | UNC. |
|--------|-----------|------|--------|------|--------|------|
| ☐1902 | Napier-McClung | Blue | 22.00 | 30.00 | 70.00 | 290.00 |
| ☐1902 | Napier-Thompson | Blue | 22.00 | 30.00 | 75.00 | 300.00 |
| ☐1902 | Napier-Burke | Blue | 22.00 | 30.00 | 70.00 | 290.00 |
| ☐1902 | Parker-Burke | Blue | 22.00 | 30.00 | 70.00 | 290.00 |
| ☐1902 | Teehee-Burke | Blue | 22.00 | 30.00 | 70.00 | 290.00 |
| ☐1902 | Elliott-Burke | Blue | 22.00 | 30.00 | 70.00 | 290.00 |
| ☐1902 | Elliott-White | Blue | 22.00 | 30.00 | 70.00 | 290.00 |
| ☐1902 | Speelman-White | Blue | 22.00 | 30.00 | 70.00 | 290.00 |
| ☐1902 | Woods-White | Blue | 22.00 | 30.00 | 70.00 | 290.00 |
| ☐1902 | Woods-Tate | Blue | 22.00 | 42.00 | 160.00 | 500.00 |
| ☐1902 | Jones-Woods | Blue | 175.00 | 400.00 | 1100.00 | 5200.00 |

## TWENTY DOLLAR NOTES (1929)
### NATIONAL BANK NOTES

(Small Size)                                    **NOTE NO. 90**

**Face Design: TYPE I**—Portrait of President Jackson in center, name of bank to left, brown seal right. Charter number in black.

**Face Design: TYPE II.**

**Back Design:** The White House, similar to all $20.00 small notes.

| SERIES | SIGNATURES | SEAL | A.B.P. | GOOD | V.FINE | UNC. |
|---|---|---|---|---|---|---|
| ☐1929 —Type I Jones-Woods | | Brown | 21.00 | 22.00 | 40.00 | 100.00 |
| ☐1929 —Type II Jones-Woods | | Brown | 21.00 | 22.00 | 42.00 | 110.00 |

**TWENTY DOLLAR NOTES** (1880)
SILVER CERTIFICATES

(Large Size)                                                **NOTE NO. 91**

**Face Design:** Portrait of Stephen Decatur right. "TWENTY SILVER DOLLARS" in center.

**Back Design:** "SILVER" in large block letters.

| SERIES | SIGNATURES | SEAL | A.B.P. | GOOD | V.FINE | UNC. |
|--------|------------|------|--------|------|--------|------|
| ☐1880 | Scofield-Gilfillan | Brown | 90.00 | 400.00 | 1500.00 | 5600.00 |
| ☐1880 | Bruce-Gilfillan | Brown | 90.00 | 400.00 | 1500.00 | 5600.00 |
| ☐1880 | Bruce-Wyman | Brown | 90.00 | 400.00 | 1500.00 | 5600.00 |
| ☐1880 | Bruce-Wyman | Red Sm | 400.00 | 1500.00 | 2400.00 | 6300.00 |

This note was also issued in series of 1878. They are very rare.

## TWENTY DOLLAR NOTES (1886)
### SILVER CERTIFICATES

(Large Size) **NOTE NO. 92**

**Face Design:** Portrait of Daniel Manning center, Agriculture left, Industry right.

**Back Design:** Double diamond design center.

| SERIES | SIGNATURES | SEAL | A.B.P. | GOOD | V.FINE | UNC. |
|--------|------------|------|--------|------|--------|------|
| ☐1886 | Rosecrans-Hyatt | Red Lg | 160.00 | 350.00 | 2200.00 | 6400.00 |
| ☐1886 | Rosecrans-Huston | Brown Lg | 160.00 | 350.00 | 2200.00 | 6400.00 |
| ☐1886 | Rosecrans-Nebeker | Brown Lg | 160.00 | 350.00 | 2200.00 | 6400.00 |
| ☐1886 | Rosecrans-Nebeker | Red Sm | 225.00 | 700.00 | 2400.00 | 6700.00 |

## TWENTY DOLLAR NOTES (1891)
### SILVER CERTIFICATES
### (NOT ISSUED IN SMALL SIZE NOTES)
(Large Size)                                                   **NOTE NO. 93**

**Face Design:** Same as Note No. 92.

**Back Design:** Revised.

| SERIES | SIGNATURES | SEAL | A.B.P. | GOOD | V.FINE | UNC. |
|--------|------------|------|--------|------|--------|------|
| ☐1891 | Rosecrans-Nebeker | Red | 46.00 | 90.00 | 600.00 | 2500.00 |
| ☐1891 | Tillman-Morgan | Red | 46.00 | 90.00 | 600.00 | 2500.00 |
| ☐1891 | Bruce-Roberts | Red | 46.00 | 90.00 | 600.00 | 2500.00 |
| ☐1891 | Lyons-Roberts | Red | 46.00 | 90.00 | 600.00 | 2500.00 |
| ☐1891 | Parker-Burke | Blue | 46.00 | 90.00 | 600.00 | 2500.00 |
| ☐1891 | Teehee-Burke | Blue | 46.00 | 90.00 | 600.00 | 2500.00 |

**TWENTY DOLLAR NOTES** (1882) GOLD CERTIFICATES
(Large Size)                                    **NOTE NO. 94**

**Face Design:** Portrait of President Garfield right, "TWENTY
DOLLARS IN GOLD COIN" center.

**Back Design:** Large "20" left, eagle and arrows center,
bright orange color.

| SERIES | SIGNATURES | SEAL | A.B.P. | GOOD | V.FINE | UNC. |
|--------|-----------|------|--------|------|--------|------|
| ☐1882 | Bruce-Gilfillan | Brown | | | | VERY RARE |

The above Note has a countersigned signature.

| SERIES | SIGNATURES | SEAL | A.B.P. | GOOD | V.FINE | UNC. |
|--------|-----------|------|--------|------|--------|------|
| ☐1882 | Bruce-Gilfillan | Brown | 260.00 | 1100.00 | 3500.00 | 7200.00 |
| ☐1882 | Bruce-Wyman | Brown | 160.00 | 800.00 | 2200.00 | 4000.00 |
| ☐1882 | Rosecrans-Huston | Brown | 160.00 | 450.00 | 2500.00 | 5000.00 |
| ☐1882 | Lyons-Roberts | Red | 80.00 | 90.00 | 500.00 | 1500.00 |

**TWENTY DOLLAR NOTES** (1905) GOLD CERTIFICATES
(Large Size) **NOTE NO. 95**

**Face Design:** Portrait of President Washington center, "XX" left, Treasury Seal right.

**Back Design:** Eagle and Shield center, printed in bright orange color.

| SERIES | SIGNATURES | SEAL | A.B.P. | GOOD | V.FINE | UNC. |
|--------|-----------|------|--------|------|--------|------|
| ☐1905 | Lyons-Roberts | Red | 100.00 | 350.00 | 1500.00 | 8000.00 |
| ☐1905 | Lyons-Treat | Red | 100.00 | 350.00 | 1100.00 | 6800.00 |
| ☐1906 | Vernon-Treat | Gold | 32.00 | 70.00 | 130.00 | 500.00 |
| ☐1906 | Vernon-McClung | Gold | 32.00 | 70.00 | 130.00 | 525.00 |
| ☐1906 | Napier-McClung | Gold | 32.00 | 70.00 | 130.00 | 525.00 |
| ☐1906 | Napier-Thompson | Gold | 32.00 | 100.00 | 200.00 | 750.00 |
| ☐1906 | Parker-Burke | Gold | 32.00 | 70.00 | 120.00 | 550.00 |
| ☐1906 | Tehee-Burke | Gold | 32.00 | 70.00 | 120.00 | 550.00 |
| ☐1922 | Speelman-White | Gold | 32.00 | 70.00 | 120.00 | 450.00 |

## TWENTY DOLLAR NOTES (1928) GOLD CERTIFICATES
(Small Size)                                    **NOTE NO. 96**

**Face Design:** Portrait of President Jackson center, gold seal left, gold serial numbers.

**Back Design:** The White House, printed green, similar to all small size $20s.

| SERIES | SIGNATURES | SEAL | A.B.P. | V.FINE | UNC. |
|--------|-----------|------|--------|--------|------|
| ☐1928 | Woods-Mellon | Gold | 23.00 | 55.00 | 190.00 |

## TWENTY DOLLAR NOTES (1890) TREASURY NOTES
(Large Size)                                    **NOTE NO. 97**

**Face Design:** Portrait of John Marshall, Supreme Court Chief Justice left, "20" center.

**Back Design**

| SERIES | SIGNATURES | SEAL | A.B.P. | GOOD | V.FINE | UNC. |
|--------|-----------|------|--------|------|--------|------|
| ☐ 1890 | Rosecrans-Huston | Brown | 110.00 | 380.00 | 2200.00 | 8200.00 |
| ☐ 1890 | Rosecrans-Nebeker | Brown | 110.00 | 380.00 | 2200.00 | 8200.00 |
| ☐ 1890 | Rosecrans-Nebeker | Red | 110.00 | 380.00 | 2200.00 | 8200.00 |

(Large Size)                                                **NOTE NO. 97A**

**Back Design**

**Face Design:** Same as previous note.

| SERIES | SIGNATURES | SEAL | A.B.P. | GOOD | V.FINE | UNC. |
|--------|-----------|------|--------|------|--------|------|
| ☐ 1891 | Tillman-Morgan | Red | 400.00 | 850.00 | 2400.00 | 8800.00 |
| ☐ 1891 | Bruce-Roberts | Red | 400.00 | 850.00 | 2400.00 | 8800.00 |

**TWENTY DOLLAR NOTES** (1914)
FEDERAL RESERVE NOTES

(Large Size)                                                **NOTE NO. 98**

**Face Design:** Portrait of President Cleveland center,
Federal Reserve Seal left, Treasury Seal right.

**Back Design:** Scenes of transportation. Locomotive left, steamship right.

### SERIES OF 1914—SIGNATURES OF BURKE-McADOO, RED TREASURY SEAL

| BANK | A.B.P. | V.FINE | UNC. | BANK | A.B.P. | V.FINE | UNC. |
|---|---|---|---|---|---|---|---|
| ☐Boston | 35.00 | 200.00 | 920.00 | ☐Chicago | 35.00 | 200.00 | 920.00 |
| ☐New York | 35.00 | 200.00 | 920.00 | ☐St. Louis | 35.00 | 200.00 | 920.00 |
| ☐Philadelphia | 35.00 | 200.00 | 920.00 | ☐Minneapolis | 35.00 | 200.00 | 920.00 |
| ☐Cleveland | 35.00 | 200.00 | 920.00 | ☐Kansas City | 35.00 | 200.00 | 920.00 |
| ☐Richmond | 35.00 | 200.00 | 920.00 | ☐Dallas | 35.00 | 200.00 | 920.00 |
| ☐Atlanta | 35.00 | 200.00 | 920.00 | ☐San Francisco | 35.00 | 200.00 | 920.00 |

### SERIES OF 1914—WITH BLUE TREASURY SEAL AND BLUE SERIAL NUMBERS

This note was issued with signatures of BURKE-McADOO, BURKE-GLASS, BURKE-HUSTON and WHITE-MELLON.

| | A.B.P. | V.FINE | UNC. |
|---|---|---|---|
| Issued to all Federal Reserve Banks | 30.00 | 60.00 | 150.00 |

## TWENTY DOLLAR NOTES (1928)
### FEDERAL RESERVE NOTES

(Small Size)                                    **NOTE NO. 99**

**Face Design:** Portrait of President Jackson center, black Federal Reserve Seal with numeral for district in center. City of issuing bank in seal circle. Green Treasury Seal right.

**Back Design:** Picture of the White House, similar to all small size $20.00 notes.

### SERIES OF 1928—SIGNATURES OF TATE-MELLON, GREEN SEAL

| BANK | A.B.P. | V.FINE | UNC. | BANK | A.B.P. | V.FINE | UNC. |
|---|---|---|---|---|---|---|---|
| ☐Boston | 22.00 | 40.00 | 83.00 | ☐Chicago | 22.00 | 40.00 | 83.00 |
| ☐New York | 22.00 | 40.00 | 83.00 | ☐St. Louis | 22.00 | 40.00 | 83.00 |
| ☐Philadelphia | 22.00 | 40.00 | 83.00 | ☐Minneapolis | 22.00 | 40.00 | 83.00 |
| ☐Cleveland | 22.00 | 40.00 | 83.00 | ☐Kansas City | 22.00 | 40.00 | 83.00 |
| ☐Richmond | 22.00 | 40.00 | 83.00 | ☐Dallas | 22.00 | 40.00 | 83.00 |
| ☐Atlanta | 22.00 | 40.00 | 83.00 | ☐San Francisco | 22.00 | 40.00 | 83.00 |

### SERIES OF 1928A—
### SIGNATURES OF WOODS-MELLON, GREEN SEAL

| CITY | A.B.P. | V.FINE | UNC. | CITY | A.B.P. | V.FINE | UNC. |
|---|---|---|---|---|---|---|---|
| ☐Boston | 22.00 | 40.00 | 83.00 | ☐Chicago | 22.00 | 40.00 | 83.00 |
| ☐New York | 22.00 | 40.00 | 83.00 | ☐St. Louis | 22.00 | 40.00 | 83.00 |
| ☐Philadelphia | 22.00 | 40.00 | 83.00 | ☐Minneapolis | | NOT ISSUED | |
| ☐Cleveland | 22.00 | 40.00 | 83.00 | ☐Kansas City | 22.00 | 40.00 | 83.00 |
| ☐Richmond | 22.00 | 40.00 | 83.00 | ☐Dallas | 22.00 | 40.00 | 83.00 |
| ☐Atlanta | 22.00 | 40.00 | 83.00 | ☐San Francisco | | NOT ISSUED | |

## TWENTY DOLLAR NOTES (1928)
### FEDERAL RESERVE NOTES

(Small Size)                                        **NOTE NO. 100**

### SERIES OF 1928B—
### SIGNATURES OF WOODS-MELLON, GREEN SEAL
**Face and Back Design similar to Previous Note. Numeral in Federal Reserve Seal is now changed to a Letter.**

| BANK | A.B.P. | V.FINE | UNC. | BANK | A.B.P. | V.FINE | UNC. |
|---|---|---|---|---|---|---|---|
| ☐Boston | 22.00 | 29.00 | 40.00 | ☐Chicago | 22.00 | 29.00 | 40.00 |
| ☐New York | 22.00 | 29.00 | 40.00 | ☐St. Louis | 22.00 | 29.00 | 40.00 |
| ☐Philadelphia | 22.00 | 29.00 | 40.00 | ☐Minneapolis | 22.00 | 29.00 | 40.00 |
| ☐Cleveland | 22.00 | 29.00 | 40.00 | ☐Kansas City | 22.00 | 29.00 | 40.00 |
| ☐Richmond | 22.00 | 29.00 | 40.00 | ☐Dallas | 22.00 | 29.00 | 40.00 |
| ☐Atlanta | 22.00 | 29.00 | 40.00 | ☐San Fran | 22.00 | 29.00 | 40.00 |

### SERIES OF 1928C—SIGNATURES OF WOODS-MILLS, GREEN SEAL
### Only two banks issued this note.

| BANK | A.B.P. | V.FINE | UNC. | BANK | A.B.P. | V.FINE | UNC. |
|---|---|---|---|---|---|---|---|
| ☐Chicago | 75.00 | 200.00 | 600.00 | ☐San Francisco | 75.00 | 200.00 | 700.00 |

## TWENTY DOLLAR NOTES (1934)
### FEDERAL RESERVE NOTES

**NOTE NO. 100A**

### SIGNATURES OF JULIAN-MORGENTHAU, GREEN SEAL
**Face and Back Design similar to Previous Note. "Redeemable in Gold" removed from obligation over Federal Reserve Seal.**

| BANK | GOOD | V.FINE | UNC. | BANK | GOOD | V.FINE | UNC. |
|---|---|---|---|---|---|---|---|
| ☐Boston | 24.00 | 30.00 | 45.00 | ☐St. Louis | 24.00 | 30.00 | 45.00 |
| ☐New York | 24.00 | 30.00 | 45.00 | ☐Minneapolis | 24.00 | 30.00 | 45 00 |
| ☐Philadelphia | 24.00 | 30.00 | 45.00 | ☐Kansas City | 24.00 | 30.00 | 45.00 |
| ☐Cleveland | 24.00 | 30.00 | 45.00 | ☐Dallas | 24.00 | 30.00 | 45.00 |
| ☐Richmond | 24.00 | 30.00 | 45.00 | ☐San Fran | 24.00 | 30.00 | 45.00 |
| ☐Atlanta | 24.00 | 30.00 | 45.00 | ☐* San Francisco | | | |
| ☐Chicago | 24.00 | 30.00 | 45.00 | (HAWAII) | 56.00 | 145.00 | 750.00 |

\* The San Francisco Federal Reserve Note with brown seal and brown serial numbers, and overprinted "HAWAII" on face and back, was a special issue for the Armed Forces in the Pacific area during World War II.

## TWENTY DOLLAR NOTES (1934A)
### FEDERAL RESERVE NOTES

(Small Size)                                          **NOTE NO. 101**
#### SERIES OF 1934A—SIGNATURES OF JULIAN-MORGENTHAU

| BANK | A.B.P. | V.FINE | UNC. | BANK | A.B.P. | V.FINE | UNC. |
|------|--------|--------|------|------|--------|--------|------|
| ☐ Boston | 24.00 | 30.00 | 45.00 | ☐ St. Louis | 24.00 | 30.00 | 45.00 |
| ☐ New York | 24.00 | 30.00 | 45.00 | ☐ Minneapolis | 24.00 | 30.00 | 45 00 |
| ☐ Philadelphia | 24.00 | 30.00 | 45.00 | ☐ Kansas City | 24.00 | 30.00 | 45.00 |
| ☐ Cleveland | 24.00 | 30.00 | 45.00 | ☐ Dallas | 24.00 | 30.00 | 45.00 |
| ☐ Richmond | 24.00 | 30.00 | 45.00 | ☐ San Fran | 24.00 | 30.00 | 45.00 |
| ☐ Atlanta | 24.00 | 30.00 | 45.00 | ☐ \* San Francisco | | | |
| ☐ Chicago | 24.00 | 30.00 | 45.00 | (HAWAII) | 26.00 | 45.00 | 335.00 |

#### SERIES OF 1934B—
#### SIGNATURES OF JULIAN-VINSON, GREEN SEAL

| BANK | A.B.P. | V.FINE | UNC. | BANK | A.B.P. | V.FINE | UNC. |
|------|--------|--------|------|------|--------|--------|------|
| ☐ Boston | 24.00 | 29.00 | 44.00 | ☐ Chicago | 24.00 | 29.00 | 44.00 |
| ☐ New York | 24.00 | 29.00 | 44.00 | ☐ St. Louis | 24.00 | 29.00 | 44.00 |
| ☐ Philadelphia | 24.00 | 29.00 | 44.00 | ☐ Minneapolis | 24.00 | 29.00 | 44.00 |
| ☐ Cleveland | 24.00 | 29.00 | 44.00 | ☐ Kansas City | 24.00 | 29.00 | 44.00 |
| ☐ Richmond | 24.00 | 29.00 | 44.00 | ☐ Dallas | 24.00 | 29.00 | 44.00 |
| ☐ Atlanta | 24.00 | 29.00 | 44.00 | ☐ San Fran | 24.00 | 29.00 | 44.00 |

## SERIES OF 1934C—
### SIGNATURES OF JULIAN-SNYDER, GREEN SEAL

**Back Design:** This has been modified with this series, balcony added to the White House.

| BANK | A.B.P. | V.FINE | UNC. | BANK | A.B.P. | V.FINE | UNC. |
|------|--------|--------|------|------|--------|--------|------|
| ☐Boston | 22.00 | 29.00 | 44.00 | ☐Chicago | 22.00 | 29.00 | 44.00 |
| ☐New York | 22.00 | 29.00 | 44.00 | ☐St. Louis | 22.00 | 29.00 | 44.00 |
| ☐Philadelphia | 22.00 | 29.00 | 44.00 | ☐Minneapolis | 22.00 | 29.00 | 44.00 |
| ☐Cleveland | 22.00 | 29.00 | 44.00 | ☐Kansas City | 22.00 | 29.00 | 44.00 |
| ☐Richmond | 22.00 | 29.00 | 44.00 | ☐Dallas | 22.00 | 29.00 | 44.00 |
| ☐Atlanta | 22.00 | 29.00 | 44.00 | ☐San Fran | 22.00 | 29.00 | 44.00 |

## SERIES OF 1934D—
### SIGNATURES OF CLARK-SNYDER, GREEN SEAL

| BANK | A.B.P. | V.FINE | UNC. | BANK | A.B.P. | V.FINE | UNC. |
|------|--------|--------|------|------|--------|--------|------|
| ☐Boston | 22.00 | 28.00 | 42.00 | ☐Chicago | 22.00 | 28.00 | 42.00 |
| ☐New York | 22.00 | 28.00 | 42.00 | ☐St. Louis | 22.00 | 28.00 | 42.00 |
| ☐Philadelphia | 22.00 | 28.00 | 42.00 | ☐Minneapolis | 22.00 | 28.00 | 42.00 |
| ☐Cleveland | 22.00 | 28.00 | 42.00 | ☐Kansas City | 22.00 | 28.00 | 42.00 |
| ☐Richmond | 22.00 | 28.00 | 42.00 | ☐Dallas | 22.00 | 28.00 | 42.00 |
| ☐Atlanta | 22.00 | 28.00 | 42.00 | ☐San Fran | 22.00 | 28.00 | 42.00 |

## TWENTY DOLLAR NOTES (1950)
### FEDERAL RESERVE NOTES

(Small Size)                                    **NOTE NO. 102**

## SERIES OF 1950—
### SIGNATURES OF CLARK-SNYDER, GREEN SEAL
**Black Federal Seal and Green Treasury Seal are slightly smaller.**

| BANK | A.B.P. | UNC. | BANK | A.B.P. | UNC. |
|------|--------|------|------|--------|------|
| ☐Boston | 22.00 | 40.00 | ☐Chicago | 22.00 | 40.00 |
| ☐New York | 22.00 | 40.00 | ☐St. Louis | 22.00 | 40.00 |
| ☐Philadelphia | 22.00 | 40.00 | ☐Minneapolis | 22.00 | 40.00 |
| ☐Cleveland | 22.00 | 40.00 | ☐Kansas City | 22.00 | 40.00 |

| BANK | A.B.P. | UNC. | BANK | A.B.P. | UNC. |
|------|--------|------|------|--------|------|
| ☐ Richmond | 22.00 | 40.00 | ☐ Dallas | 22.00 | 40.00 |
| ☐ Atlanta | 22.00 | 40.00 | ☐ San Francisco | 22.00 | 40.00 |

## SERIES OF 1950A—
## SIGNATURES OF PRIEST-HUMPHREY, GREEN SEAL

Issued for all Federal Reserve Banks                                    35.00

## SERIES OF 1950B—
## SIGNATURES OF PRIEST-ANDERSON, GREEN SEAL

Issued for all Federal Reserve Banks                                    35.00

## SERIES OF 1950C—SIGNATURES OF SMITH-DILLON, GREEN SEAL

Issued for all Federal Reserve Banks                                    34.00

## SERIES OF 1950D—
## SIGNATURES OF GRANAHAN-DILLON, GREEN SEAL

Issued for all Federal Reserve Banks                                    35.00

## SERIES OF 1950E—
## SIGNATURES OF GRANAHAN-FOWLER, GREEN SEAL

Issued only for New York, Chicago and San Francisco        35.00

## TWENTY DOLLAR NOTES (1963)
### FEDERAL RESERVE NOTES

(Small Size)                                             **NOTE NO. 102A**

## SERIES OF 1963—
## SIGNATURES OF GRANAHAN-DILLON, GREEN SEAL

Issued for all banks except Minneapolis                          34.00

## SERIES OF 1963A—
## SIGNATURES OF GRANAHAN-FOWLER, GREEN SEAL

Issued for all Federal Reserve Banks                             35.00

## SERIES OF 1969—
## SIGNATURES OF ELSTON-KENNEDY, GREEN SEAL

Issued for all Federal Reserve Banks                             35.00

## SERIES OF 1969A—
## SIGNATURES OF KABIS-CONNALLY, GREEN SEAL

Issued for all Federal Reserve Banks                             34.00

## SERIES OF 1969B—SIGNATURES OF BANUELOS-CONNALLY

Issued for all Federal Reserve Banks                             32.00

## SERIES OF 1969C—
## SIGNATURES OF BANUELOS-SHULTZ, GREEN SEAL

Issued for all Federal Reserve Banks                             32.00

## SERIES OF 1974—SIGNATURES OF NEFF-SIMON, GREEN SEAL

Issued for all Federal Reserve Banks                             33.00

## SERIES OF 1977—
## SIGNATURES OF MORTON-BLUMENTHAL, GREEN SEAL

Issued for all Federal Reserve Banks                             28.00

### SERIES OF 1977A—
### SIGNATURES OF MORTON-MILLER, GREEN SEAL
Issued for all Federal Reserve Banks     29.00
### SERIES OF 1981—
### SIGNATURES OF BUCHANAN-REGAN, GREEN SEAL
Issued for all Federal Reserve Banks     27.00
### SERIES OF 1981A—
### SIGNATURES OF ORTEGA-REGAN, GREEN SEAL
Issued for all Federal Reserve Banks     25.00
### SERIES OF 1985—
### SIGNATURES OF ORTEGA-BAKER, GREEN SEAL
Issued for all Federal Reserve Banks     24.00

### TWENTY DOLLAR NOTES (1915-1918)
### FEDERAL RESERVE BANK NOTES
### (ALL HAVE BLUE SEALS)
(Large Size)     **NOTE NO. 103**

**Face Design:**
Portrait of President Cleveland left, name of bank and city center, blue Seal right.

**Back Design:**
Locomotive and steamship, similar to Note No. 98.

| BANK & CITY | SERIES | GOV'T SIGNATURES | BANK SIGNATURES | A.B.P. | GOOD | V.FINE | UNC. |
|---|---|---|---|---|---|---|---|
| ☐Atlanta | 1915 | Teehee-Burke | Bell-Wellborn | 55.00 | 100.00 | 500.00 | 2000.00 |
| ☐Atlanta | 1918 | Elliott-Burke | Bell-Wellborn | 55.00 | 100.00 | 500.00 | 2000.00 |
| ☐Chicago | 1915 | Teehee-Burke | McLallen-McDougal | 55.00 | 100.00 | 500.00 | 2000.00 |
| ☐St. Louis | 1918 | Teehee-Burke | Attebery-Wells | 55.00 | 200.00 | 750.00 | 3600.00 |
| ☐Kan. City | 1915 | Teehee-Burke | Anderson-Miller | 55.00 | 100.00 | 600.00 | 2000.00 |

| BANK & CITY | SERIES | GOV'T SIGNATURES | BANK SIGNATURES | A.B.P. | GOOD | V.FINE | UNC. |
|---|---|---|---|---|---|---|---|
| ☐Kan. City | 1915 | Teehee-Burke | Cross-Miller | 55.00 | 100.00 | 600.00 | 2000.00 |
| ☐Dallas | 1915 | Teehee-Burke | Hoopes-Van Zandt | 55.00 | 100.00 | 600.00 | 2000.00 |
| ☐Dallas | 1915 | Teehee-Burke | Gilbert-Van Zandt | 55.00 | 115.00 | 600.00 | 2000.00 |
| ☐Dallas | 1915 | Teehee-Burke | Talley-Van Zandt | 55.00 | 115.00 | 600.00 | 2000.00 |

## TWENTY DOLLAR NOTES (1929)
## FEDERAL RESERVE BANK NOTES

(Small Size)                                      **NOTE NO. 103A**

**Face Design:**
Portrait of
President
Jackson center,
name of bank
and city left,
blue seal right.

**Back Design:** The White House.

| BANK | A.B.P. | V.FINE | UNC. | BANK | A.B.P. | V.FINE | UNC. |
|---|---|---|---|---|---|---|---|
| ☐Boston | 22.00 | 30.00 | 85.00 | ☐Chicago | 22.00 | 30.00 | 70.00 |
| ☐New York | 22.00 | 30.00 | 70.00 | ☐St. Louis | 22.00 | 30.00 | 70.00 |
| ☐Philadelphia | 22.00 | 30.00 | 70.00 | ☐Minneapolis | 22.00 | 30.00 | 70.00 |
| ☐Cleveland | 22.00 | 30.00 | 70.00 | ☐Kansas City | 22.00 | 30.00 | 70.00 |
| ☐Richmond | 22.00 | 30.00 | 75.00 | ☐Dallas | 22.00 | 30.00 | 375.00 |
| ☐Atlanta | 22.00 | 30.00 | 82.00 | ☐San Francisco | 22.00 | 40.00 | 190.00 |

# FIFTY DOLLAR NOTES

## FIFTY DOLLAR NOTES (1862-1863)
### UNITED STATES NOTES
### (ALSO KNOWN AS LEGAL TENDER NOTES)
(Large Size)                                    **NOTE NO. 104**

**Face Design:** Portrait of Hamilton to left.

## Back Design

| SERIES | SIGNATURES | SEAL | A.B.P. | GOOD | V.FINE | UNC. |
|--------|------------|------|--------|------|--------|------|
| ☐1862 | Chittenden-Spinner* | Red | 1300.00 | 2800.00 | 9000.00 | 18,000.00 |
| ☐1862 | Chittenden-Spinner** | Red | 1300.00 | 2800.00 | 8500.00 | 18,000.00 |
| ☐1863 | Chittenden-Spinner** | Red | 1300.00 | 2800.00 | 8500.00 | 18,000.00 |

*First Obligation: Similar to Note No. 33.
**Second Obligation: Shown above.

**FIFTY DOLLAR NOTES** (1869) UNITED STATES NOTES
(ALSO KNOWN AS LEGAL TENDER NOTES)
(Large Size)                                    **NOTE NO. 105**

**Face Design:** Portrait of Henry Clay to right.

**Back Design**

| SERIES | SIGNATURES | SEAL | A.B.P. | GOOD | V.FINE | UNC. |
|--------|-----------|------|--------|------|--------|------|
| ☐1869 | Allison-Spinner | Red | 2000.00 | 2800.00 | 8000.00 | 22,000.00 |

Note: Only 24 pieces of this note remain unredeemed.

## FIFTY DOLLAR NOTES (1874-1880)
### UNITED STATES NOTES

(Large Size) **NOTE NO. 106**

**Face Design:** Franklin to left.

**Back Design**

| SERIES | SIGNATURES | SEAL | A.B.P. | GOOD | V.FINE | UNC. |
|--------|-----------|------|--------|------|--------|------|
| ☐1874 Allison-Spinner | | Sm. Red | 300.00 | 700.00 | 4400.00 | 12,000.00 |
| ☐1875 Allison-Wyman | | Sm. Red | 300.00 | 650.00 | 4000.00 | 8500.00 |
| ☐1878 Allison-Gilfillan | | Sm. Red | 300.00 | 650.00 | 4000.00 | 8500.00 |
| ☐1880 Bruce-Gilfillan | | Lg. Brown | 140.00 | 500.00 | 2200.00 | 6800.00 |
| ☐1880 Bruce-Wyman | | Lg. Brown | 140.00 | 500.00 | 2200.00 | 6800.00 |
| ☐1880 Rosecrans-Jordan | | Lg. Red | 140.00 | 500.00 | 2000.00 | 5200.00 |
| ☐1880 Rosecrans-Hyatt | | Lg. Red | 140.00 | 500.00 | 2000.00 | 5200.00 |
| ☐1880 Rosecrans-Hyatt | | Lg. Red | 140.00 | 500.00 | 2000.00 | 5200.00 |
| ☐1880 Rosecrans-Huston | | Lg. Red | 140.00 | 500.00 | 2000.00 | 5200.00 |
| ☐1880 Rosecrans-Huston | | Lg. Brown | 140.00 | 500.00 | 2000.00 | 5200.00 |
| ☐1880 Tillman-Morgan | | Sm. Red | 140.00 | 500.00 | 2000.00 | 4600.00 |
| ☐1880 Bruce-Roberts | | Sm. Red | 140.00 | 500.00 | 2000.00 | 4600.00 |
| ☐1880 Lyons-Roberts | | Sm. Red | 140.00 | 500.00 | 2000.00 | 4600.00 |

**FIFTY DOLLAR NOTES** (1875) NATIONAL BANK NOTES
FIRST CHARTER PERIOD (Large Size)          **NOTE NO. 107**

**Face Design:** Washington crossing Delaware left,
Washington at Valley Forge, right.

**Back Design:** Embarkation of the Pilgrims.

| SERIES | SIGNATURES | SEAL | A.B.P. | V.FINE | UNC. |
|---|---|---|---|---|---|
| ☐Original | Chittenden-Spinner | Red/rays | 1600.00 | 3200.00 | 12,000.00 |
| ☐Original | Colby-Spinner | Red/rays | 1600.00 | 3200.00 | 12,000.00 |
| ☐Original | Allison-Spinner | Red/rays | 1600.00 | 3200.00 | 12,000.00 |
| ☐1875 | Allison-New | Red/Scals | 1500.00 | 3000.00 | 10,000.00 |
| ☐1875 | Allison-Wyman | Red/Scals | 1500.00 | 3000.00 | 10,000.00 |
| ☐1875 | Allison-Gilfillan | Red/Scals | 1500.00 | 3000.00 | 10,000.00 |
| ☐1875 | Scofield-Gilfillan | Red/Scals | 1500.00 | 3000.00 | 10,000.00 |
| ☐1875 | Bruce-Gilfillan | Red/Scals | 1500.00 | 3000.00 | 10,000.00 |
| ☐1875 | Bruce-Wyman | Red/Scals | 1500.00 | 3000.00 | 10,000.00 |
| ☐1875 | Rosecrans-Huston | Red/Scals | 1500.00 | 3000.00 | 10,000.00 |
| ☐1875 | Rosecrans-Nebeker | Red/Scals | 1500.00 | 3000.00 | 10,000.00 |
| ☐1875 | Tillman-Morgan | Red/Scals | 1500.00 | 3000.00 | 10,000.00 |

## FIFTY DOLLAR NOTES (1882) NATIONAL BANK NOTES
SECOND CHARTER PERIOD (Large Size)          **NOTE NO. 108**

**First Issue**—Brown seal and brown back.
**Back Design** of Note No. 108
**Face Design:** Similar to Note No. 107.

| SERIES | SIGNATURES | SEAL | A.B.P. | GOOD | V.FINE | UNC. |
|--------|-----------|------|--------|------|--------|------|
| ☐1882 | Bruce-Gilfillan | Brown | 125.00 | 280.00 | 550.00 | 3400.00 |
| ☐1882 | Bruce-Wyman | Brown | 125.00 | 280.00 | 550.00 | 3400.00 |
| ☐1882 | Bruce-Jordan | Brown | 125.00 | 280.00 | 550.00 | 3400.00 |
| ☐1882 | Rosecrans-Jordan | Brown | 125.00 | 280.00 | 550.00 | 3400.00 |
| ☐1882 | Rosecrans-Hyatt | Brown | 125.00 | 280.00 | 550.00 | 3400.00 |
| ☐1882 | Rosecrans-Huston | Brown | 125.00 | 280.00 | 550.00 | 3400.00 |
| ☐1882 | Rosecrans-Nebeker | Brown | 125.00 | 280.00 | 550.00 | 3400.00 |
| ☐1882 | Rosecrans-Morgan | Brown | 300.00 | 500.00 | 1300.00 | 3900.00 |
| ☐1882 | Tillman-Morgan | Brown | 125.00 | 280.00 | 550.00 | 3400.00 |
| ☐1882 | Tillman-Roberts | Brown | 125.00 | 280.00 | 550.00 | 3400.00 |
| ☐1882 | Bruce-Roberts | Brown | 125.00 | 280.00 | 550.00 | 3400.00 |
| ☐1882 | Lyons-Roberts | Brown | 125.00 | 280.00 | 550.00 | 3400.00 |
| ☐1882 | Vernon-Treat | Brown | 300.00 | 600.00 | 1300.00 | 3600.00 |

**FIFTY DOLLAR NOTES** (1882) NATIONAL BANK NOTES
SECOND CHARTER PERIOD (Large Size)  **NOTE NO. 108A**

**Second Issue**—Blue seal, green back with date 1902-1908.
**Face Design:** Washington crossing Delaware left,
Washington at Valley Forge, right.

**Back Design**

| SERIES | SIGNATURES | SEAL | A.B.P. | GOOD | V.FINE | UNC. |
|--------|-----------|------|--------|------|--------|------|
| ☐1882 | Rosecrans-Huston | Blue | 120.00 | 250.00 | 700.00 | 2800.00 |
| ☐1882 | Rosecrans-Nebeker | Blue | 120.00 | 250.00 | 700.00 | 2800.00 |
| ☐1882 | Tillman-Morgan | Blue | 120.00 | 250.00 | 700.00 | 2800.00 |
| ☐1882 | Tillman-Roberts | Blue | 120.00 | 250.00 | 700.00 | 2800.00 |
| ☐1882 | Bruce-Roberts | Blue | 120.00 | 250.00 | 700.00 | 2800.00 |
| ☐1882 | Lyons-Roberts | Blue | 120.00 | 250.00 | 700.00 | 2800.00 |
| ☐1882 | Vernon-Treat | Blue | 120.00 | 250.00 | 700.00 | 2800.00 |
| ☐1882 | Napier-McClung | Blue | 120.00 | 250.00 | 700.00 | 2800.00 |

## FIFTY DOLLAR NOTES (1902) NATIONAL BANK NOTES
THIRD CHARTER PERIOD (Large Size)          **NOTE NO. 109**

**First Issues**—Red seal and numbers.
**Face Design:** Portrait of Sherman left. Name of bank center. Treasury Seal and numbers.

| SERIES | SIGNATURES | SEAL | A.B.P. | GOOD | V.FINE | UNC. |
|---|---|---|---|---|---|---|
| ☐1902 | Lyons-Roberts | Red | 210.00 | 325.00 | 1900.00 | 7200.00 |
| ☐1902 | Lyons-Treat | Red | 210.00 | 325.00 | 1900.00 | 7200.00 |
| ☐1902 | Vernon-Treat | Red | 210.00 | 325.00 | 1900.00 | 7200.00 |

**Second Issue**—Treasury Seal
Numbers remain blue, date 1902-1908 added on back.

| | | | | | | |
|---|---|---|---|---|---|---|
| ☐1902 | Lyons-Roberts | Blue | 60.00 | 65.00 | 140.00 | 1250.00 |
| ☐1902 | Lyons-Treat | Blue | 60.00 | 65.00 | 140.00 | 1250.00 |
| ☐1902 | Vernon-Treat | Blue | 60.00 | 65.00 | 140.00 | 1250.00 |
| ☐1902 | Vernon-McClung | Blue | 60.00 | 65.00 | 140.00 | 1250.00 |
| ☐1902 | Napier-McClung | Blue | 60.00 | 65.00 | 140.00 | 1250.00 |
| ☐1902 | Napier-Thompson | Blue | 60.00 | 65.00 | 140.00 | 1250.00 |
| ☐1902 | Napier-Burke | Blue | 60.00 | 65.00 | 140.00 | 1250.00 |
| ☐1902 | Parker-Burke | Blue | 60.00 | 65.00 | 140.00 | 1250.00 |
| ☐1902 | Teehee-Burke | Blue | 60.00 | 65.00 | 140.00 | 1250.00 |

**Third Issue**—Treasury Seal
Numbers remain blue, date of 1902-1908 removed from back.

| | | | | | | |
|---|---|---|---|---|---|---|
| ☐1902 | Lyons-Roberts | Blue | 60.00 | 75.00 | 250.00 | 1200.00 |
| ☐1902 | Lyons-Treat | Blue | 60.00 | 75.00 | 250.00 | 1200.00 |
| ☐1902 | Vernon-Treat | Blue | 60.00 | 75.00 | 250.00 | 1200.00 |
| ☐1902 | Vernon-McClung | Blue | 60.00 | 75.00 | 250.00 | 1200.00 |
| ☐1902 | Napier-McClung | Blue | 60.00 | 75.00 | 250.00 | 1200.00 |
| ☐1902 | Napier-Thompson | Blue | 60.00 | 75.00 | 250.00 | 1200.00 |
| ☐1902 | Napier-Burke | Blue | 60.00 | 75.00 | 250.00 | 1200.00 |
| ☐1902 | Parker-Burke | Blue | 60.00 | 75.00 | 250.00 | 1200.00 |
| ☐1902 | Teehee-Burke | Blue | 60.00 | 75.00 | 250.00 | 1200.00 |
| ☐1902 | Elliott-Burke | Blue | 60.00 | 75.00 | 250.00 | 1200.00 |
| ☐1902 | Elliott-White | Blue | 60.00 | 75.00 | 250.00 | 1200.00 |

| SERIES | SIGNATURES | SEAL | A.B.P. | GOOD | V.FINE | UNC. |
|---|---|---|---|---|---|---|
| ☐1902 | Speelman-White | Blue | 60.00 | 75.00 | 250.00 | 1200.00 |
| ☐1902 | Woods-White | Blue | 60.00 | 75.00 | 250.00 | 1200.00 |

## FIFTY DOLLAR NOTES (1929) NATIONAL BANK NOTES
(Small Size)                                        **NOTE NO. 110**

**Face Design:** Portrait of President Grant center. Bank left, brown seal right. Brown serial numbers, black charter numbers.

**Back Design:** The Capitol.

| SERIES | SIGNATURES | SEAL | A.B.P. | V.FINE | UNC. |
|---|---|---|---|---|---|
| ☐1929 TYPE I* | Jones-Wood | Brown | 60.00 | 100.00 | 240.00 |
| ☐1929 TYPE II* | Jones-Wood | Brown | 62.00 | 175.00 | 700.00 |

*See Page 78. TYPE I—Charter number in black. TYPE II—Similar. Charter number added in brown.

## FIFTY DOLLAR NOTES (1878-1880)
### SILVER CERTIFICATES

(Large Size)                                    **NOTE NO. 111**

**Face Design:** Portrait of Edward Everett.

**Back Design**

| SERIES | SIGNATURES | SEAL | A.B.P. | GOOD | V.FINE |
|--------|-----------|------|--------|------|--------|
| ☐1878 | Varied | Red | | | VERY RARE |
| ☐1880 | Scofield-Gilfillan | Brown | 1000.00 | 3000.00 | 9300.00 |
| ☐1880 | Bruce-Gilfillan | Brown | 1000.00 | 3000.00 | 9300.00 |
| ☐1880 | Bruce-Wyman | Brown | 1000.00 | 3000.00 | 9300.00 |
| ☐1880 | Rosecrans-Huston | Brown | 1000.00 | 3000.00 | 9300.00 |
| ☐1880 | Rosecrans-Nebeker | Red | 1000.00 | 3000.00 | 9300.00 |

## FIFTY DOLLAR NOTES (1891) SILVER CERTIFICATES
(Large Size) **NOTE NO. 111A**

**Face Design:** Portrait of Edward Everett

**Back Design**

| SERIES | SIGNATURES | SEAL | A.B.P. | GOOD | V.FINE | UNC. |
|--------|------------|------|--------|------|--------|------|
| ☐1891 | Rosecrans-Nebeker | Red | 220.00 | 450.00 | 1800.00 | 6500.00 |
| ☐1891 | Tillman-Morgan | Red | 220.00 | 450.00 | 1800.00 | 6500.00 |
| ☐1891 | Bruce-Roberts | Red | 220.00 | 450.00 | 1800.00 | 6500.00 |
| ☐1891 | Lyons-Roberts | Red | 220.00 | 450.00 | 1800.00 | 6500.00 |
| ☐1891 | Vernon-Treat | Red | 220.00 | 450.00 | 1800.00 | 6500.00 |
| ☐1891 | Parker-Burke | Blue | 220.00 | 450.00 | 1800.00 | 6500.00 |

**FIFTY DOLLAR NOTES** (1882) GOLD CERTIFICATES
(Large Size)                                    **NOTE NO. 112**

**Face Design:** Portrait of Silas Wright to left.

**Back Design:** Bright yellow color.

| SERIES | SIGNATURES | SEAL | A.B.P. | GOOD | V.FINE | UNC. |
|--------|-----------|------|--------|------|--------|------|
| ☐1882 | Bruce-Gilfillan | Brown | 230.00 | 800.00 | 3600.00 | 14,000.00 |
| ☐1882 | Bruce-Wyman | Brown | 230.00 | 800.00 | 3600.00 | 14,000.00 |
| ☐1882 | Rosecrans-Hyatt | Red | 230.00 | 800.00 | 3600.00 | 14,000.00 |
| ☐1882 | Rosecrans-Huston | Brown | 230.00 | 800.00 | 3600.00 | 14,000.00 |
| ☐1882 | Lyons-Roberts | Red | 230.00 | 400.00 | 800.00 | 5500.00 |
| ☐1882 | Lyons-Treat | Red | 230.00 | 400.00 | 800.00 | 5500.00 |
| ☐1882 | Vernon-Treat | Red | 230.00 | 400.00 | 800.00 | 5500.00 |
| ☐1882 | Vernon-McClung | Red | 230.00 | 400.00 | 800.00 | 5500.00 |
| ☐1882 | Napier-McClung | Red | 230.00 | 400.00 | 800.00 | 5500.00 |

**FIFTY DOLLAR NOTES** (1913) GOLD CERTIFICATES
(Large Size)                                    **NOTE NO. 113**

**Face Design:** Portrait of President Grant.

**Back Design:** Bright yellow color.

| SERIES | SIGNATURES | SEAL | A.B.P. | GOOD | V.FINE | UNC. |
|--------|------------|------|--------|------|--------|------|
| ☐1913 | Parker-Burke | Gold | 90.00 | 210.00 | 600.00 | 3200.00 |
| ☐1913 | Teehee-Burke | Gold | 90.00 | 210.00 | 600.00 | 4100.00 |
| ☐1922 | Speelman-White | Gold | 68.00 | 170.00 | 325.00 | 1300.00 |

**FIFTY DOLLAR NOTES** (1928) GOLD CERTIFICATES
(Small Size) **NOTE NO. 114**

**Back Design:** Same as Note No. 110.

| SERIES | SIGNATURES | SEAL | A.B.P. | GOOD | V.FINE | UNC. |
|--------|-----------|------|--------|------|--------|------|
| ☐1928 | Woods-Mellon | Gold | 65.00 | 75.00 | 95.00 | 600.00 |

**FIFTY DOLLAR NOTES** (1891) TREASURY NOTES
(Large Size) **NOTE NO. 114A**
**Face Design:** Portrait of William H. Seward. Only 25 pieces remain unredeemed.

**Back Design:** Green.

| SERIES | SIGNATURES | SEAL | A.B.P. | GOOD | V.FINE | UNC. |
|--------|-----------|------|--------|------|--------|------|
| ☐1891 | Rosecrans-Nebeker | Red | 3000.00 | 6000.00 | 16,000.00 | RARE |

## FIFTY DOLLAR NOTES (1914)
### FEDERAL RESERVE NOTES

(Large Size)                                          **NOTE NO. 115**

### SERIES OF 1914—
### SIGNATURES OF BURKE-McADOO, RED SEAL AND
### RED SERIAL NUMBERS*

| CITY | A.B.P. | GOOD | V.FINE | UNC. | CITY | A.B.P. | GOOD | V.FINE | UNC. |
|------|--------|------|--------|------|------|--------|------|--------|------|
| ☐ Boston | 67.00 | 150.00 | 600.00 | 1600.00 | ☐ Chicago | 65.00 | 150.00 | 600.00 | 1600.00 |
| ☐ NYC | 67.00 | 150.00 | 600.00 | 1600.00 | ☐ St. Louis | 65.00 | 150.00 | 600.00 | 1600.00 |
| ☐ Phila | 67.00 | 150.00 | 600.00 | 1600.00 | ☐ Minneap | 65.00 | 150.00 | 600.00 | 1600.00 |
| ☐ Cleveland | 67.00 | 150.00 | 600.00 | 1600.00 | ☐ Kansas C | 65.00 | 150.00 | 600.00 | 1600.00 |
| ☐ Richmd | 67.00 | 150.00 | 600.00 | 1600.00 | ☐ Dallas | 65.00 | 150.00 | 600.00 | 1600.00 |
| ☐ Atlanta | 67.00 | 150.00 | 600.00 | 1600.00 | ☐ San Fran. | 65.00 | 150.00 | 600.00 | 1600.00 |

### SERIES OF 1914—DESIGN CONTINUES AS PREVIOUS NOTE.
### THE SEAL AND SERIAL NUMBERS ARE NOW BLUE.
**(This note was issued with various signatures for each bank.)**

| BANK | A.B.P. | GOOD | V.FINE | UNC. | BANK | A.B.P. | GOOD | V.FINE | UNC. |
|------|--------|------|--------|------|------|--------|------|--------|------|
| ☐ Boston | 55.00 | 70.00 | 140.00 | 600.00 | ☐ Chicago | 55.00 | 70.00 | 140.00 | 600.00 |
| ☐ NYC | 55.00 | 70.00 | 140.00 | 600.00 | ☐ St. Louis | 55.00 | 70.00 | 140.00 | 600.00 |
| ☐ Phila | 55.00 | 70.00 | 140.00 | 600.00 | ☐ Minneap | 55.00 | 70.00 | 140.00 | 600.00 |
| ☐ Cleveland | 55.00 | 70.00 | 140.00 | 600.00 | ☐ Kansas C | 55.00 | 70.00 | 140.00 | 600.00 |
| ☐ Richmd | 55.00 | 70.00 | 140.00 | 600.00 | ☐ Dallas | 55.00 | 70.00 | 140.00 | 600.00 |
| ☐ Atlanta | 55.00 | 70.00 | 140.00 | 600.00 | ☐ San Fran | 55.00 | 70.00 | 140.00 | 600.00 |

*Signatures: Burke-McAdoo, Burke-Glass, Burke-Huston, White-Mellon.

## FIFTY DOLLAR NOTES (1928)
### FEDERAL RESERVE NOTES

(Small Size)                                          **NOTE NO. 116**

**Face Design:** Portrait of President Grant center. Black Federal Reserve Seal with number to left. Green Treasury Seal to right.
**Back Design:** Same as Note No. 110.

### SERIES OF 1928—
### SIGNATURES OF WOODS-MELLON, GREEN SEAL

|                                   | A.B.P. | UNC.   |
| --------------------------------- | ------ | ------ |
| Issued for all Federal Reserve Banks | 75.00  | 125.00 |

(Small Size)                                          **NOTE NO. 116A**
### SERIES OF 1928A—
### SIGNATURES OF WOODS-MELLON, GREEN SEAL
### LETTER REPLACES NUMERAL IN FEDERAL RESERVE, SEAL

| Issued for all Federal Reserve Banks | 75.00 | 115.00 |
| --- | --- | --- |

(Small Size)                                          **NOTE NO. 116B**
### SERIES OF 1934—
### SIGNATURES OF JULIAN-MORGENTHAU, GREEN SEAL

| Issued for all Federal Reserve Banks | 68.00 | 95.00 |
| --- | --- | --- |

### SERIES OF 1934A—
### SIGNATURES OF JULIAN-MORGENTHAU, GREEN SEAL

| Issued for all Federal Reserve Banks except Philadelphia | 67.00 | 90.00 |
| --- | --- | --- |

### SERIES OF 1934B—
### SIGNATURES OF JULIAN-VINSON, GREEN SEAL

| Issued for all Federal Reserve Banks except Boston and New York | 67.00 | 100.00 |
| --- | --- | --- |

### SERIES OF 1934C—
### SIGNATURES OF JULIAN-SNYDER, GREEN SEAL

| Issued for all Federal Reserve Banks except San Francisco | 67.00 | 90.00 |
| --- | --- | --- |

## SERIES OF 1934D—
## SIGNATURES OF CLARK-SNYDER, GREEN SEAL

Issued for Cleveland, St. Louis, Minneapolis, Kansas City,
San Francisco                                          67.00       85.00

## FIFTY DOLLAR NOTES (1950)
### FEDERAL RESERVE NOTES
(Small Size)                                            **NOTE NO. 116C**
## SERIES OF 1950—
## SIGNATURES OF CLARK-SNYDER, FEDERAL
## RESERVE AND TREASURY SEALS ARE NOW SMALLER

|                                                        | UNC. |
|---|---|
| Issued for all Federal Reserve Banks | 75.00 |

### SERIES OF 1950A—SIGNATURES OF PRIEST-HUMPHREY
Issued for all Federal Reserve Banks except Minneapolis    74.00
### SERIES OF 1950B—SIGNATURES OF PRIEST-ANDERSON
Issued for all Federal Reserve Banks except Atlanta and Minneapolis   70.00
### SERIES OF 1950C—SIGNATURES OF SMITH-DILLON
Issued for all Federal Reserve Banks except Atlanta       73.00
### SERIES OF 1950D—SIGNATURES OF GRANAHAN-DILLON
Issued for all Federal Reserve Banks                      70.00
### SERIES OF 1950E—SIGNATURES OF GRANAHAN-FOWLER
Issued only for New York, Chicago, San Francisco          82.00

## FIFTY DOLLAR NOTES (1963)
### FEDERAL RESERVE NOTES
("IN GOD WE TRUST" ADDED ON BACK)
(Small Size)                                            **NOTE NO. 116D**
## SERIES OF 1963, NO NOTES WERE PRINTED; SERIES OF
## 1963A—SIGNATURES OF GRANAHAN-FOWLER
Issued for all Federal Reserve Banks                      65.00

## FIFTY DOLLAR NOTES (1969)
### FEDERAL RESERVE NOTES
(WORDING IN GREEN SEAL CHANGED
FROM LATIN TO ENGLISH)

**NOTE NO. 116E**
### SERIES OF 1969—SIGNATURES OF ELSTON-KENNEDY
Issued for all Federal Reserve Banks                      62.00
### SERIES OF 1969A—SIGNATURES OF KABIS-CONNALLY
Issued for all Federal Reserve Banks                      62.00
### SERIES OF 1969B—SIGNATURES OF BANUELOS-CONNALLY
Issued for Boston, New York, Philadelphia, Richmond, Atlanta,
Chicago, Dallas                                           60.00

### SERIES OF 1969C—SIGNATURES OF BANUELOS-SHULTZ

Issued for all Federal Reserve Banks 60.00

### SERIES OF 1974—SIGNATURES OF NEFF-SIMON

Issued for all Federal Reserve Banks 60.00

### SERIES OF 1977—SIGNATURES OF MORTON-BLUMENTHAL

Issued for all Federal Reserve Banks 60.00

### SERIES OF 1977A—SIGNATURES OF MORTON-MILLER

Issued for all Federal Reserve Banks 60.00

### SERIES OF 1981—BUCHANAN-REGAN, GREEN SEAL

Issued for all Federal Reserve Banks 61.00

### SERIES OF 1981A— SIGNATURES OF ORTEGA-REGAN, GREEN SEAL

Issued for all Federal Reserve Banks 61.00

### SERIES OF 1985— SIGNATURES OF ORTEGA-BAKER, GREEN SEAL

Issued for all Federal Reserve Banks 60.00

### SERIES OF 1988— SIGNATURES OF ORTEGA-BAKER, GREEN SEAL

Issued for all Federal Reserve Banks 60.00

## FIFTY DOLLAR NOTES (1918)
### FEDERAL RESERVE BANK NOTES

(Large Size) **NOTE NO. 117**

**Face Design:** Portrait of President Grant to left, Federal Reserve Bank in center, blue seal right.

**Back Design:** Female figure of Panama between merchant ship and battleship. Plates were made for all 12 Federal Reserve Districts. Only St. Louis bank issued. Less than 30 notes are known today.

| CITY | SERIES | GOV'T SIGNATURES | BANK SIGNATURES | A.B.P. | FINE | UNC. |
|------|--------|------------------|-----------------|--------|------|------|
| ☐ St. Louis | 1918 | Teehee-Burke | Attebery-Wells | 2400.00 | 4000.00 | 11,000.00 |

## FIFTY DOLLAR NOTES (1929)
### FEDERAL RESERVE BANK

(Small Size)                                          **NOTE NO. 117A**

**Face Design:**
Portrait of
Grant center,
name of bank
left, brown
serial numbers,
black letter for
Federal Reserve
District.

**Back Design:**
Same as Note
No. 110.

| BANK | SERIES | SIGNATURES | SEAL | A.B.P. | V.FINE | UNC. |
|------|--------|-----------|------|--------|--------|------|
| ☐New York | 1929 | Jones-Woods | Brown | 55.00 | 100.00 | 140.00 |
| ☐Cleveland | 1929 | Jones-Woods | Brown | 55.00 | 100.00 | 140.00 |
| ☐Chicago | 1929 | Jones-Woods | Brown | 55.00 | 100.00 | 140.00 |
| ☐Minneapolis | 1929 | Jones-Woods | Brown | 55.00 | 100.00 | 185.00 |
| ☐Kansas City | 1929 | Jones-Woods | Brown | 55.00 | 100.00 | 160.00 |
| ☐Dallas | 1929 | Jones-Woods | Brown | 55.00 | 100.00 | 300 00 |
| ☐San Francisco | 1929 | Jones-Woods | Brown | 55.00 | 115.00 | 250.00 |

# ONE HUNDRED DOLLAR NOTES

## ONE HUNDRED DOLLAR NOTES (1862-1863)
### U.S. NOTES
### (ALSO KNOWN AS LEGAL TENDER NOTES)

(Large Size)                                    **NOTE NO. 118**

**Face Design:** Eagle with spread wings left, three discs with "100," red seal numbers.

**Back Design:** Green, two variations of the wording in obligation.

| SERIES | SIGNATURES | SEAL | A.B.P. | GOOD | V.FINE | UNC. |
|--------|-----------|------|--------|------|--------|------|
| □1862 | Chittenden-Spinner* | Red | 1000.00 | 2000.00 | 7500.00 | 21,000.00 |
| □1862 | Chittenden-Spinner** | Red | 1000.00 | 2000.00 | 7500.00 | 21,000.00 |
| □1863 | Chittenden-Spinner** | Red | 1000.00 | 2000.00 | 8000.00 | 21,000.00 |

*First Obligation: Similar to Note No. 33.
**Second Obligation: Shown above.

## ONE HUNDRED DOLLAR NOTES (1869-1880)
### U.S. NOTES

(Large Size)                                    **NOTE NO. 119**

**Face Design:** Portrait of President Lincoln.

**Back Design:** No. 119.

**Back Design:** No. 119A.

| SERIES | SIGNATURES | SEAL | A.B.P. | GOOD | V.FINE | UNC. |
|--------|-----------|------|--------|------|--------|------|
| ☐1869 | Allison-Spinner | Red | 2000.00 | 4000.00 | 14,000.00 | 48,000.00 |

**THE FOLLOWING NOTES HAVE A MODIFIED BACK DESIGN**

(Small Size)                                    **NOTE NO. 119A**

| SERIES | SIGNATURES | SEAL | A.B.P. | GOOD | V.FINE | UNC. |
|--------|-----------|------|--------|------|--------|------|
| ☐1875 | Allison-New | Sm. Red | 1200.00 | 2800.00 | 10,000.00 | 19,000.00 |
| ☐1875 | Allison-Wyman | Sm. Red | 1200.00 | 2800.00 | 10,000.00 | 19,000.00 |
| ☐1878 | Allison-Gilfillan | Sm. Red | 1200.00 | 2800.00 | 10,000.00 | 19,000.00 |
| ☐1880 | Bruce-Gilfillan | Lg. Brown | 500.00 | 900.00 | 3500.00 | 11,000.00 |
| ☐1880 | Bruce-Wyman | Lg. Brown | 500.00 | 900.00 | 3500.00 | 11,000.00 |
| ☐1880 | Rosecrans-Jordan | Lg. Red | 500.00 | 900.00 | 3500.00 | 11,000.00 |
| ☐1880 | Rosecrans-Hyatt | Lg. Red | 500.00 | 900.00 | 3500.00 | 11,000.00 |
| ☐1880 | Rosecrans-Hyatt | Lg. Red | 500.00 | 900.00 | 3500.00 | 11,000.00 |
| ☐1880 | Rosecrans-Huston | Lg. Red | 500.00 | 900.00 | 3500.00 | 11,000.00 |
| ☐1880 | Rosecrans-Huston | Lg. Brown | 500.00 | 900.00 | 3500.00 | 11,000.00 |
| ☐1880 | Tillman-Morgan | Sm. Red | 500.00 | 900.00 | 3500.00 | 11,000.00 |
| ☐1880 | Bruce-Roberts | Sm. Red | 500.00 | 900.00 | 3500.00 | 11,000.00 |
| ☐1880 | Lyons-Roberts | Sm. Red | 500.00 | 900.00 | 3500.00 | 11,000.00 |

## ONE HUNDRED DOLLAR NOTES (1966) U.S. NOTES
## (ALSO KNOWN AS LEGAL TENDER NOTES)
(Small Size)                                    **NOTE NO. 119B**

**Face Design:** Portrait of Franklin, red seal, red serial numbers.

**Back Design:** Independence Hall.

| SERIES | SIGNATURES | SEAL | V.FINE | UNC. |
|--------|-----------|------|--------|------|
| ☐1966* | Granahan-Fowler | Red | 110.00 | 190.00 |
| ☐1966A | Elston-Kennedy | Red | 150.00 | 650.00 |

*This is the first note to be issued with the new Treasury Seal with wording in English instead of Latin.

**ONE HUNDRED DOLLAR NOTES** (1875)
NATIONAL BANK NOTES
(ALL HAVE RED SEAL)
FIRST CHARTER PERIOD (Large Size)          **NOTE NO. 120**

**Face Design:** Perry leaving the Lawrence, left.

**Face Design:** Border green, center black, Signing of the Declaration of Independence.

| SERIES | SIGNATURES | SEAL | A.B.P. | GOOD | V.FINE |
|---|---|---|---|---|---|
| ☐Original | Chittenden-Spinner | Red | 650.00 | 1600.00 | 3800.00 |
| ☐Original | Colby-Spinner | Red | 650.00 | 1600.00 | 3800.00 |
| ☐Original | Allison-Spinner | Red | 650.00 | 1600.00 | 3800.00 |
| ☐1875 | Allison-New | Red | 650.00 | 1400.00 | 3500.00 |
| ☐1875 | Allison-Wyman | Red | 650.00 | 1400.00 | 3500.00 |
| ☐1875 | Allison-Gilfillan | Red | 650.00 | 1400.00 | 3500.00 |
| ☐1875 | Scofield-Gilfillan | Red | 650.00 | 1400.00 | 3500.00 |
| ☐1875 | Bruce-Gilfillan | Red | 650.00 | 1400.00 | 3500.00 |
| ☐1875 | Bruce-Wyman | Red | 650.00 | 1400.00 | 3500.00 |
| ☐1875 | Rosecrans-Huston | Red | 650.00 | 1400.00 | 3500.00 |
| ☐1875 | Tillman-Morgan | Red | 650.00 | 1400.00 | 3500.00 |

## ONE HUNDRED DOLLAR NOTES (1882)
### NATIONAL BANK NOTES

SECOND CHARTER PERIOD (Large Size)          **NOTE NO. 120A**

**First Issue**—Brown seal and brown backs.
**Face Design:** Similar to Note No. 120.
**Back Design:** Similar to Note No. 39

| SERIES | SIGNATURES | SEAL | A.B.P. | GOOD | V.FINE | UNC. |
|--------|------------|------|--------|------|--------|------|
| ☐1882 | Bruce-Gilfillan | Brown | 140.00 | 500.00 | 1000.00 | 4100.00 |
| ☐1882 | Bruce-Wyman | Brown | 140.00 | 500.00 | 1000.00 | 4100.00 |
| ☐1882 | Bruce-Jordan | Brown | 140.00 | 500.00 | 1000.00 | 4100.00 |
| ☐1882 | Rosecrans-Jordan | Brown | 140.00 | 500.00 | 1000.00 | 4100.00 |
| ☐1882 | Rosecrans-Hyatt | Brown | 140.00 | 500.00 | 1000.00 | 4100.00 |
| ☐1882 | Rosecrans-Huston | Brown | 140.00 | 500.00 | 1000.00 | 4100.00 |
| ☐1882 | Rosecrans-Nebeker | Brown | 140.00 | 500.00 | 1000.00 | 4100.00 |
| ☐1882 | Rosecrans-Morgan | Brown | 140.00 | 500.00 | 1000.00 | 4100.00 |
| ☐1882 | Tillman-Morgan | Brown | 140.00 | 500.00 | 1000.00 | 4100.00 |
| ☐1882 | Tillman-Roberts | Brown | 140.00 | 500.00 | 1000.00 | 4100.00 |
| ☐1882 | Bruce-Roberts | Brown | 140.00 | 500.00 | 1000.00 | 4100.00 |
| ☐1882 | Lyons-Roberts | Brown | 140.00 | 500.00 | 1000.00 | 4100.00 |

SECOND CHARTER PERIOD (Large Size)          **NOTE NO. 121**

**Second Issue**—Blue seal, green back with date 1902-1908.
**Face Design:** Similar to Note No. 120.
**Back Design:** Green with date 1882-1908, center.

| SERIES | SIGNATURES | SEAL | A.B.P. | V.FINE | UNC. |
|--------|------------|------|--------|--------|------|
| ☐1882 | Rosecrans-Huston | Blue | 150.00 | 800.00 | 3400.00 |
| ☐1882 | Rosecrans-Nebeker | Blue | 150.00 | 800.00 | 3400.00 |
| ☐1882 | Tillman-Morgan | Blue | 150.00 | 800.00 | 3400.00 |
| ☐1882 | Tillman-Roberts | Blue | 150.00 | 800.00 | 3400.00 |
| ☐1882 | Bruce-Roberts | Blue | 150.00 | 800.00 | 3400.00 |
| ☐1882 | Lyons-Roberts | Blue | 150.00 | 800.00 | 3400.00 |
| ☐1882 | Vernon-Treat | Blue | 150.00 | 800.00 | 3400.00 |
| ☐1882 | Napier-McClung | Blue | 150.00 | 800.00 | 3400.00 |

This note was also issued with (value) "ONE HUNDRED DOLLARS" on the
back. Very rare.

## ONE HUNDRED DOLLAR NOTES (1902)
### NATIONAL BANK NOTES
THIRD CHARTER PERIOD (Large Size)          **NOTE NO. 122**

**Face Design:** Portrait of John J. Knox, left.

**First Issue**—Red seal.
**Back Design:** Male figures with shield and flags.

| SERIES | SIGNATURES | SEAL | A.B.P. | GOOD | V.FINE | UNC. |
|---|---|---|---|---|---|---|
| ☐ 1902 | Lyons-Roberts | Red | 200.00 | 500.00 | 1600.00 | 7400.00 |
| ☐ 1902 | Lyons-Treat | Red | 200.00 | 500.00 | 1600.00 | 7400.00 |
| ☐ 1902 | Vernon-Treat | Red | 200.00 | 500.00 | 1600.00 | 7400.00 |

**Second Issue**—Design is similar to previous note. Seal and serial numbers are now blue, back of note has date 1902-1908 added.

| | | | | | | |
|---|---|---|---|---|---|---|
| ☐ | | Blue | 125.00 | 150.00 | 400.00 | 1200.00 |

**Third Issue**—Design continues as previous notes. Seal and serial numbers remain blue, date 1902-1908 removed from back.

The notes of the **Second and Third Issue** appeared with various signatures: Lyons-Roberts, Lyons-Treat, Vernon-Treat, Vernon-McClung, Napier-McClung, Parker-Burke, Teehee-Burke, Elliott-Burke, Elliott-White, Speelman-White, Woods-White.

| | | | | | | |
|---|---|---|---|---|---|---|
| ☐ | | Blue | 130.00 | 140.00 | 350.00 | 1100.00 |

## ONE HUNDRED DOLLAR NOTES (1929)
### NATIONAL BANK NOTES
(Small Size)                                              **NOTE NO. 123**

**Face Design:** Portrait of Franklin, center. Name of bank and city, left. Brown seal, right.

| SERIES SIGNATURES | SEAL | A.B.P. | V.FINE | UNC. |
|---|---|---|---|---|
| ☐1929 TYPE I Jones-Woods | Brown | 100.00 | 125.00 | 300.00 |
| ☐1929 TYPE II Jones-Woods | Brown | 120.00 | 200.00 | 700.00 |

## ONE HUNDRED DOLLAR NOTES (1878)
### SILVER CERTIFICATES

| SERIES | SIGNATURES | SEAL | A.B.P. | GOOD | V.FINE | UNC. |
|---|---|---|---|---|---|---|
| ☐1878 | Scofield-Gilfillan-White | Red | | | | UNIQUE |
| ☐1878 | Scofield-Gilfillan-Hopper | Red | | NO SPECIMENS KNOWN | | |
| ☐1878 | Scofield-Gilfillan-Hillhouse | Red | | NO SPECIMENS KNOWN | | |
| ☐1878 | Scofield-Gilfillan-Anthony | Red | | | | UNIQUE |
| ☐1878 | Scofield-Gilfillan-Wyman (printed signature of Wyman) | | | | | |
| | | Red | | NO SPECIMENS KNOWN | | |
| ☐1878 | Scofield-Gilfillan | Red | | | | VERY RARE |
| ☐1880 | Scofield-Gilfillan | Brown | | EXTREMELY RARE | | |
| ☐1880 | Bruce-Gilfillan | Brown | 1100.00 | 3000.00 | 9000.00 | 18,000.00 |
| ☐1880 | Bruce-Wyman | Brown | 1100.00 | 3000.00 | 9000.00 | 18,000.00 |
| ☐1880 | Rosecrans-Huston | Brown | 1100.00 | 3000.00 | 10,000.00 | 19,000.00 |
| ☐1880 | Rosecrans-Nebeker | Brown | 1100.00 | 3000.00 | 10,000.00 | 20,000.00 |

## ONE HUNDRED DOLLAR NOTES (1891)
### SILVER CERTIFICATES

(Large Size) **NOTE NO. 124**

**Face Design:** Portrait of President Monroe.

| SERIES | SIGNATURES | SEAL | A.B.P. | GOOD | V.FINE | UNC. |
|--------|-----------|------|--------|------|--------|------|
| ☐1891 | Rosecrans-Nebeker | Red | 400.00 | 1000.00 | 6000.00 | 15,000.00 |
| ☐1891 | Tillman-Morgan | Red | 400.00 | 1000.00 | 6000.00 | 15,000.00 |

This note was also issued in the Series of 1878 and 1880. They are very rare.

## ONE HUNDRED DOLLAR NOTES (1882-1922)
### GOLD CERTIFICATES

(Large Size) **NOTE NO. 125**

**Face Design:** Portrait of Thomas H. Benton.

| SERIES | SIGNATURES | SEAL | A.B.P. | GOOD | V.FINE | UNC. |
|--------|------------|------|--------|------|--------|------|
| ☐1882 | Bruce-Gilfillan | Lg. Brown | 300.00 | 750.00 | 6000.00 | RARE |
| ☐1882 | Bruce-Wyman | Lg. Brown | 300.00 | 750.00 | 6000.00 | RARE |
| ☐1882 | Rosecrans-Hyatt | Lg. Red | 300.00 | 750.00 | 6000.00 | RARE |
| ☐1882 | Rosecrans-Huston | Lg. Brown | 300.00 | 750.00 | 6000.00 | RARE |
| ☐1882 | Lyons-Roberts | Sm. Red | 130.00 | 300.00 | 500.00 | 6000.00 |
| ☐1882 | Lyons-Treat | Sm. Red | 130.00 | 300.00 | 500.00 | 6000.00 |
| ☐1882 | Vernon-Treat | Sm. Red | 130.00 | 300.00 | 500.00 | 6000.00 |
| ☐1882 | Vernon-McClung | Sm. Red | 130.00 | 300.00 | 500.00 | 6000.00 |
| ☐1882 | Napier-McClung | Sm. Red | 130.00 | 300.00 | 500.00 | 6000.00 |
| ☐1882 | Napier-Thompson | Sm. Red | 130.00 | 300.00 | 500.00 | 6000.00 |
| ☐1882 | Napier-Burke | Sm. Red | 130.00 | 300.00 | 500.00 | 6000.00 |
| ☐1882 | Parker-Burke | Sm. Red | 130.00 | 300.00 | 500.00 | 6000.00 |
| ☐1882 | Teehee-Burke | Sm. Red | 130.00 | 300.00 | 500.00 | 6000.00 |
| ☐1922 | Speelman-White | Sm. Red | 130.00 | 300.00 | 500.00 | 3000.00 |

## ONE HUNDRED DOLLAR NOTES (1928)
### GOLD CERTIFICATES

(Small Size)                                                    **NOTE NO. 126**

**Face Design:** Portrait of Franklin, center. Yellow seal to left.
Yellow numbers.

| SERIES | SIGNATURES | SEAL | A.B.P. | GOOD | V.FINE | UNC. |
|--------|------------|------|--------|------|--------|------|
| ☐1928 | Woods-Mellon | Gold | 115.00 | 110.00 | 160.00 | 700.00 |

## ONE HUNDRED DOLLAR NOTES (1890-1891)
### TREASURY NOTES
(Large Size) **NOTE NO. 127**

**Face Design:** Portrait of Commodore Farragut to right.

**Back Design:** Large "100," called "Watermelon Note."

**Back Design:** "One Hundred" in scalloped medallion.

| SERIES | SIGNATURES | SEAL | A.B.P. | GOOD | V.FINE | UNC. |
|--------|------------|------|--------|------|--------|------|
| ☐1890 | Rosecrans-Huston | Brown | 3000.00 | 7500.00 | 18,000.00 | RARE |
| ☐1890 | Rosecrans-Nebeker | Red | 3000.00 | 10,000.00 | 26,000.00 | RARE |

## ONE HUNDRED DOLLAR NOTES (1914)
### FEDERAL RESERVE NOTES

(Large Size)                                          **NOTE NO. 128**

**Face Design:** Portrait of Franklin in center.
**Back Design:** Group of five allegorical figures.

### SERIES OF 1914—
### SIGNATURES OF BURKE-McADOO, RED SEAL
### AND RED SERIAL NUMBERS

| CITY | A.B.P. | GOOD | V.FINE | UNC. | CITY | A.B.P. | GOOD | V.FINE | UNC. |
|------|--------|------|--------|------|------|--------|------|--------|------|
| ☐ Boston | 120.00 | 200.00 | 750.00 | 2400.00 | ☐ Chicago | 120.00 | 200.00 | 750.00 | 2400.00 |
| ☐ NYC | 120.00 | 200.00 | 750.00 | 2400.00 | ☐ St. Louis | 120.00 | 200.00 | 750.00 | 2400.00 |
| ☐ Phila | 120.00 | 200.00 | 750.00 | 2400.00 | ☐ Minneap | 120.00 | 200.00 | 750.00 | 2400.00 |
| ☐ Cleveld | 120.00 | 200.00 | 750.00 | 2400.00 | ☐ Kansas C | 120.00 | 200.00 | 750.00 | 2400.00 |
| ☐ Richmd | 120.00 | 200.00 | 750.00 | 2400.00 | ☐ Dallas | 120.00 | 200.00 | 750.00 | 2400.00 |
| ☐ Atlanta | 120.00 | 200.00 | 750.00 | 2400.00 | ☐ San Fran | 120.00 | 200.00 | 750.00 | 2400.00 |

### SERIES OF 1914—DESIGN CONTINUES AS PREVIOUS NOTE.
### THE SEAL AND SERIAL NUMBERS ARE NOW BLUE.

*(This note was issued with various signatures for each bank.)

| BANK | A.B.P. | V.FINE | UNC. | BANK | A.B.P. | V.FINE | UNC. |
|------|--------|--------|------|------|--------|--------|------|
| ☐ Boston | 120.00 | 220.00 | 575.00 | ☐ Chicago | 120.00 | 220.00 | 575.00 |
| ☐ New York | 120.00 | 220.00 | 575.00 | ☐ St. Louis | 120.00 | 220.00 | 575.00 |
| ☐ Philadelphia | 120.00 | 220.00 | 575.00 | ☐ Minneapolis | 120.00 | 220.00 | 575.00 |
| ☐ Cleveland | 120.00 | 220.00 | 575.00 | ☐ Kansas City | 120.00 | 220.00 | 575.00 |
| ☐ Richmond | 120.00 | 220.00 | 575.00 | ☐ Dallas | 120.00 | 220.00 | 575.00 |
| ☐ Atlanta | 120.00 | 220.00 | 575.00 | ☐ San Fran | 120.00 | 220.00 | 575.00 |

*Signatures: Burke-McAdoo, Burke-Glass, Burke-Huston, White-Mellon.

## ONE HUNDRED DOLLAR NOTES (1928)
### FEDERAL RESERVE NOTES
(Small Size)                                    **NOTE NO. 129**

**Face Design:** Portrait of Franklin, Black Federal Reserve
Seal left with number, green Treasury Seal right.

### SERIES OF 1928—
### SIGNATURES OF WOODS-MELLON, GREEN SEAL

| CITY | A.B.P. | V.FINE | UNC. | CITY | A.B.P. | V.FINE | UNC. |
|---|---|---|---|---|---|---|---|
| ☐ Boston | 110.00 | 140.00 | 195.00 | ☐ Chicago | 110.00 | 140.00 | 195.00 |
| ☐ New York | 110.00 | 140.00 | 195.00 | ☐ St. Louis | 110.00 | 140.00 | 195.00 |
| ☐ Philadelphia | 110.00 | 140.00 | 195.00 | ☐ Minneapolis | 110.00 | 140.00 | 195.00 |
| ☐ Cleveland | 110.00 | 140.00 | 195.00 | ☐ Kansas City | 110.00 | 140.00 | 195.00 |
| ☐ Richmond | 110.00 | 140.00 | 195.00 | ☐ Dallas | 110.00 | 140.00 | 195.00 |
| ☐ Atlanta | 110.00 | 140.00 | 195.00 | ☐ San Fran | 110.00 | 140.00 | 195.00 |

### SERIES OF 1928A—
### SIGNATURES OF WOODS-MELLON, GREEN SEAL
### NUMBER IN BLACK, FEDERAL RESERVE SEAL
### IS CHANGED TO A LETTER

(Small Size)                                    **NOTE NO. 129A**

| CITY | A.B.P. | V.FINE | UNC. | CITY | A.B.P. | V.FINE | UNC. |
|---|---|---|---|---|---|---|---|
| ☐ Boston | 110.00 | 145.00 | 200.00 | ☐ Chicago | 110.00 | 145.00 | 200.00 |
| ☐ New York | 110.00 | 145.00 | 200.00 | ☐ St. Louis | 110.00 | 145.00 | 200.00 |
| ☐ Philadelphia | 110.00 | 145.00 | 200.00 | ☐ Minneapolis | 110.00 | 145.00 | 200.00 |
| ☐ Cleveland | 110.00 | 145.00 | 200.00 | ☐ Kansas City | 110.00 | 145.00 | 200.00 |
| ☐ Richmond | 110.00 | 145.00 | 200.00 | ☐ Dallas | 110.00 | 145.00 | 210.00 |
| ☐ Atlanta | 110.00 | 145.00 | 200.00 | ☐ San Fran | 110.00 | 145.00 | 200.00 |

### SERIES OF 1934*—
### SIGNATURES OF JULIAN-MORGENTHAU, GREEN SEAL
### SERIES OF 1934A*—
### SIGNATURES OF JULIAN-MORGENTHAU, GREEN SEAL

*(The above two notes were issued on all Federal Reserve Districts.)
### SERIES OF 1934B*—
### SIGNATURES OF JULIAN-VINSON, GREEN SEAL

### SERIES OF 1934C*—
### SIGNATURES OF JULIAN-SNYDER, GREEN SEAL
### SERIES OF 1934D*—
### SIGNATURES OF CLARK-SNYDER, GREEN SEAL

*(Not all Districts issued these series.)

|  | A.B.P. | V.FINE | UNC. |
|---|---|---|---|
| AVERAGE PRICES ARE FOR ABOVE FIVE ISSUES | 110.00 | 120.00 | 185.00 |

## ONE HUNDRED DOLLAR NOTES (1950)
### FEDERAL RESERVE NOTES, GREEN SEAL
(Small Size)                                      **NOTE NO. 129C**
### SERIES OF 1950—SIGNATURES OF CLARK-SNYDER
Issued for all Federal Reserve Banks                         150.00
### SERIES OF 1950A—SIGNATURES OF PRIEST-HUMPHREY
Issued for all Federal Reserve Banks                         140.00
### SERIES OF 1950B—SIGNATURES OF PRIEST-ANDERSON
Issued for all Federal Reserve Banks                         140.00
### SERIES OF 1950C—SIGNATURES OF SMITH-DILLON
Issued for all Federal Reserve Banks                         146.00
### SERIES OF 1950D—SIGNATURES OF GRANAHAN-DILLON
Issued for all Federal Reserve Banks                         146.00
### SERIES OF 1950E—SIGNATURES OF GRANAHAN-FOWLER
Issued for New York, Chicago, San Francisco only             185.00

## ONE HUNDRED DOLLAR NOTES (1963)
### FEDERAL RESERVE NOTES

**NOTE NO. 129D**
### SERIES OF 1963—NO NOTES WERE PRINTED FOR THIS SERIES
### SERIES OF 1963A—"IN GOD WE TRUST" ADDED ON BACK
### SERIES OF 1963B—SIGNATURES OF GRANAHAN-FOWLER
Issued for all Federal Reserve Banks                         135.00

## ONE HUNDRED DOLLAR NOTES (1969)
### FEDERAL RESERVE NOTES

**NOTE NO. 129E**
### SERIES OF 1969—ENGLISH WORDING IN TREASURY SEAL
### SERIES OF 1969—SIGNATURES OF ELSTON-KENNEDY
Issued for all Federal Reserve Banks                         130.00
### SERIES OF 1969A—SIGNATURES OF KABIS-CONNALLY
Issued for all Federal Reserve Banks                         125.00
### SERIES OF 1969B—NO NOTES WERE PRINTED
### SERIES OF 1969C—SIGNATURES OF BANUELOS-SHULTZ
Issued for all Federal Reserve Banks                         120.00

### SERIES OF 1974—SIGNATURES OF NEFF-SIMON
Issued for all Federal Reserve Banks      120.00
### SERIES OF 1977—SIGNATURES OF MORTON-BLUMENTHAL
Issued for all Federal Reserve Banks      120.00
### SERIES OF 1977A—SIGNATURES OF MORTON-MILLER
Issued for all Federal Reserve Banks      120.00
### SERIES OF 1981—
### SIGNATURES OF BUCHANAN-REGAN, GREEN SEAL
Issued for all Federal Reserve Banks      110.00
### SERIES OF 1981A—
### SIGNATURES OF ORTEGA-REGAN, GREEN SEAL
Issued for all Federal Reserve Banks      110.00
### SERIES OF 1985—
### SIGNATURES OF ORTEGA-BAKER, GREEN SEAL
Issued for all Federal Reserve Banks      110.00
### SERIES OF 1988—
### SIGNATURES OF ORTEGA-BAKER, GREEN SEAL
Issued for all Federal Reserve Banks      110.00

### ONE HUNDRED DOLLAR NOTES (1929)
### FEDERAL RESERVE BANK NOTES
### (ISSUED ONLY IN SERIES OF 1929)
(Small Size)      **NOTE NO. 129F**

**Face Design:** Portrait of Franklin, brown seal and numbers.

**Back Design**

| BANK & CITY | SIGNATURES | SEAL | A.B.P. | V.FINE | UNC. |
|---|---|---|---|---|---|
| ☐New York | Jones-Woods | Brown | 110.00 | 130.00 | 225.00 |
| ☐Cleveland | Jones-Woods | Brown | 110.00 | 130.00 | 240.00 |
| ☐Richmond | Jones-Woods | Brown | 110.00 | 130.00 | 240.00 |
| ☐Chicago | Jones-Woods | Brown | 110.00 | 130.00 | 225.00 |
| ☐Minneapolis | Jones-Woods | Brown | 110.00 | 130.00 | 225.00 |
| ☐Kansas City | Jones-Woods | Brown | 110.00 | 130.00 | 250.00 |
| ☐Dallas | Jones-Woods | Brown | 110.00 | 130.00 | 250.00 |

# FIVE HUNDRED, ONE THOUSAND, FIVE THOUSAND, AND TEN THOUSAND DOLLAR NOTES

*(Production of notes in denominations above one hundred dollars was discontinued in 1969.)

# SPECIAL REPORT: UNCUT SHEETS

As very few notes exist in the form of full uncut sheets, this is a limited area for the collector. Also, the prices are high, well out of range for most hobbyists.

Uncut sheets available on the market are of small-size notes exclusively. In most instances it is not known precisely how they reached public hands. Some were undoubtedly presented as souvenir gifts to Treasury Department officials. In any event, uncut sheets have never been illegal to own, since the notes they comprise are precisely the same as those released into general circulation.

The sheets differ in the number of notes, from a low of six in National Currency sheets to a high of eighteen for some sheets of United States (Legal Tender) Notes and Silver Certificates. Others have twelve notes. These differences are due entirely to the printing method being used at their time of manufacture. Any given note was always printed in sheets of the same size, with the same number of specimens per sheet. If you have an uncut sheet with twelve notes, it means that all notes from the series were printed twelve to a sheet.

The condition standards for uncut sheets are the same as those for single notes. Obviously, an uncut sheet did not circulate as money, but some specimens became worn or damaged as a result of careless storage, accident, or other causes. These impaired sheets do turn up in the market, but there is not much demand for them. Almost every buyer of uncut sheets wants uncirculated condition. Quite often an uncut sheet will be framed when you buy it. This should be considered a plus, as the frame has probably kept the sheet in immaculate condition. Just to be entirely safe, however, it is wise to examine the reverse side of the sheet for possible staining or other problems.

The following prices were current for uncut sheets in uncirculated grade at publication time. Gem uncirculated sheets in absolutely pristine condition command higher prices than those shown.

# SILVER CERTIFICATES

| DENOMINATION | SERIES | NUMBER OF NOTES PER SHEET | CURRENT PRICE RANGE IN UNCIRCULATED CONDITION |
|---|---|---|---|
| $1 | 1928 | 12 | 1700.00—4800.00 |
| $1 | 1934 | 12 | 4300.00—6500.00 |
| $5 | 1934 | 12 | 2000.00—3500.00 |
| $10 | 1934 | 12 | 3000.00—4000.00 |
| $1 | 1935 | 12 | 750.00—2000.00 |
| $5 | 1953 | 18 | 2000.00—3000.00 |
| $10 | 1953 | 18 | 4000.00—5000.00 |

# UNITED STATES NOTES
# (LEGAL TENDER NOTES)

| DENOMINATION | SERIES | NUMBER OF NOTES PER SHEET | CURRENT PRICE RANGE IN UNCIRCULATED CONDITION |
|---|---|---|---|
| $1 | 1928 | 12 | 20,000.00 & UP |
| $2 | 1928 | 12 | 1500.00—3500.00 |
| $5 | 1928 | 12 | 2000.00—3500.00 |
| $2 | 1953 | 18 | 1000.00—2000.00 |
| $5 | 1953 | 18 | 1500.00—2800.00 |

# NATIONAL CURRENCY

| DENOMINATION | SERIES | NUMBER OF NOTES PER SHEET | CURRENT PRICE RANGE IN UNCIRCULATED CONDITION |
|---|---|---|---|
| $5 | 1929 | 6 | 1000.00—2400.00 |
| $10 | 1929 | 6 | 1100.00—2500.00 |
| $20 | 1929 | 6 | 1200.00—2500.00 |
| $50 | 1929 | 6 | 4000.00—8000.00 |

# MULES
# (MIXED PLATE NUMBERS)

All United States currency have plate numbers on the face and back. These plate numbers are in the lower right corner somewhat close to the fine scroll design. They refer to the number of the engraved plate used to print the sheet of notes. Each plate can be used for about 100,000 impressions. It is then destroyed and a new plate with the next number in sequence is put into use.

During the term of Treasury officials Julian and Morgenthau, the plate numbers were changed from almost a microscopic to a larger size, far easier to read. Due to this improvement the series designation then in use was an advance on United States Notes, Silver Certificates and Federal Reserve Notes. The signatures remained Julian-Morgenthau. National currency and gold certificates were not affected, as these were discontinued earlier.

During the changeover period in printing, plates were sometimes mixed up, producing a note with a large number on one side and a small number on the other side. Notes of this variety are called mules, or mule notes. This is from a term applied to coins struck with the obverse or reverse die of one year and the opposite side from a die of another year.

Many collectors are eager to add one or more of these mule notes to their collection. Some of the most common mule notes are:

| | |
|---|---|
| **$2.00 UNITED STATES NOTES** | **$1.00 SILVER CERTIFICATES** |
| 1928-C 1928-D | 1935 1935-A |
| **$5.00 UNITED STATES NOTES** | **$5.00 SILVER CERTIFICATES** |
| 1928-B 1928-C 1928-D 1928-E | 1934 1934-A 1934-B 1934-C |

### $10.00 SILVER CERTIFICATES
1934 1934-A

Mules were also issued in the Federal Reserve Note series. However, these are not as popular with collectors as the United States Notes and Silver Certificates because of the higher denominations and the 12 districts involved.

The schedule below shows some of the most common mule notes and their values in new condition. The combination of the prefix and suffix letters of the serial numbers on notes is known as "Blocks." For instance: A—A Block, B—A Block.

| | | | UNC. |
|---|---|---|---|
| **$2.00 UNITED STATES NOTE** | 1928-D | B—A | 500.00 |
| | | C—A | 70.00 |
| | | *—A | 75.00 |
| **$5.00 UNITED STATES NOTE** | 1928-B | E—A | 100.00 |
| | | *—A | 550.00 |
| | 1928-C | E—A | 85.00 |
| | | *—A | 125.00 |
| **$1.00 SILVER CERTIFICATE** | 1935 | N—A | |
| | | Thru | 160.00 |
| | | P—A | |
| | 1935-A | M—A | |
| | | Thru | 75.00 |
| | | V—A | |
| | | C—B | 78.00 |
| **$5.00 SILVER CERTIFICATE** | 1934-A | D—A | |
| | | Thru | 80.00 |
| | | G—A | |
| | | *—A | 160.00 |
| **$10.00 SILVER CERTIFICATE** | 1934 | A—A | 85.00 |
| | | *—A | 125.00 |
| | 1934-A | A—A | 200.00 |

Front      SIZES DIFFERENT      Back

# INTRODUCTION TO UNITED STATES FRACTIONAL CURRENCY

Events following the outbreak of the Civil War resulted in a shortage of circulating coinage. Trade was hampered as many merchants, especially in large cities, were unable to make change and only customers presenting the exact amount for a purchase could buy—but they were generally as short on coins as the shop proprietors. Various attempts were made to solve this problem by issuing credit slips (which most customers didn't care for), tokens (which they also didn't care for), and using postage stamps as money. Finally in 1862 the government stepped in, recocnizing that the economy was being seriously hurt, and issued a series of small paper notes as equivalents of coinage denominations. They carried designs adapted from the current postage stamps of the day and were known as Postage Currency or Postal Currency. The more popular title is now Fractional Currency. There were five separate issues of fractional currency, three of which occurred during the Civil War and two thereafter, the final one as late as 1874. That a need existed for coin substitutes as late as the 1870s demonstrates the drain placed upon coinage during the war and the long period of recovery. A total of six denominations were issued, from 3¢ to 59¢, comprising 23 designs and more than 100 varieties. Because of its small size and lack of visual impact, fractional currency was long shunned by collectors. In recent years it has enjoyed an unprecedented surge of popularity, which, if continued, promises to drive prices beyond present levels. All told, more than $360,000,000 worth of fractional currency was circulated. It would be extremely plentiful today but for the fact that most notes were redeemed, leaving only about $2,000,000 outstanding. This is what collectors have to work with, and a good deal of these are badly preserved.

**FIRST ISSUE**—Postage Currency August 21st, 1862
5-10-25-50

**SECOND ISSUE**—Fractional Currency October 10th, 1863
5-10-25-50

**THIRD ISSUE**—Fractional Currency December 5th, 1864
3-5-10-15-25-50

**FOURTH ISSUE**—Fractional Currency July 14th, 1869
10-15-25-50

**FIFTH ISSUE**—Fractional Currency February 26th, 1874
10-25-50

# THE FRACTIONAL CURRENCY SHIELD

Fractional currency shields were sold by the Treasury Department in 1866. Specimen notes printed only on one side were used. Very good condition shields are valued at $2500 to $3500. Choice condition shields in contemporary frames can sell for $4200. Shields with pink, green or other backgrounds are more valuable.

# UNITED STATES FRACTIONAL CURRENCY

**These notes may be collected by issue
or by denomination. We list them here
by denomination for convenience.**

NOTE: Since most of these notes were hastily cut from
large sheets, the margin size can vary. Specimens with
larger than normal margins command premium prices.

## THREE-CENT NOTES

THIRD ISSUE                                    NOTE NO. 142

**Face Design:**
Portrait of
President
Washington.

**Back Design:**
Large "3"
green.

|  | A.B.P. | GOOD | V.FINE | UNC. |
|---|---|---|---|---|
| ☐With Light Portrait | 6.00 | 7.00 | 19.00 | 70.00 |
| ☐With Dark Portrait | 6.50 | 8.00 | 20.00 | 98.00 |

## FIVE-CENT NOTES

FIRST ISSUE                                    NOTE NO. 143

**Face Design:**
Portrait of
President
Jefferson,
brown.

**Back
Design:**
"5" black.

|  | A.B.P. | GOOD | V.FINE | UNC. |
|---|---|---|---|---|
| ☐Perforated edges. Monogram ABNCO on back | 4.00 | 6.00 | 20.00 | 110.00 |
| ☐Perforated edges. Without monogram on back | 5.00 | 7.00 | 16.00 | 130.00 |
| ☐Straight edges. Monogram ABNCO on back | 4.50 | 6.00 | 10.00 | 65.00 |
| ☐Straight edges. Without monogram on back | 7.00 | 11.00 | 21.00 | 155.00 |

## FIVE-CENT NOTES

SECOND ISSUE                                NOTE NO. 144

**Face Design:**
Portrait of
President
Washington.

**Back Design:**
Shield and
brown, "5s".

|  | A.B.P. | GOOD | V.FINE | UNC. |
|---|---|---|---|---|
| ☐Value only in bronze on back | 4.00 | 6.00 | 11.00 | 50.00 |
| ☐Surcharges 18-63 on back | 4.00 | 6.00 | 11.00 | 54.00 |
| ☐Surcharges S-18-63 on back | 6.00 | 10.00 | 12.50 | 80.00 |
| ☐Surcharges R-1-18-63 on back—fiber paper | 8.00 | 13.00 | 42.00 | 250.00 |

## FIVE-CENT NOTES

THIRD ISSUE                                 NOTE NO. 145

**Face Design:**
Portrait of
Spencer M.
Clark.

**Back Design:**
Green or
red.

|  | A.B.P. | GOOD | V.FINE | UNC. |
|---|---|---|---|---|
| ☐Without letter "A" on face. Green back | 5.00 | 8.00 | 20.00 | 115.00 |
| ☐With letter "A" on face. Green back | 6.00 | 9.00 | 26.00 | 145.00 |
| ☐Without letter "A" on face. Red back | 4.00 | 6.00 | 15.00 | 60.00 |
| ☐With letter "A" on face. Red back | 4.00 | 6.00 | 16.00 | 62.00 |

NOTE: This note was authorized to have the portraits of the explorers Lewis and Clark on the face. Mr. Spencer M. Clark, who was then head of the Bureau of Currency, flagrantly placed his own portrait on this note. This caused Congress to pass legislation forbidding the likeness of any living person on U.S. currency.

## TEN-CENT NOTES

FIRST ISSUE                                 NOTE NO. 146

**Face Design:**
Portrait of
President
Washington

**Back Design:**
"10,"
black.

|  | A.B.P. | GOOD | V.FINE | UNC. |
|---|---|---|---|---|
| ☐Perforated edges. Monogram ABNCO on back | 4.00 | 6.00 | 26.00 | 120.00 |
| ☐Perforated edges. Without monogram on back | 4.00 | 6.00 | 28.00 | 140.00 |
| ☐Plain edges. Monogram ABNCO on back | 4.00 | 5.50 | 11.00 | 65.00 |
| ☐Plain edges. Without monogram on back | 6.00 | 11.00 | 36.00 | 155.00 |

## TEN-CENT NOTES

SECOND ISSUE                                       **NOTE NO. 147**

**Face Design:**
Portrait of
President
Washington

**Back Design:**
"10,"
green.

| | A.B.P. | GOOD | V.FINE | UNC. |
|---|---|---|---|---|
| ☐Value only surcharge on back | 4.00 | 7.00 | 13.00 | 55.00 |
| ☐Surcharge 18-63 on back | 4.00 | 7.00 | 14.00 | 57.00 |
| ☐Surcharge S-18-63 on back | 5.00 | 8.00 | 15.00 | 70.00 |
| ☐Surcharge I-18-63 on back | 9.00 | 21.00 | 42.00 | 215.00 |
| ☐Surcharge O-63 on back | 150.00 | 410.00 | 1100.00 | 2100.00 |
| ☐Surcharge T-1-18-63 on back—fiber paper | 7.00 | 14.00 | 65.00 | 230.00 |

## TEN-CENT NOTES

THIRD ISSUE                                        **NOTE NO. 148**

**Face Design:**
Portrait of
President
Washington.

**Back Design:**
"10," green
or red.

| | A.B.P. | GOOD | V.FINE | UNC. |
|---|---|---|---|---|
| ☐Printed signatures Colby-Spinner. Green back | 4.00 | 9.00 | 14.00 | 70.00 |
| ☐As above. Figure "1" near left margin on face | 4.00 | 10.00 | 14.00 | 70.00 |
| ☐Printed signatures Colby-Spinner. Red back | 4.00 | 10.00 | 21.00 | 150.00 |
| ☐As above. Figure "1" near left margin. Red back | | | | |
| | 5.00 | 13.00 | 20.00 | 64.00 |
| ☐Autographed signatures Colby-Spinner. Red back | | | | |
| | 7.00 | 17.00 | 26.00 | 150.00 |
| ☐Autographed signatures Jeffries-Spinner. Red back | | | | |
| | 7.00 | 17.00 | 50.00 | 200.00 |

## TEN-CENT NOTES

FOURTH ISSUE                                       **NOTE NO. 149**

**Face Design:**
Bust of
Liberty.

**Back Design:**
Green with
"Ten" &
"10."

| | A.B.P. | GOOD | V.FINE | UNC. |
|---|---|---|---|---|
| ☐Large red seal. Watermarked paper | 3.50 | 6.00 | 14.00 | 50.00 |
| ☐Large red seal. Pink fibers in paper | 3.50 | 6.00 | 15.00 | 50.00 |
| ☐Large seal. Pink fibers in paper. Right end blue | 4.00 | 6.50 | 18.00 | 68.00 |
| ☐Large brown seal | 13.00 | 28.00 | 80.00 | 200.00 |
| ☐Small red seal. Pink fibers. Right end blue | 4.00 | 7.00 | 24.00 | 80.00 |

## TEN-CENT NOTES

FIFTH ISSUE                                    **NOTE NO. 150**

**Face Design:**
William
Meredith.

**Back Design:**
Green.

| | A.B.P. | GOOD | V.FINE | UNC. |
|---|---|---|---|---|
| ☐Green seal. Long narrow key | 4.00 | 6.00 | 11.00 | 55.00 |
| ☐Red seal. Long narrow key | 3.00 | 5.00 | 10.00 | 40.00 |
| ☐Red seal. Short stubby key | 4.00 | 6.00 | 10.00 | 40.00 |

## FIFTEEN-CENT NOTES
### FACES AND BACKS PRINTED SEPARATELY
THIRD ISSUE                                    **NOTE NO. 151**

**Face Design:**
Sherman and
President
Grant.

**Back Design:**
Green
or red.

| | NARROW MARGIN | WIDE MARGIN |
|---|---|---|
| ☐With printed signatures Colby-Spinner* | 200.00 | 310.00 |
| ☐With autographed signatures Colby-Spinner** | 1150.00 | RARE |
| ☐With autographed signatures Jeffries-Spinner** | 250.00 | 375.00 |
| ☐With autographed signatures Allison-Spinner** | 285.00 | 400.00 |
| ☐*Green back | 170.00 | 225.00 |
| ☐*Red back | 165.00 | 220.00 |

## FIFTEEN-CENT NOTES

FOURTH ISSUE

NOTE NO. 152

**Face Design:**
Bust
of Columbia.

**Back Design:**
Green
with "15s."

| | A.B.P. | GOOD | V.FINE | UNC. |
|---|---|---|---|---|
| ☐ Large seal. Watermarked paper | 6.00 | 11.00 | 22.00 | 110.00 |
| ☐ Large seal. Pink fibers in paper | 6.00 | 12.00 | 30.00 | 140.00 |
| ☐ Large seal. Pink fibers in paper. Right end blue | | | | |
| | 6.00 | 12.00 | 27.00 | 138.00 |
| ☐ Large brown seal | 18.00 | 36.00 | 160.00 | RARE |
| ☐ Smaller red seal. Pink fibers. Right end blue | 6.00 | 11.00 | 28.00 | 140.00 |

## TWENTY-FIVE-CENT NOTES

FIRST ISSUE

NOTE NO. 153

**Face Design:**
Five 5¢
Jefferson
Stamps.

**Back Design:**
Black,
large "25."

| | A.B.P. | GOOD | V.FINE | UNC. |
|---|---|---|---|---|
| ☐ Perforated edges. Monogram ABNCO on back | 5.00 | 10.00 | 21.00 | 165.00 |
| ☐ Perforated edges. Without monogram on back | 5.00 | 11.00 | 55.00 | 280.00 |
| ☐ Straight edges. Monogram ABNCO on back | 5.00 | 9.00 | 16.00 | 85.00 |
| ☐ Straight edges. Without monogram on back | 6.00 | 14.00 | 65.00 | 310.00 |

**A.B.P.**—*Average Buying Price in better than good condition.*

## TWENTY-FIVE-CENT NOTES

SECOND ISSUE

NOTE NO. 154

(Time and climatic condition have changed the purple color on the back of this note into many variations.)

**Face Design:**
Portrait of
President
Washington.

**Back Design:**
Purple with
"25."

|  | A.B.P. | GOOD | V.FINE | UNC. |
|---|---|---|---|---|
| ☐Value only surcharge on back | 4.00 | 8.00 | 20.00 | 82.00 |
| ☐Surcharge 18-63 on back | 6.00 | 12.00 | 20.00 | 90.00 |
| ☐Surcharge A-18-63 on back | 6.00 | 11.00 | 20.00 | 90.00 |
| ☐Surcharge 1-18-63 on back | 18.00 | 36.00 | 90.00 | 260.00 |
| ☐Surcharge 2-18-63 on back | 6.00 | 11.00 | 25.00 | 115.00 |
| ☐Surcharge S-18-63 on back | 8.00 | 15.00 | 25.00 | 115.00 |
| ☐Surcharge T-1-18-63 on back, fiber paper | 10.00 | 15.00 | 25.00 | 220.00 |
| ☐Surcharge T-2-18-63 on back, fiber paper | 7.00 | 15.00 | 25.00 | 210.00 |
| ☐Surcharge S-2-18-63, fiber paper |  |  |  | RARE |

## TWENTY-FIVE-CENT NOTES

THIRD ISSUE                                          **NOTE NO. 155**

(All notes have printed signatures of Colby-Spinner.)

**Face Design:**
Portrait of
Fessenden.

**Back Design:**
Green or
red with "25
CENTS."

|  | A.B.P. | GOOD | V.FINE | UNC. |
|---|---|---|---|---|
| ☐Face—Bust of Fessenden between solid bronze surcharges. Fiber paper. Back—Green. Surcharge M-2-6-5 in corners | 100.00 | 185.00 | 410.00 | 1000.00 |
| ☐As above. With letter "A" in lower left corner of face | 110.00 | 300.00 | 700.00 | 1600.00 |
| ☐Face—Fessenden. Open scroll bronze surcharges Fiber paper. Back—Green. Surcharges M-2-6-5 in corners | 11.00 | 20.00 | 48.00 | 300.00 |
| ☐As above with letter "A" in lower left corner of face | 8.00 | 17.00 | 45.00 | 225.00 |
| ☐Face—Fessenden. Open scroll surcharges. Plain paper. Back—Green. Value surcharges only | 7.50 | 14.00 | 30.00 | 140.00 |
| ☐As before. Letter "A" in lower left corner of face. Back—Green. Plain paper | 10.00 | 17.00 | 42.00 | 125.00 |
| ☐Face—Fessenden. Red back. Value surcharge only | 9.00 | 13.00 | 32.00 | 130.00 |
| ☐As above. Letter "A" in lower left corner of face | 9.00 | 13.00 | 30.00 | 130.00 |

## TWENTY-FIVE-CENT NOTES

FOURTH ISSUE                              **NOTE NO. 156**

**Face Design:**
Portrait of
President
Washington
and Treasury Seal.

**Back
Design:**
Green.

| | A.B.P. | GOOD | V.FINE | UNC. |
|---|---|---|---|---|
| ☐Large seal. Plain watermarked paper | 4.00 | 7.50 | 20.00 | 75.00 |
| ☐Large seal. Pink silk fiber in paper | 4.00 | 7.50 | 20.00 | 75.00 |
| ☐Large seal. Pink fibers in paper. Right end blue | 4.00 | 7.50 | 21.00 | 85.00 |
| ☐Large brown seal. Right end blue | 35.00 | 70.00 | 280.00 | 1100.00 |
| ☐Smaller red seal. Right end blue | 4.00 | 8.00 | 20.00 | 75.00 |

## TWENTY-FIVE-CENT NOTES

FIFTH ISSUE                               **NOTE NO. 157**

**Face Design:**
Portrait of
Walker and
red seal.

**Back
Design:**
Black.

| | A.B.P. | GOOD | V.FINE | UNC. |
|---|---|---|---|---|
| ☐With long narrow key in Treasury Seal. | 4.00 | 6.00 | 11.00 | 45.00 |
| ☐With short stubby key in Treasury Seal | 4.00 | 6.00 | 11.00 | 40.00 |

**A.B.P.**—*Average Buying Price in better than good condition.*

## FIFTY-CENT NOTES

FIRST ISSUE                               **NOTE NO. 158**

**Face Design:**
Five 10¢
Washington
Stamps.

**Back
Design:**
Green.

| | A.B.P. | GOOD | V.FINE | UNC. |
|---|---|---|---|---|
| ☐Perforated edges. Monogram ABNCO on back | 8.00 | 11.00 | 76.00 | 200.00 |
| ☐Perforated edges. Without monogram on back | 10.00 | 18.00 | 70.00 | 310.00 |
| ☐Straight edges. Monogram ABNCO on back | 6.00 | 9.00 | 25.00 | 110.00 |
| ☐Straight edges. Without monogram | 11.00 | 18.00 | 80.00 | 310.00 |

## FIFTY-CENT NOTES

SECOND ISSUE                                    **NOTE NO. 159**

**Face Design:**
Portrait of
President
Washington.

**Back
Design:**
Red.

|  | A.B.P. | GOOD | V.FINE | UNC. |
|---|---|---|---|---|
| ☐ Value surcharge only on back | 44.00 | 100.00 | 350.00 | 1000.00 |
| ☐ Surcharge 18-63 on back | 7.00 | 9.00 | 35.00 | 165.00 |
| ☐ Surcharge A-18-63 on back | 6.00 | 9.00 | 26.00 | 150.00 |
| ☐ Surcharge I-18-63 | 6.00 | 9.00 | 26.00 | 150.00 |
| ☐ Surcharge O-1-18-63. Fiber paper | 7.00 | 18.00 | 60.00 | 235.00 |
| ☐ Surcharge R-2-18-63. Fiber paper | 10.00 | 16.00 | 46.00 | 240.00 |
| ☐ Surcharge T-1-18-63. Fiber paper | 7.00 | 14.00 | 46.00 | 225.00 |
| ☐ Surcharge T-18-63. Fiber paper | 45.00 | 90.00 | 190.00 | 500.00 |

## FIFTY-CENT NOTES

THIRD ISSUE                                     **NOTE NO. 160**

(Notes with Printed Signatures of Colby-Spinner, Green Backs.)

**Face Design:**
Justice with
Sword,
Shield,
Scales.

**Back
Design:**
Green
or red.

|  | A.B.P. | GOOD | V.FINE | UNC. |
|---|---|---|---|---|
| ☐ Value surcharge and S-2-6-4 on back. Fiber paper | | | | VERY RARE |
| ☐ Value surcharge and A-2-6-5 on back. Fiber paper | 16.00 | 32.00 | 75.00 | 500.00 |
| ☐ As above with "1" and letter "A" on face. A-2-6-5 on back | 26.00 | 75.00 | 350.00 | 1600.00 |
| ☐ As above with "1" only on face. A-2-6-5 on back | 16.00 | 32.00 | 75.00 | 325.00 |
| ☐ As above with letter "A" only on face. A-2-6-5 on back | 16.00 | 37.00 | 80.00 | 325.00 |
| ☐ A-2-6-5 on back, narrowly spaced. Plain paper | 7.00 | 10.00 | 35.00 | 275.00 |
| ☐ As above. Numeral "1" and letter "A" on face | 11.00 | 20.00 | 70.00 | 750.00 |

| | A.B.P. | GOOD | V.FINE | UNC. |
|---|---|---|---|---|
| ☐As above. Numeral "1" only on face | 6.00 | 12.00 | 35.00 | 270.00 |
| ☐As above. Letter "A" only on face | 11.00 | 18.00 | 41.00 | 300.00 |
| ☐A-2-6-5 on back, widely spaced. Plain paper | 10.00 | 18.00 | 41.00 | 310.00 |
| ☐As above. Numeral "1" and letter "A" on face | | | | |
| | 10.00 | 30.00 | 100.00 | 550.00 |
| ☐As above. Numeral "1" only on face | 7.00 | 13.00 | 50.00 | 450.00 |
| ☐As above. Letter "A" only on face | 6.00 | 12.00 | 50.00 | 450.00 |
| ☐Without position letters or back surcharges | 6.00 | 12.00 | 33.00 | 310.00 |
| ☐As above with numeral "1" and letter "A" on face | | | | |
| | 15.00 | 26.00 | 50.00 | 450.00 |
| ☐As above with numeral "1" only on face | 5.00 | 11.00 | 30.00 | 310.00 |
| ☐As above with letter "A" only on face | 6.00 | 12.00 | 36.00 | 300.00 |

### (Notes with Printed Signatures of Colby-Spinner, Red Backs.)

| | A.B.P. | GOOD | V.FINE | UNC. |
|---|---|---|---|---|
| ☐Value surcharge and S-2-6-4 on back. Fiber | | | | |
| | 40.00 | 60.00 | 350.00 | 1200.00 |
| ☐As above. Numeral "1" and letter "A" | 125.00 | 350.00 | 700.00 | RARE |
| ☐As above. Numeral "1" only on face | 100.00 | 200.00 | 400.00 | 1600.00 |
| ☐As above. Letter "A" only on face | 95.00 | 200.00 | 500.00 | 1600.00 |
| ☐Value surcharge and A-2-6-5 on back. Plain | 7.00 | 16.00 | 45.00 | 325.00 |
| ☐As above. Numeral "1" and letter "A" | 15.00 | 31.00 | 70.00 | 350.00 |
| ☐As above. Numeral "1" only on face | 8.00 | 17.00 | 36.00 | 350.00 |
| ☐As above. Letter "A" only on face | 9.00 | 18.00 | 46.00 | 265.00 |
| ☐Value surcharge only on back. Plain paper | 9.00 | 18.00 | 42.00 | 325.00 |
| ☐As above. Numeral "1" and letter "A" on face | | | | |
| | 13.00 | 26.00 | 55.00 | 410.00 |
| ☐As above. Numeral "1" only on face | 10.00 | 22.00 | 42.00 | 260.00 |
| ☐As above. Letter "A" only on face | 10.00 | 25.00 | 60.00 | 360.00 |

### (Notes with Autographed Signatures of Colby-Spinner, Red Backs.)

| | A.B.P. | GOOD | V.FINE | UNC. |
|---|---|---|---|---|
| ☐Value surcharge and S-2-6-4 on back. Fiber | 32.00 | 75.00 | 200.00 | 1100.00 |
| ☐Value surcharge and A-2-6-5 on back. Fiber | 14.00 | 24.00 | 80.00 | 600.00 |
| ☐Value surcharge only on back. Plain paper | 10.00 | 22.00 | 80.00 | 315.00 |

## FIFTY-CENT NOTES

THIRD ISSUE                                              **NOTE NO. 161**

**Face Design:** Bust of Spinner with surcharges.
**Back Design:** Green or red.

(Notes with Printed Signatures of Colby-Spinner, Green Backs.)

|  | A.B.P. | GOOD | V.FINE | UNC. |
|---|---|---|---|---|
| ☐Value surcharge and A-2-6-5 on back | 8.00 | 17.00 | 72.00 | 290.00 |
| ☐As above. Numeral "1" and letter "A" on face | 20.00 | 39.00 | 110.00 | 650.00 |
| ☐As above. Numeral "1" only on face | 6.00 | 17.00 | 42.00 | 325.00 |
| ☐As above. Letter "A" only on face | 6.00 | 16.00 | 65.00 | 400.00 |
| ☐Value surcharge only on back | 6.00 | 10.00 | 35.00 | 350.00 |
| ☐As above. Numeral "1" and letter "A" on face | 10.00 | 26.00 | 45.00 | 350.00 |
| ☐As above. Numeral "1" only on face | 6.00 | 12.00 | 32.00 | 370.00 |
| ☐As above. Letter "A" only on face | 6.00 | 12.00 | 32.00 | 400.00 |

### (TYPE II BACK DESIGN)

|  | A.B.P. | GOOD | V.FINE | UNC. |
|---|---|---|---|---|
| ☐Value surcharge only on back | 7.00 | 15.00 | 32.00 | 300.00 |
| ☐Numeral "1" and letter "A" on face | 18.00 | 35.00 | 75.00 | 350.00 |
| ☐Numeral "1" only on face | 8.00 | 15.00 | 42.00 | 315.00 |
| ☐Letter "A" only on face | 8.00 | 18.00 | 60.00 | 350.00 |

(Notes with Portrait of Spinner, Printed Signatures of
Colby-Spinner, Red Backs, Type I.)

|  | A.B.P. | GOOD | V.FINE | UNC. |
|---|---|---|---|---|
| ☐Value surcharge and A-2-6-5 on back | 8.00 | 16.00 | 45.00 | 330.00 |
| ☐As above with numeral "1" and letter "A" | 18.00 | 39.00 | 130.00 | 400.00 |
| ☐As above with numeral "1" only on face | 10.00 | 15.00 | 45.00 | 330.00 |
| ☐As above with letter "A" only on face | 10.00 | 22.00 | 58.00 | 340.00 |

(Notes with Autographed Signatures, Red Backs, Type I.)

|  | A.B.P. | GOOD | V.FINE | UNC. |
|---|---|---|---|---|
| ☐Autographed signatures COLBY-SPINNER. | | | | |
| Back surcharged Value and A-2-6-5 | 9.00 | 26.00 | 60.00 | 460.00 |
| ☐Autographed signatures ALLISON-SPINNER. | | | | |
| Back surcharged Value and A-2-6-5 | 9.00 | 26.00 | 75.00 | 610.00 |
| ☐Autographed signatures ALLISON-NEW. | | | | |
| Back surcharged Value and A-2-6-5 | 300.00 | 600.00 | 1000.00 | 2600.00 |

**A.B.P.**—*Average Buying Price in better than good condition.*

## FIFTY-CENT NOTES

FOURTH ISSUE                                              **NOTE NO. 162**

**Face Design:**                                          **Back**
Bust                                                      **Design:**
of Lincoln.                                               Green.

|  | A.B.P. | GOOD | V.FINE | UNC. |
|---|---|---|---|---|
| ☐ Plain paper | 8.00 | 16.00 | 46.00 | 185.00 |
| ☐ Paper with pink fibers | 8.00 | 16.00 | 52.00 | 190.00 |

## FIFTY-CENT NOTES

FOURTH ISSUE                                              **NOTE NO. 163**

**Face Design:**                                          **Back**
Bust                                                      **Design:**
of Stanton.                                               Green
                                                          with "50."

|  | A.B.P. | GOOD | V.FINE | UNC. |
|---|---|---|---|---|
| ☐ Red Seal and signatures ALLISON-SPINNER. Paper with pink fibers. Blue ends | 6.00 | 11.00 | 35.00 | 170.00 |

## FIFTY-CENT NOTES

FOURTH ISSUE                                              **NOTE NO. 164**

**Face Design:**                                          **Back**
Bust of                                                   **Design:**
Samuel                                                    Green with
Dexter.                                                   "50."

|  | A.B.P. | GOOD | V.FINE | UNC. |
|---|---|---|---|---|
| ☐ Green seal. Pink fibers. Blue ends | 6.00 | 10.00 | 22.00 | 115.00 |

## FIFTY-CENT NOTES

FIFTH ISSUE                                               **NOTE NO. 165**

**Face Design:**                                          **Back**
Bust                                                      **Design:**
of Crawford.                                              Green with
                                                          "50."

|  | A.B.P. | GOOD | V.FINE | UNC. |
|---|---|---|---|---|
| ☐ Signatures ALLISON-NEW. Paper with pink fibers. Blue ends | 4.00 | 6.00 | 18.00 | 65.00 |

**A.B.P.**—*Average Buying Price in better than good condition.*

# ERROR OR FREAK NOTES

Notes have been misprinted from time to time since the earliest days of currency. The frequency of misprintings and other abnormalities has increased in recent years, due to heavier production and high-speed machinery. This has provided a major sub-hobby for note collectors. Freaks and errors have become very popular, their appeal and prices showing upward movement each year.

On the following pages we have pictured and described most of the more familiar and collectible error notes. Pricing is approximate only because many notes bearing the same general type of error differ in severity of error from one specimen to another. As a general rule, the less glaring or obvious errors carry a smaller premium value. Very valuable error notes include double denominations, or bills having the face of one denomination and reverse side of another.

Error and freak notes do turn up in everyday change. Specimens are located either in that fashion or from bank packs. As far as circulated specimens are concerned, some error notes have passed through so many hands before being noticed that the condition is not up to collector standards. This, of course, results in a very low premium valuation.

Values given below are for the specimens pictured and described. Different premiums may be attached to other specimens with similar errors, or notes showing the same errors but of different denominations.

## 1. MISMATCHED SERIAL NUMBERS

On ordinary notes, the serial number in the lower left of the obverse matches that in the upper right. When it fails to, even by the difference of a single digit, this is known as a MISMATCHED SERIAL NUMBER. It occurs as the result of a cylinder or cylinders in the high-speed numbering machine becoming jammed. If more than one digit is mismatched, the value will be greater.

|  | V.FINE | UNC. |
|---|---|---|
| ☐$1 Federal Reserve Note, Series 1969, Signatures Elston-Kennedy | 45.00 | 145.00 |

|  | V.FINE | UNC. |
|---|---|---|
| ☐$1 Silver Certificate, Series 1957B, Signatures Granahan-Dillon | 50.00 | 145.00 |

|  | V.FINE | UNC. |
|---|---|---|
| ☐$1 Federal Reserve Note, Series 1977A, Signatures Morton-Miller | 75.00 | 150.00 |

## 2. INVERTED THIRD PRINT

The inverted third print is also known as Inverted Overprint. The Treasury Seal, District Seal, Serial Numbers and District Number are inverted on the obverse side of the note, or printed upside-down, caused by the sheet of notes (having already received the primary design on front and back) being fed upside-down into the press for this so-called "third print." (The back design is the "first print," the front is the "second print," and these various additions comprise the "third print." It is not possible to print these "third print" items at the same time as the obverse design, since they are not standard on every bill. At one time the signatures were included in the "third print," but these are now engraved directly into the plate and are part of the "second print.")

Though very spectacular, inverted third print errors are not particularly scarce and are especially plentiful in 1974 and 1976 series notes.

|  | V.FINE | UNC. |
|---|---|---|
| ☐ $5 Federal Reserve Note, Series 1974, Signatures Neff-Simon | 100.00 | 185.00 |

|  | V.FINE | UNC. |
|---|---|---|
| ☐ $2 Federal Reserve Note, Series 1976, Signatures Neff-Simon | 200.00 | 500.00 |

|  | **V.FINE** | **UNC.** |
|---|---|---|
| ☐ $1 Federal Reserve Note, Series 1974, Signatures Neff-Simon | 85.00 | 210.00 |

|  | **V.FINE** | **UNC.** |
|---|---|---|
| ☐ $50 Federal Reserve Note, Series 1977, Signatures Morton-Blumenthal | 250.00 | 500.00 |

|  | **V.FINE** | **UNC.** |
|---|---|---|
| ☐ $20 Federal Reserve Note, Series 1974, Signatures Neff-Simon | 140.00 | 280.00 |

|  | **V.FINE** | **UNC.** |
|---|---|---|
| ☐ $10 Federal Reserve Note, Series 1974, Signatures Neff-Simon | 120.00 | 250.00 |

## 3. COMPLETE OFFSET TRANSFER

Offset transfers are not, as is often believed, caused by still-wet printed sheets coming into contact under pressure. Though very slight offsetting can occur in that manner, it would not create notes as spectacular as those pictured here, in which the offset impression is almost as strong as the primary printing. These happen as a result of the printing press being started up an instant or so before the paper is fed in. Instead of contacting the paper, the inked plate makes its impression upon the machine bed. When the paper is then fed through, it picks up this "ghost" impression from the bed, in addition to the primary impression it is supposed to receive. Each successive sheet going through the press will acquire the impression until all ink is totally removed from the machine bed. But, naturally, the first sheet will show the transfer strongest, and the others will be weaker and weaker. Obviously, the market value of such notes depends largely on the strength of the offset impression. The heavier and more noticeable it is, the more valuable the note will be—all other things being equal.

|  | V.FINE | UNC. |
|---|---|---|
| ☐ $5 Federal Reserve note, Series 1977, Signatures Morton-Blumenthal Offset of reverse side of face | | |
| ☐ Dark | 45.00 | 160.00 |
| ☐ Light | 28.00 | 85.00 |

|  | V.FINE | UNC. |
|---|---|---|
| ☐ $1 Federal Reserve note, Series 1974, Signatures Neff-Simon. Offset of reverse side of face. | | |
| ☐ Dark | 70.00 | 182.00 |
| ☐ Light | 42.00 | 95.00 |

## 4. PARTIAL OFFSET TRANSFER

The most logical explanation for this error is that a sheet of paper fed into the press incorrectly became mangled or torn, and part of the inked plate contacted the printing press bed. Therefore, wet ink was left on those portions of the press bed not covered by paper. When the next sheet was fed through, it received the correct impression, plus it acquired a partial offset transfer by contacting this wet area of the press bed. Just as with #3, the first sheet going through the press following an accident of this kind will receive the strongest transfer, and it will become gradually less noticeable on succeeding sheets.

|  | V.FINE | UNC. |
|---|---|---|
| ☐ $1 Federal Reserve Note, Series 1969D, Signatures Banuelos-Schultz. Offset of a portion of reverse side on face. | | |
| ☐ Dark | 21.00 | 56.00 |
| ☐ Light | 20.00 | 45.00 |

## 5. PRINTED FOLD

Notes showing printed folds occur as the result of folds in the paper before printing, which probably happen most often when the sheet is being fed into the press. If the sheet is folded in such a manner that a portion of the reverse side is facing upward, as shown here, it will receive a part of the impression intended for its obverse. Naturally the positioning of these misplaced portions of printing is very random, depending on the nature and size of the fold.

|  | V.FINE | UNC. |
|---|---|---|
| ☐ $20 Federal Reserve Note, Series 1977, Signatures Morton-Blumenthal Federal Reserve district seal and district number printed on reverse | 80.00 | 185.00 |

## 6. THIRD PRINT ON REVERSE

The cause of this error is obvious, the sheet having been fed through the press on the wrong side (back instead of front) for the third impression or "third print." In the so-called "third print," the note receives the Treasury and Federal Reserve District seals, district numbers, and serial numbers.

|  | V.FINE | UNC. |
|---|---|---|
| ☐ $1 Federal Reserve Note. Third print on reverse | 80.00 | 180.00 |

## 7. BOARD BREAKS

The terminology of this error is misleading. It suggests that the fern-like unprinted areas were caused by a broken printing plate. Actually they must have resulted from something, probably linty matter, sticking to the printing ink. The assumption reached by the public, when it encounters such a note, is that the blank streaks were caused by the paper being folded in printing. This, however, is not possible, as that would yield an error of a much different kind (see **PRINTED FOLD**).

It should be pointed out that Board Breaks are easily created by counterfeiters by erasing portions of the printed surface, and that the collector ought to examine such specimens closely.

|  | V.FINE | UNC. |
|---|---|---|
| ☐ $20 Federal Reserve Note. Board breaks on reverse | 40.00 | 95.00 |

## 8. MISSING SECOND PRINT

The "second print" is the front face, or obverse of the note—the "first" print being the reverse or back. A note with a Missing Second Print has not received the primary impression on its obverse, though the back is normal and the front carries the standard "third print" matter (Treasury seal, serial numbers, etc.). These errors, while they probably occur frequently, are so easily spotted by B.E.P. checkers that such notes are very scarce on the market.

|  | V.FINE | UNC. |
|---|---|---|
| ☐$10 Federal Reserve Note. Missing second print | 175.00 | 325.00 |

## 9. PRINTED FOLD

This note was folded nearly in half before receiving the Third Print, which fell across the waste margin on the reverse side. Had the note not been folded, this waste margin would have been removed in the cutting process. This note, when unfolded, is grotesque in shape.

|  | V.FINE | UNC. |
|---|---|---|
| ☐$1 Federal Reserve Note. Printed fold with Federal Reserve District seal, district numbers, and serial numbers on reverse. (Naturally, this note lacks the "third print" matter, such as the Treasury seal, that was supposed to appear on the righthand side of the obverse.) | 85.00 | 185.00 |

**V.FINE        UNC.**

☐ $5 Federal Reserve Note. Printed fold with entire Federal
Reserve District seal, portion of another Federal Reserve
District seal, and portion of two different serial numbers
on the reverse. It may be hard to imagine how a freak of
this nature occurs. This note was folded diagonally along a
line bisecting the Lincoln Memorial building slightly to the
right of center. The lefthand portion of the reverse side
was thereby drawn down across the lefthand side of the
obverse, extending well below the bottom of the note. It
reached far enough down to catch the district seal intended
for the note beneath it, as well as a bit of the serial number. This is why the two serial numbers are different; they
were supposed to go on two different notes. Obviously,
when something this dramatic happens in printing, not
only one error note is created but several—at least—at the
same time. Not all necessarily reach circulation, however

130.00     375.00

## 10. THIRD PRINT BLACK INK MISSING OR LIGHT

Though the machinery used is ultra-modern, U.S. currency notes are printed by the same basic technique used
when printing was first invented more than 500 years ago.
Ink is spread on the metal plates and these are pressed on
the sheets as they go through the press. Because the inking
is manually fed (as is the paper), an even flow is usually
achieved. When an under-inked note is found, it is generally
merely "light," giving a faded appearance. But sometimes
the plate will be very improperly inked, due to mechanical
misfunction or some other cause, resulting in whole areas
being unprinted or so lightly printed that they cannot be
seen with-out close inspection. These are not especially

valuable notes but counterfeit specimens are frequently made.

|  | V.FINE | UNC. |
|---|---|---|
| ☐$1 Federal Reserve Note, Series 1977, Signatures of Morton-Blumenthal. Federal Reserve district seal and district numbers missing from lefthand side, remainder of "third print" material light but distinct. If the lefthand serial number was strong, there might be suspicion of this being a counterfeit | 26.00 | 65.00 |

## 11. THIRD PRINT GREEN INK MISSING OR LIGHT

In this case, the green, rather than the black, ink was applied too lightly to the printing plate.

|  | V.FINE | UNC. |
|---|---|---|
| ☐$5 Federal Reserve Note, Series 1977, Signatures of Morton-Blumenthal | 26.00 | 45.00 |

## 12. NOTE FOLDED DURING OVERPRINT

This note was folded as it was being overprinted and failed to receive the district seal and district numbers at the left side of its obverse. This kind of error, like all involving missing portions of printing, has been extensively counterfeited.

|  | V.FINE | UNC. |
|---|---|---|
| ☐$2 Federal Reserve Note, Series 1976, Signatures of Neff-Simon | 35.00 | 100.00 |

## 13. FAULTY ALIGNMENT

Notes of this kind were formerly called "miscut," and sometimes still are. "Faulty alignment" is a more inclusive term which encompasses not only bad cutting but accidents in printing. If the sheet shifts around in the press, it will not receive the printed impressions exactly where they should be. Even if the cutting is normal, the resulting note will be misaligned; the cutting machine cannot correct botched printing. It is very easy to determine where the fault lies. If one side of the note has its design higher than the opposite side, this is a printing error. If the misalignment occurs equally on both sides, the problem was in cutting. Since the two sides are not printed in the same operation, it would be a one-in-a-million chance for them to become equally misaligned.

The value of such notes depends upon the degree of misalignment. Collectors are especially fond of specimens showing a portion—even if very slight, as with the one pictured of an adjoining note.

|  | V.FINE | UNC. |
|---|---|---|
| ☐$5 Federal Reserve Note. Bottom left of reverse shaved (or "bled"), corresponding portion of adjoining note just visible at top. This ranks as a "dramatic" specimen. | | |
| ☐Slight | 17.00 | 46.00 |
| ☐Dramatic | 40.00 | 150.00 |

## 14. INSUFFICIENT PRESSURE

Under-inking of the printing plate is not the only cause of weak or partially missing impressions. If the press is not operating correctly and the inked plate meets the sheet with insufficient pressure, the result is similar to under-inking. This probably happens as a result of a sheet going through just as the press is being turned off for the day, or at other intervals. Supposedly all action ceases at the instant of turn-off, but considering the rapidity of this operation, it is likely that a random sheet could pass through and be insufficiently impressed. The note pictured here received normal "third prints," as is generally the case with notes whose first or second print is made with insufficient pressure.

|  | V.FINE | UNC. |
|---|---|---|
| □ $20 Federal Reserve Note, Series 1977, Signatures of Morton-Blumenthal | 72.00 | 150.00 |

## 15. PRINTED FOLD

This note, along with a large portion of the adjoining note, became folded after the second print. When it passed through the press to receive the third print or overprints (seals, serial numbers, etc.), these naturally failed to appear on the folded area.

|  | V.FINE | UNC. |
|---|---|---|
| □ $1 Federal Reserve Note. Printed fold with overprints partially missing. | | |
| □ Small | 32.00 | 95.00 |
| □ Large | 90.00 | 210.00 |

## 16. DOUBLE IMPRESSION

Double impressions have traditionally been traced to the sheet of notes passing through the press twice, which would be the logical explanation. However, in considering the method by which currency is printed, it would seem more likely that double impression notes have not made two trips through the press. They probably result from the automatic paper feed jamming. The sheet just printed fails to be ejected, and the printing plate falls upon it a second time instead of on a fresh sheet. This does not merely create a strong impression, but a twin, or a ghost, impression, since the sheet is not positioned exactly the same way for the second strike. Though the paper feed may not be operating properly, there will still be some slight movement—enough to prevent the second impression from falling directly atop the first.

|  | V.FINE | UNC. |
|---|---|---|
| ☐$1 Federal Reserve Note, Series 1977A | | |
| Signatures of Morton-Miller. Double "second print" impression. | | |
| ☐Partial | 115.00 | 200.00 |
| ☐Complete | 250.00 | 600.00 |

## 17. DOUBLE IMPRESSION OF OVERPRINTS ("DOUBLE THIRD PRINT")

This note is normal as far as the primary obverse and reverse printings are concerned. It received twin impressions of the overprints or "third print." This was not caused by jamming of the paper feed as discussed above. Naturally, the serial numbers are different, as the automatic numbering machine turns with every rise and fall of the press.

|                                                                                             | V.FINE  | UNC.   |
|---------------------------------------------------------------------------------------------|---------|--------|
| ☐ $20 Federal Reserve Note, Series 1950. Signatures of Priest-Humphrey. Double impression of overprints. |         |        |
| ☐ Partial                                                                                   | 90.00   | 325.00 |
| ☐ Complete                                                                                  | 210.00  | 600.00 |

## 18. THIRD PRINT (OR OVERPRINTS) SHIFTED

Whenever the overprints (serial number, seals, etc.) are out of position, vertically or horizontally, this is known as "third print shifted" or "overprints shifted." In the example pictured, shifting is extreme. This is a premium value specimen which would command the higher of the two sums quoted. Normally, the overprinting on a "shifted" note fails to touch the portrait, or touches it only slightly. The cause of this kind of error is a sheet feeding incorrectly into the press for the overprinting operation. As striking and desirable as these notes are to collectors, they often go unnoticed by the public.

|                                                                                     | V.FINE  | UNC.   |
|-------------------------------------------------------------------------------------|---------|--------|
| ☐ $100 Federal Reserve Note, Series 1969C, Signatures of Banuelos-Schultz. Third print shifted. |         |        |
| ☐ Slight                                                                            | 120.00  | 210.00 |
| ☐ Dramatic                                                                          | 180.00  | 260.00 |

## 19. INK SMEARS

Ink smearing is one of the more common abnormalities of currency notes. Generally it can be attributed to malfunction of the automatic inking device which inks the printing plate. When performing properly, ink is applied at a steady, controlled pace to the printing plate. A very minor disorder in the machine can dispense enough extra ink to yield very spectacular "smeared notes," such as the one illustrated. The value of ink smear notes depends upon the area and intensity of the smear. They are quite easily faked, so the buyer should be cautious.

|  | V.FINE | UNC. |
|---|---|---|
| ☐$1 Federal Reserve Note. Ink smear. | | |
| ☐Small | 18.00 | 35.00 |
| ☐Large | 30.00 | 60.00 |

## 20. PRINTING FOLD

This note was crumpled along the right side prior to the third printing or application of overprints. Hence the "third print" matter on the lefthand side is normal, but portions of the overprint on the right appear on the note's reverse side.

|  | V.FINE | UNC. |
|---|---|---|
| ☐$20 Federal Reserve Note, Series 1977, Signatures Morton-Blumenthal | 70.00 | 165.00 |

## 21. BLANK CREASE

It occasionally happens that a note becomes creased prior to the reverse or obverse printing in such a way that a small fold is created. During the printing procedure this fold hides a portion of the note's surface, which fails to receive the impression. These notes are actually double errors—the cutting machine cuts them without knowledge of the fold, and when the fold is opened out the bill is then of larger than normal size. Since "crease errors" are difficult to spot in the B.E.P.'s checking, they find their way into circulation in rather sizable numbers. It is difficult to place standard values on them because the price depends on the exact nature of the specimen. The wider the crease, the more valuable the note will be. Premium values are attached to notes with multiple creases that cause the blank unprinted area to fall across the portrait.

| | V.FINE | UNC. |
|---|---|---|
| ☐Blank crease note, any denomination. Value stated is collector premium over and above face value (if note has additional value because of series,signatures, etc., this too must be added) | | |
| ☐Single crease | 12.00 | 35.00 |
| ☐Multiple crease | 21.00 | 38.00 |

## 22. MIXED DENOMINATION

The two notes pictured are normal in themselves, and if they were not owned together as a set, no premium value would be attached to them. The error (which may be dubious to term as such) lies with their serial numbers. The $5 note has a serial number one digit higher than the $1, suggesting that it was fed into the printing machine intended to print overprints (or "third prints") on $1 bills. Even when this does happen (probably infrequently), it is very difficult to obtain "matching" notes of the kind illustrated, in which the serial numbers are only a single digit apart. Even if you had a $5 note and $1 note (or other combination of denominations) from sheets that were fed one after the other, the odds on getting one-digit-apart serial numbers are extremely small.

The value is given for an uncirculated set only, as there would be no possibility of finding such matched notes except in a bank pack. Once released into circulation, they can never again be mated.

UNC.

☐ Mixed denomination pair from bank pack, $5 Federal
Reserve Note within pack of $1 Federal Reserve notes          1600.00

## 23. BLANK REVERSE

U.S. currency has its reverse printed before the obverse—in other words, back before front. The only logical explanation for blank reverse notes is that blank paper found its way into the batch of sheets on which reverses had already been printed. They were then fed—without detection—into the press for application of the obverse. They continued to escape notice during printing of the overprints, and miraculously got into circulation.

|  | V.FINE | UNC. |
|---|---|---|
| ☐ $100 Federal Reserve Note. Blank reverse | 180.00 | 370.00 |

|  | V.FINE | UNC. |
|---|---|---|
| ☐ $20 Federal Reserve Note, Series 1977, Signatures of Morton-Blumenthal Blank reverse | 90.00 | 200.00 |

|  | V.FINE | UNC. |
|---|---|---|
| ☐ $10 Federal Reserve Note, Series 1974, Signatures of Neff-Simon Blank reverse | 100.00 | 200.00 |

|  | V.FINE | UNC. |
|---|---|---|
| ☐ $1 Federal Reserve Note, Series 1977, Signatures of Morton-Blumenthal Blank reverse | 75.00 | 185.00 |

## 24. DOUBLE DENOMINATION COUNTERFEIT

This is a counterfeit or faked error. We include it to show the kind of work done by counterfeiters, and how such items can be made to resemble genuine errors. This happens to be a counterfeit of an error note that cannot exist in its genuine state. Thus, there can be no hesitancy in proclaiming it a fake. Anyone who is even slightly familiar with the way currency is printed should instantly recognize this item as a fraud. Nevertheless, fakers succeed in selling (often at high prices) specimens of this kind, probably because some collectors want the impossible for their albums. Genuine double or twin denomination notes have the obverse of one denomination and the reverse of a different denomination. They do not consist of two obverses or two reverses, such as the one pictured. The note illustrated carries four serial numbers. For it to be genuine, it would have had to pass through the "third print" (overprinting) process twice. Obviously it was made by gluing a $1 and $5 note together. Much more deceptive paste-ups are created with the notes correctly paired so that the obverse of one and reverse of the other shows. Beware!

## 25. INVERTED OBVERSE

U.S. currency is printed reverse first. Therefore, when the back and front do not face in the same vertical direction (as they should), the note is known as an INVERTED OBVERSE. The term "inverted reverse" is never used. This, of course, results from the sheet being fed through upside-down for the obverse or second print. Though these specimens are scarce in uncirculated condition, they often pass through many hands in circulation before being spotted. The uninformed public is not even aware that a note with faces in opposite directions is an error and has premium value.

|  | V.FINE | UNC. |
|---|---|---|
| ☐ $2 Federal Reserve Note, Series 1976, Signatures of Neff-Simon. Inverted obverse | 200.00 | 450.00 |

## 26. MISSING THIRD PRINT

Also known as missing overprint. Note released into circulation without having gone through the "third print" operation.

|  | V.FINE | UNC. |
|---|---|---|
| ☐ $1 Federal Reserve Note, Series 1977, Signatures Morton-Blumenthal. Missing third print | 100.00 | 210.00 |

## 27. FOREIGN MATTER ON OBVERSE

Sometimes foreign matter, usually paper scraps of one kind or another, gets between the printing plate and the sheet. This naturally results in the area covered being blank on the note. Because of the extreme pressure exerted in printing, the foreign matter is occasionally "glued" to the note and travels with it into circulation. If the appendage is paper, it will normally be found to be of the same stock from which the note is made—apparently a shred from one of the sheet margins that worked its way into a batch of sheets awaiting printing. The value of such notes varies greatly, depending on the size of the foreign matter and its placement. It's rare to find notes in which foreign matter became attached before the first or second print. Nearly always, they found their way to the note after the second print and before the third.

|  | V.FINE | UNC. |
|---|---|---|
| ☐$1 Federal Reserve Note, Series 1974, Signatures Neff-Simon. Foreign matter on obverse | 100.00 | 140.00 |

|  | V.FINE | UNC. |
|---|---|---|
| ☐$1 Silver Certificate, Series 1935E. Signatures of Priest-Humphrey. Foreign matter on obverse. More valuable than the preceding because of the note's age and the foreign matter being larger | 190.00 | 400.00 |

## 28. MISSING PORTION OF REVERSE DESIGN (DUE TO ADHERENCE OF SCRAP PAPER)

In this instance, the foreign matter got in the way of the first print, or reverse printing. It prevented the covered area from being printed, but it later became dislodged and is no longer present. What appears on the illustration to be a strip of paper on the note is really the blank unprinted area once covered by the strip. Obviously a note that merely had a random strip of paper attached, over a normally printed design, would have no collector interest.

|                                                                                      | V.FINE | UNC.   |
| ------------------------------------------------------------------------------------ | ------ | ------ |
| ☐ $1 Federal Reserve Note. Missing portion of reverse design due to adherence of scrap paper | 60.00  | 140.00 |

## 29. OVERPRINT PARTIALLY MISSING

The overprint or third print on this note is normal on the righthand side and missing entirely on the left. This was caused by the note being folded (more or less in half, vertically) immediately before overprinting. Had the lefthand side been folded over the face, this would have interfered with the overprints on the righthand side. Instead, this specimen was folded over the reverse side, or downward, with the result that the missing portion of overprint did not strike the note at all—it simply hit the printing press bed. The reverse side of this note is normal.

|                                                                  | V.FINE | UNC.   |
| ---------------------------------------------------------------- | ------ | ------ |
| ☐ $1 Federal Reserve Note, Series 1963A. Overprint partially missing | 45.00  | 100.00 |

## 30. THIRD PRINT OFFSET ON REVERSE

This note is normal on the obverse but carries an "offset" of the third print or overprints on its reverse. It would appear that the overprints are showing through to the reverse, as if the note were printed on very thin paper. Actually, this "mirror image" is caused by a malfunction in the printing or paper-feeding machinery. The inked plate for printing the overprints contacted the machine bed without a sheet of paper being in place. Therefore, as the next sheet came through it received the normal overprint on its face and picked up the offset impression on its reverse from the machine bed. Each successive sheet going through the press also received an offset, but it naturally became fainter and fainter as the ink was absorbed. The value of a note of this kind depends on the intensity of the impression.

| | V.FINE | UNC. |
|---|---|---|
| ☐$5 Federal Reserve Note. Offset impression of overprints on reverse | 75.00 | 160.00 |

# CONFEDERATE MONEY

The Civil War Centennial of 1961-65 has generally been credited with sparking an interest in the collecting and study of Confederate or C.S.A. notes. This, however, is not totally borne out by facts, as C.S.A. currency had advanced steadily in value since the 1940s. It rides a crest of popularity today surpassing the early 1960s. This is due in part to the exhaustive research carried out since that time and numerous books and articles published. Even today, some C.S.A. notes would still appear to be undervalued based on their availability vs. regular U.S. issues.

**History.** It became apparent upon the outbreak of the Civil War that both sides would experience extreme coinage shortages, and each took to the printing of notes that could be exchanged in lieu of bullion or "real money" (which always meant coined money until the 1860s). The South suffered more serious difficulties than the North, as it did not have as many skilled printers or engravers at its command. Also, with the war being fought on its territory rather than the North's, there was an ever-present danger of sabotage to plants printing money or engaging in related activities. The Confederacy tried by all available means to satisfy the currency demand and succeeded in distributing quite a large quantity of notes. Its shortage was taken up by notes issued by private banks, individual states, counties, railroads, and private merchants. Merchant tokens, to take the place of rapidly disappearing small change, poured forth in abundance during this period. All told, the Confederate Congress authorized the printing of about one and a half billion dollars' worth of paper currency. It is impossible to determine the total actually produced, but it would appear that this figure was far surpassed. At the war's conclusion, these notes were worthless, as the C.S.A. no longer existed and the federal government refused to redeem them. Many were discarded as scrap, but a surprising number were held faithfully by their owners who believed "the South will rise again." The South did indeed rise, industrially and economically, and those old C.S.A. notes rose, too. They still aren't spendable, but many are worth sums in excess of face value as collectors' pieces. Until about 1900, however, practically no value was placed on Confederate currency—even by collectors.

**Designs.** Some surprising designs will be observed, including mythological gods and goddesses that seem to relate very little to the Southern artistic or cultural climate of the 1860s. Many scholarly efforts have been made to explain away the use of such motifs, but the simple fact is that they appeared not so much by choice as necessity. Southern printers, not having the facilities of their Northern counterparts, were compelled to make do with whatever engravings or "stock cuts" were already on hand, as inappropriate as they might have proved. However, a number of original designs were created reflecting unmistakably regional themes and at times picturing heroes or leaders of the Confederacy. Slaves at labor, used as a symbol of the South's economic strength and its supposed advantage over the North, where labor was hired, was a frequent motif. Sailors were also depicted, as well as railroad trains and anything else that appeared symbolic of Southern industry. Probably the most notable single design, not intended to carry the satirical overtones it now possesses, is "General Francis Marion's Sweet Potato Breakfast" on the $10 1861 issue note. In general, the C.S.A. notes are not so badly designed a group as might be anticipated in light of conditions. The designing was, in fact, several leagues improved over the printing, which often left much to be desired. George Washington is depicted—not for being the first U.S. President but as a native son of Virginia. Jefferson Davis, President of the C.S.A., is among the more common portraits. He became even more disliked in the North than he otherwise might have been because of his picture turning up on currency. But after the war he took a moderate stand and erased the old ill feelings; he even had words of praise for Lincoln. Other individuals whose portraits (not necessarily very faithful) will be encountered are:

John C. Calhoun, U.S. Senator who led the battle for slavery and Southern Rights (later called "states rights")
Alexander H. Stephen, Davis' Vice-President of the C.S.A.
Judah P. Benjamin, holder of various official titles in the Southern government
C. G. Memminger, Secretary of the Treasury and Secretary of War
Lucy Pickens, wife of South Carolina's governor and the only woman (aside from mythological types) shown on C.S.A. currency
John E. Ward
R. M. T. Hunter

**Printers.** The study of printers of C.S.A. notes is complex, made no less so by the fact that some contractors produced only plates, others did only printing (from plates procured elsewhere), while some did both. The principal Southern printer was the lithography firm of Hoyer & Ludwig of Richmond, Virginia. Also located in Richmond were Keatinge & Ball, which did commendable, if not exactly inspired, work, and B. Duncan, who also worked in Columbia, South Carolina. Another firm involved in quite a bit of note printing was J. T. Paterson of Columbia. The so-called "Southern Bank Note Company" was a fictitious name used to disguise the origin of notes prepared in the North. Some early notes were marked "National Bank Note Co., New York," but it was subsequently decided to remove correct identification from the notes of this printer, undoubtedly on the latter's request (fearing prosecution for aiding the enemy).

**Cancellations.** Two varieties of cancels are commonly found on C.S.A. notes. First is the cut cancel (CC), in which a knife or similar instrument has been used to make piercings in a design or pattern. Unless roughly executed, such cuts do not materially reduce a specimen's value. In the case of some notes, examples without cancellation are almost impossible to find. The COC or Cut-Out Cancel is more objectionable because, instead of merely leaving slits, a portion of the paper was removed. The reduction of value for a Cut-Out Cancel averages around 25 percent. These are considered "space fillers" if the issue is fairly common, but a rare note with a COC may be very desirable. Pen Cancellations (PC) are far less frequently encountered. These show the word "Canceled" written out by hand across the note's face, in ink. Unless the ink is heavy or blotchy, a pen cancel will not have too much bearing on value. As the note is not physically injured, it would seem to be the least offensive of the three varieties. Whenever a note is being sold, presence of a cancel, of whatever type, should be plainly spelled out. Some collectors are not interested in canceled specimens. In time, as the scarce issues become even scarcer, they will probably have to be accepted as a fact of life.

**Signatures.** There are so many signature combinations on C.S.A. notes that utter confusion would await anyone attempting to collect them on this basis. The names are unknown and in most instances difficult to trace, representing not government officials but employees authorized to sign for the Treasurer and Registrar of the Treasury. Only the first six notes bear the actual signatures of these officials.

**Condition Grades.** While condition standards are basically the same for Confederate currency as other notes of their age, some allowance must be made for paper quality and deficiencies in printing and cutting. These matters have nothing to do with the preservation or wear and can be observed just as frequently in uncirculated specimens as in those in average condition. Without a source of good paper, printers were obliged to use whatever was most easily and quickly obtainable. Often the paper was thin, or stiff, or contained networks of minute wrinkles which interfered with printing. Cutting was generally not done by machine, as in the North, but by hand with a pair of scissors—workers actually took the sheets and cut apart notes individually. When paper-cutting devices were employed, they were apparently not of the best quality. In any case, regular edges on C.S.A. notes are uncommon, and their absence does not constitute grounds for classifying an otherwise perfect specimen in a condition grade below Uncirculated. When the occasional gem is located—a well-printed, well-preserved note on good paper, decently cut—its value is sure to be higher than those listed. The collector is not advised to confine himself to such specimens, as his activities would become seriously limited.

**UNCIRCULATED—UNC.** An uncirculated note shows no evidence of handling and is as close to "new condition" as possible. An uncirculated specimen may, however, have pinholes or a finger smudge, which should be mentioned in a sales offering. If these are readily noticeable, the note deserves to be classified as "almost uncirculated." Crispness is hardly a criterion of uncirculation as this quality is expected in notes graded as low as Very Fine.

**ALMOST UNCIRCULATED—A.U.** Similar to the above grade, but not quite as good as an uncirculated specimen. The note bears no indication of having actually circulated but has minor flaws resulting from accident or mishandling, such an individuals' counting crinkles.

**EXTREMELY FINE—X.F.** An X.F. note is on the borderline between uncirculated and circulated. It has not been heavily handled but may reveal several imperfections: a pinhole, finger smudge, counting crinkles, or a light wallet fold. The fold is not so heavy as to be termed a crease.

**VERY FINE—V.F.** Has been in circulation but is not worn or seriously creased. It must still be clean and crisp, without stains or tears. Fine to Very Fine condition is considered the equivalent of "average circulated" but not "average condition" (which is another term for poor).

**FINE—F.** A note that has been in circulation and shows it, but has no physical injuries or just slight ones.

**VERY GOOD—V.G.** A well-circulated note bearing evidence of numerous foldings. It may possibly have creased corners and wrinkles as well as light staining, smudging, or pinholes, but major defects (such as a missing corner) would place it into an even lower category.

**GOOD—G.** Good notes heavily circulated, worn, possibly stained or scribbled on edges, could be frayed or "dog-eared." There may be holes larger than pin punctures, but not on the central portion of design. This is the lowest grade of condition acceptable to a collector, and only when nothing better is available. Unless very rare, such specimens are considered space-fillers only.

**A.B.P.—AVERAGE BUYING PRICES.** The average buying prices given here are the approximate sums paid by retail dealers for specimens in good condition. As selling prices vary, so do buying prices, and in fact they usually vary a bit more. A dealer who is overstocked on a certain note is sure to offer less than one who has no specimens on hand. The dealer's location, size of operation, and other circumstances will also influence the buying price. We present these figures merely as approximate guides to what sellers should expect.

## FOR MORE INFORMATION

Considered to be the foremost authority on confederate currency, Col. Grover Criswell has a variety of books available. His newest release, *Confederate and Southern States Currency* ($45), covers all the currency issued by the Confederate States Central Government, the Southern States, the Indian Territories, the Florida Republic and Territory, and the Republic and Independent Government of Texas. This edition also gives interesting discovery information that you are sure to enjoy. There are also current market values listed, as well as rarities. This is the best reference available for the serious collector, libraries, and the casual reader.

To order this book or for a complete list of books that are available, write Criswell's Publications, Salt Springs, Florida 32134-6000 or call (904) 685-2287.

## CONFEDERATE STATES OF AMERICA—
### 1861 ISSUE MONTGOMERY, ALABAMA
$1,000,000 Authorized by "Act of March 9th."
Written Dates "1861."
"NATIONAL BANK NOTE CO., NY"

**Face Design:** Green and black, bears "Interest Ten Cents Per Day," 607 issued. John C. Calhoun left, Andrew Jackson right.

| CRISWELL | NOTE | A.B.P. | GOOD | UNC. |
|----------|------|--------|------|------|
| ☐1 | $1000 | 1800.00 | 3000.00 | 16,000.00 |

### "NATIONAL BANK NOTE CO., NY"

**Face Design:** Green and black, bears "Interest Five Cents Per Day," 607 issued. Cattle crossing a brook.

| CRISWELL | NOTE | A.B.P. | GOOD | UNC. |
|----------|------|--------|------|------|
| ☐2 | $500 | 2000.00 | 3000.00 | 15,000.00 |

## CONFEDERATE STATES OF AMERICA—
## 1861 ISSUE
### "NATIONAL BANK NOTE CO., NY"

**Face Design:** Green and black, bears "Interest One Cent Per Day." Railway train, Minerva left.

| CRISWELL | NOTE | A.B.P. | GOOD | UNC. |
|---|---|---|---|---|
| ☐3 | $100 | 1200.00 | 2600.00 | 8000.00 |

### "NATIONAL BANK NOTE CO., NY"

**Face Design:** Green and black, bears "Interest Half A Cent Per Day." Negroes hoeing cotton.

| CRISWELL | NOTE | A.B.P. | GOOD | UNC. |
|---|---|---|---|---|
| ☐4 | $50 | 1200.00 | 2500.00 | 7000.00 |

## CONFEDERATE STATES OF AMERICA—1861 ISSUE
### "AMERICAN BANK NOTE CO., NY"
(Though ostensibly by the "SOUTHERN BANK NOTE CO.")

**Face Design:** Green and black, red fibre paper, bears "Interest One Cent Per Day." Railway train, Justice left and Minerva right.

| CRISWELL | NOTE | A.B.P. | GOOD | UNC. |
|----------|------|--------|------|------|
| ☐5 | $100 | 150.00 | 250.00 | 800.00 |

**Face Design:** Green and black, red fibre paper, bears "Interest Half A Cent Per Day." Pallas and Ceres seated on bale of cotton, Washington at right.

| CRISWELL | NOTE | A.B.P. | GOOD | UNC. |
|----------|------|--------|------|------|
| ☐6 | $50 | 125.00 | 200.00 | 700.00 |

## CONFEDERATE STATES OF AMERICA—1861 ISSUE
### $20,000,000 Authorized by "Act of May 16th, 1861"
### "HOYER & LUDWIG, RICHMOND, VA"
### (All Lithographic Date "July 25th, 1861")

**Face Design:** Ceres and Proserpina flying, Washington left.

| CRISWELL | NOTE | A.B.P. | GOOD | UNC. |
|---|---|---|---|---|
| ☐7-13 | $100 | 150.00 | 250.00 | 700.00 |

**Face Design:** Washington, Tellus left.

| CRISWELL | NOTE | A.B.P. | GOOD | UNC. |
|---|---|---|---|---|
| ☐14-22 | $50 | 35.00 | 60.00 | 110.00 |

## CONFEDERATE STATES OF AMERICA—1861 ISSUE

**Face Design:** Exists in a variety of colors.

| CRISWELL | NOTE | | A.B.P. | GOOD | UNC. |
|----------|------|--|--------|------|------|
| ☐21 | $20 | | 35.00 | 60.00 | 140.00 |

NOTE: The above type notes were bogus. For years it was thought they were a regular Confederate issue, and evidence exists that they were circulated as such. No collection of Confederate notes is complete without one. There is no evidence as to who the printer was, but the authors have reason to believe he was located somewhere in Ohio. It is not a product of S. C. Upham, of Philadelphia, the well-known counterfeiter of Confederate notes.

**Face Design:** Large sailing vessel, "20" at left.

| CRISWELL | NOTE | | A.B.P. | GOOD | UNC. |
|----------|------|--|--------|------|------|
| ☐23-33 | $20 | | 20.00 | 45.00 | 100.00 |

## CONFEDERATE STATES OF AMERICA—1861 ISSUE

**Face Design:** Liberty seated by Eagle, with shield and flag.

NOTE: There are at least 42 minor varieties of this note, including a supposed 10 or 11 stars on shield. Usually the stars are so indistinct that a note may show from six to 15 stars. The other differences are minute changes in the size of the "10" in the upper corners. We list only the major type.

| CRISWELL | NOTE | A.B.P. | GOOD | UNC. |
|----------|------|--------|------|------|
| ☐34-40 | $10 | 30.00 | 72.00 | 600.00 |

**Face Design:** Liberty seated by Eagle, sailor left.

| CRISWELL | NOTE | A.B.P. | GOOD | UNC. |
|----------|------|--------|------|------|
| ☐42-44 | $5 | 100.00 | 750.00 | 8000.00 |

## CONFEDERATE STATES OF AMERICA—1861 ISSUE
### "J. MANOUVRIER, NEW ORLEANS"
(Written Date "July 25th, 1861")

**Face Design:** "Confederate States of America" in blue on blue reverse.

| CRISWELL | NOTE | A.B.P. | GOOD | UNC. |
|----------|------|--------|------|------|
| ☐46-49 | $5 | 200.00 | 1800.00 | 5000.00 |

$100,000,000 authorized by "Act of Aug. 19th, 1861."
$50,000,000 authorized by "Act of Dec. 24th, 1861."

### "HOYER & LUDWIG, RICHMOND, VA"
(Lithographic Date, "September 2nd, 2d, & s, 1861")

**Face Design:** Negroes loading cotton, sailor left.

| CRISWELL | NOTE | A.B.P. | GOOD | UNC. |
|----------|------|--------|------|------|
| ☐50-58 | $100 | 20.00 | 35.00 | 100.00 |

## CONFEDERATE STATES OF AMERICA—1861 ISSUE

**Face Design:** Moneta seated by treasure chests, sailor left.

| CRISWELL | NOTE | A.B.P. | GOOD | UNC. |
|----------|------|--------|------|------|
| ☐59-78 | $50 | 20.00 | 30.00 | 80.00 |

### "SOUTHERN BANK NOTE CO., NEW ORLEANS"

**Face Design:** Black and red on red fibre paper. Railway train, Justice right, Hope with anchor left.

| CRISWELL | NOTE | A.B.P. | GOOD | UNC. |
|----------|------|--------|------|------|
| ☐79 | $50 | 300.00 | 500.00 | 4500.00 |

## CONFEDERATE STATES OF AMERICA—1861 ISSUE
### "KEATINGE & BALL, RICHMOND, VA"

**Face Design:** Black and green, red fibre paper. Portrait of Jefferson Davis.

| CRISWELL | NOTE | A.B.P. | GOOD | UNC. |
|----------|------|--------|------|------|
| ☐80-94 | $50 | 35.00 | 50.00 | 300.00 |

### "HOYER & LUDWIG, RICHMOND, VA"

**Face Design:** Black with green ornamentation, plain paper. Ceres seated between Commerce and Navigation, Liberty left.

| CRISWELL | NOTE | A.B.P. | GOOD | UNC. |
|----------|------|--------|------|------|
| ☐99-100 | $20 | 42.00 | 90.00 | 500.00 |

## CONFEDERATE STATES OF AMERICA—1861 ISSUE
### "HOYER & LUDWIG, RICHMOND, VA"

**Face Design:** Large sailing vessel, sailor at capstan left.

| CRISWELL | NOTE | A.B.P. | GOOD | UNC. |
|----------|------|--------|------|------|
| □101-136 | $20 | 10.00 | 20.00 | 70.00 |

### "SOUTHERN BANK NOTE CO., NEW ORLEANS"

**Face Design:** Black and red on red fibre paper. Navigator seated by charts, Minerva left, blacksmith right.

| CRISWELL | NOTE | A.B.P. | GOOD | UNC. |
|----------|------|--------|------|------|
| □137 | $20 | 150.00 | 500.00 | 3000.00 |

## CONFEDERATE STATES OF AMERICA—1861 ISSUE

**Face Design:** Industry seated between cupid and beehive, bust of A. H. Stevens left.

### PRINTED BY "B. DUNCAN, COLUMBIA, SC"

| CRISWELL | NOTE | A.B.P. | GOOD | UNC. |
|---|---|---|---|---|
| ☐139-140 | $20 | 10.00 | 20.00 | 75.00 |

### PRINTED BY "B. DUNCAN, RICHMOND, VA"

| CRISWELL | NOTE | A.B.P. | GOOD | UNC. |
|---|---|---|---|---|
| ☐141-143 | $20 | 10.00 | 20.00 | 75.00 |

### "KEATING & BALL, COLUMBIA, SC"

**Face Design:** Portrait of Alexander H. Stephens.

#### YELLOW-GREEN ORNAMENTATION

| CRISWELL | NOTE | A.B.P. | GOOD | UNC. |
|---|---|---|---|---|
| ☐144 | $20 | 25.00 | 50.00 | 400.00 |

#### DARK-GREEN ORNAMENTATION

| CRISWELL | NOTE | A.B.P. | GOOD | UNC. |
|---|---|---|---|---|
| ☐145-149 | $20 | 25.00 | 50.00 | 400.00 |

## CONFEDERATE STATES OF AMERICA—1861 ISSUE
### "SOUTHERN BANK NOTE CO., NEW ORLEANS"

**Face Design:** Black and red, red fibre paper. Group of Indians, Thetis left, maiden with "X" at right.

| CRISWELL | NOTE | A.B.P. | GOOD | UNC. |
|---|---|---|---|---|
| ☐150-152 | $10.00 | 50.00 | 80.00 | 450.00 |

### "LEGGETT, KEATINGE & BALL, RICHMOND, VA"

**Face Design:** Black and orange/red. Wagonload of cotton, harvesting sugar cane right. John E. Ward left.

| CRISWELL | NOTE | A.B.P. | GOOD | UNC. |
|---|---|---|---|---|
| ☐153-155 | $10 | 80.00 | 200.00 | 950.00 |

## CONFEDERATE STATES OF AMERICA—1861 ISSUE
### "LEGGETT, KEATINGE & BALL, RICHMOND, VA"

**Face Design:** Black and orange/red. R. M. T. Hunter left, vignette of child right.

| CRISWELL | NOTE | A.B.P. | GOOD | UNC. |
|----------|------|--------|------|------|
| ☐156-160 | $10 | 20.00 | 36.00 | 300.00 |

### "KEATINGE & BALL, RICHMOND, VA"

| CRISWELL | NOTE | A.B.P. | GOOD | UNC. |
|----------|------|--------|------|------|
| ☐161-167 | $10.00 | 20.00 | 36.00 | 300.00 |

### "KEATINGE & BALL, RICHMOND, VA"

**Face Design:** Hope with anchor, R. M. T. Hunter left, C. G. Memminger right.

| CRISWELL | NOTE | A.B.P. | GOOD | UNC. |
|----------|------|--------|------|------|
| ☐168-171 | $10.00 | 20.00 | 40.00 | 275.00 |

## CONFEDERATE STATES OF AMERICA—1861 ISSUE
### "KEATINGE & BALL, RICHMOND, VA"

**Face Design:** Hope with anchor, R. M. T. Hunter left, C. G. Memminger right.

NOTE: There are three types of red "X" and "X" overprints. That section of the note on which the overprints appear is illustrated in double size.

**Face Design:** Solid red "X" and "X" overprint.

| CRISWELL | NOTE | A.B.P. | GOOD | UNC. |
|---|---|---|---|---|
| ☐173-188 | $10.00 | 20.00 | 42.00 | 300.00 |

**Face Design:** Coarse lace "X" and "X" red overprint.

| CRISWELL | NOTE | A.B.P. | GOOD | UNC. |
|---|---|---|---|---|
| ☐189-210 | $10.00 | 20.00 | 40.00 | 300.00 |

## CONFEDERATE STATES OF AMERICA—1861 ISSUE

**Face Design:** Fine lace "X" and "X" red overprint.

| CRISWELL | NOTE | A.B.P. | GOOD | UNC. |
|----------|------|--------|------|------|
| ☐211–220 | $10 | 20.00 | 40.00 | 300.00 |

**Face Design:** Liberty seated by shield and eagle.

| CRISWELL | NOTE | A.B.P. | GOOD | UNC. |
|----------|------|--------|------|------|
| ☐221-229 | $10 | 600.00 | 2500.00 | 20,000.00 |

## CONFEDERATE STATES OF AMERICA—1861 ISSUE
### "HOYER & LUDWIG, RICHMOND, VA"

**Face Design:** Ceres and Commerce with an urn.

| CRISWELL | NOTE | A.B.P. | GOOD | UNC. |
|---|---|---|---|---|
| ☐230-234 | $10 | 15.00 | 25.00 | 180.00 |

### "J. T. PATERSON, COLUMBIA, SC"

| CRISWELL | NOTE | A.B.P. | GOOD | UNC. |
|---|---|---|---|---|
| ☐235-236 | $10 | 15.00 | 30.00 | 180.00 |

### "B. DUNCAN, RICHMOND, VA"

**Face Design:** Negro picking cotton.

| CRISWELL | NOTE | A.B.P. | GOOD | UNC. |
|---|---|---|---|---|
| ☐237 | $10 | 25.00 | 40.00 | 300.00 |

## CONFEDERATE STATES OF AMERICA—1861 ISSUE
### "B. DUNCAN, COLUMBIA, SC"

**Face Design:** Gen. Francis Marion's "Sweet Potato Dinner." R. M. T. Hunter left, Minerva right.

| CRISWELL | NOTE | A.B.P. | GOOD | UNC. |
|----------|------|--------|------|------|
| ☐238 | $10 | 15.00 | 25.00 | 150.00 |

### NO ENGRAVER'S NAME

| CRISWELL | NOTE | A.B.P. | GOOD | UNC. |
|----------|------|--------|------|------|
| ☐239-241 | $10 | 15.00 | 25.00 | 150.00 |

### "SOUTHERN BANK NOTE CO., NEW ORLEANS"

**Face Design:** Black and red on red fibre paper. Minerva left; Agriculture, Commerce, Industry, Justice and Liberty seated at center; statue of Washington right.

| CRISWELL | NOTE | A.B.P. | GOOD | UNC. |
|----------|------|--------|------|------|
| ☐243-245 | $5 | 50.00 | 90.00 | 350.00 |

## CONFEDERATE STATES OF AMERICA—1861 ISSUE
### "LEGGETT, KEATINGE & BALL, RICHMOND, VA"

**Face Design:** Black and orange/red. Machinist with hammer, boy in oval left.

| CRISWELL | NOTE | A.B.P. | GOOD | UNC. |
|---|---|---|---|---|
| ☐246-249 | $5 | 70.00 | 160.00 | 1500.00 |

### "LEGGETT, KEATINGE & BALL, RICHMOND, VA"

**Face Design:** Black and white note with blue-green ornamentation. C. G. Memminger, Minerva right.

| CRISWELL | NOTE | A.B.P. | GOOD | UNC. |
|---|---|---|---|---|
| ☐250-253 | $5 | 15.00 | 21.00 | 175.00 |

### "KEATINGE & BALL, RICHMOND, VA"

| CRISWELL | NOTE | A.B.P. | GOOD | UNC. |
|---|---|---|---|---|
| ☐254-257 | $5 | 15.00 | 26.00 | 175.00 |

### NO ENGRAVER'S NAME

| CRISWELL | NOTE | A.B.P. | GOOD | UNC. |
|---|---|---|---|---|
| ☐258-261 | $5 | 15.00 | 22.00 | 175.00 |

## CONFEDERATE STATES OF AMERICA—1861 ISSUE
### "KEATINGE & BALL, RICHMOND, VA"

**Face Design:** C. G. Memminger, Minerva right.

| CRISWELL | NOTE | A.B.P. | GOOD | UNC. |
|---|---|---|---|---|
| ☐262-270 | $5 | 18.00 | 35.00 | 250.00 |

### "PRINTED BY HOYER & LUDWIG, RICHMOND, VA"

**Face Design:** Loading cotton left, "Indian Princess" right.

| CRISWELL | NOTE | A.B.P. | GOOD | UNC. |
|---|---|---|---|---|
| ☐271 | $5 | 1000.00 | 2500.00 | 50,000.00 |

## CONFEDERATE STATES OF AMERICA—1861 ISSUE
### "HOYER & LUDWIG, RICHMOND, VA"

**Face Design:** Ceres seated on bale of cotton, sailor left.

| CRISWELL | NOTE | A.B.P. | GOOD | UNC. |
|---|---|---|---|---|
| ☐272 | $5 | 10.00 | 16.00 | 80.00 |

### "J. T. PATERSON & CO., COLUMBIA, SC"

| CRISWELL | NOTE | A.B.P. | GOOD | UNC. |
|---|---|---|---|---|
| ☐274 | $5 | 10.00 | 14.00 | 70.00 |

### "J. T. PATERSON & CO., COLUMBIA, SC"

| CRISWELL | NOTE | A.B.P. | GOOD | UNC. |
|---|---|---|---|---|
| ☐276-282 | $5 | 10.00 | 20.00 | 80.00 |

# CONFEDERATE STATES OF AMERICA—1861 ISSUE
## "B. DUNCAN, RICHMOND, VA"

**Face Design:** Sailor seated beside bales of cotton, C. G. Memminger left, Justice and Ceres right.

| CRISWELL | NOTE | A.B.P. | GOOD | UNC. |
|---|---|---|---|---|
| ☐284 | $5 | 20.00 | 35.00 | 150.00 |

## "B. DUNCAN, COLUMBIA, SC"

| CRISWELL | NOTE | A.B.P. | GOOD | UNC. |
|---|---|---|---|---|
| ☐285 | $5 | 20.00 | 30.00 | 150.00 |

## "B. DUNCAN, COLUMBIA, SC"

**Face Design:** Personification of South striking down Union, J. P. Benjamin left. NOTE: Dated "September 2, 1861," through an error. No Confederate note less than $5 was authorized in 1861.

| CRISWELL | NOTE | A.B.P. | GOOD | UNC. |
|---|---|---|---|---|
| ☐286 | $2 | 95.00 | 285.00 | 3000.00 |

# THE BLACKBOOKS!